Thread of Blood

HEGEMONY AND EXPERIENCE
Critical Studies in Anthropology and History

SERIES EDITORS
Hermann Rebel and William Roseberry

ANA MARÍA ALONSO

Thread of Blood

Colonialism, Revolution, and Gender

on Mexico's Northern Frontier

The University of Arizona Press · Tucson

THE UNIVERSITY OF ARIZONA PRESS

www.uapress.arizona.edu

Library of Congress Cataloging-in-Publication Data
Alonso, Ana Maria, 1995–
Thread of blood : colonialism, revolution, and gender on Mexico's northern
frontier / Ana Maria Alonso.
p.   cm. — (Hegemony and experience)
Includes bibliographical references and index.
ISBN 978-0-8165-1574-5 (paper : alk. paper)
1. Frontier and pioneer life—Mexico—Chihuahua (State) 2. Sierra Madre
Region (Mexico)—History. 3. Namiquipa (Mexico)—History. 4. Indians
of Mexico—Wars—Mexico—Chihuahua (State) 5. Government, Resistance
to—Mexico—Chihuahua (State)—History. 6. Social structure—Mexico—
Chihuahua (State)—History. 7. Chihuahua (Mexico : State)—Social life and
customs. I. Title. II. Series.
F1261.A45 1995   95-32475
972'.16—dc20   CIP

Thread of Blood is published with a generous gift from the Clara Lee Tanner
Publishing Fund, whose contribution is matched by a Challenge Grant from the
National Endowment for the Humanities to support publishing in anthropology
at the University of Arizona Press.

16   15   14   13   12   7   6   5   4   3

*To my friends in Namiquipa
and to my family.*

Y en recuerdo de Daniel Nugent.

CONTENTS

ACKNOWLEDGMENTS

I am most greatly indebted to the people of Namiquipa, Chihuahua, whose generosity, hospitality, and friendship have been overwhelming and whose insights, memories, and reflections have formed the basis of this book. Their company made the years I spent in Namiquipa some of the best of my life. This book is dedicated to them.

In addition, I would like to express my gratitude to those who so kindly took us into their homes, that is, the *familias* Morales Carrasco, Ruiz Barrera, Cano Salinas, and Salazar Cano; to the physicians who treated us without charge, Dr. Florencio Aguilera and Dr. Prisciliana Reyes; to the municipal presidents of Namiquipa, Daniel Salazar Quintano and Rafael Ruiz Barrera, and of Guerrero City, Victor Peregrino and his successor, as well as to the municipal staff, who gave us their support and cooperation, especially Professors Rascón and Gándara; to the director and students of the local high school, as well as Professor Colmenero, who helped us to organize the archives of Namiquipa; to Padre Gabriel, who put us up in Guerrero City; to Lic. González, who allowed us to use his photocopying machine in Guerrero City at cost; and to all those who shared their memories of the past with us and who aided us in our research. I would also like to acknowledge the help of four very special people who have died since 1984, whose company and conversation I miss more than I can ever express: Doña Aurelia Muñoz, Don Cruz Tena, Doña Guadalupe Casavantes, and Don Mike Maldonado. This book is also dedicated to them.

The funding for my ethnographic fieldwork and archival research was provided by the Inter-American Foundation, the Social Science Research

Council, the American Council of Learned Societies, and the Center for Latin American Studies, University of Chicago. I refer the reader to "A Note on Sources" (at the beginning of the bibliography) for a discussion of the archival sources used in preparing this book. I held a fellowship from the Pembroke Center for Research and Writing on Women, Brown University, 1987-88, and a Rockefeller fellowship from the Southwest Institute for Research and Writing on Women, University of Arizona, Tucson, 1990-91. I thank all of these institutions for their financial support.

My research was carried out in collaboration with Daniel Nugent. I would like to thank Daniel for all his help and especially for his editorial assistance, his criticisms and suggestions, and his help with computer problems. I am also grateful to Peggy and Charles Nugent for their support and friendship.

I would like to extend a special thanks to my parents, Ana María and Luis Ricardo Alonso, for their comments and suggestions, and to my brothers, Ricardo and Armando, and my son, Carlos. This book is also dedicated to them.

The cooperation and assistance of numerous people in Mexico and the United States—friends, colleagues, archivists, government officials —were essential to my research. I would like to thank all of them for their support, especially Eugenia Meyer, Adolfo Gilly, Javier Garcia-diego, Jane-Dale Lloyd, Robert Holden, Armando Ruiz, Hector Aguilar Camín, Ulises Beltrán and his wife, Estela, Chalu, Thomas Naylor, Tom Sheridan, Fritz Jandrui, Diana Hadley, César Caballero, Sergio Campos, and Apolinar Frías. In particular, I would like to acknowledge my debt to Dr. Rubén Osorio, who provided introductions to people as well as advice and who shared his own research with me.

This book is based on my dissertation (Alonso 1988), which was supervised by Professors Raymond T. Smith, Friedrich Katz, and Jean Comaroff. I am very grateful for their criticisms, suggestions, and support. I would also like to thank Professor Paul Friedrich, whose advice and insights have been valuable to my work.

A substantial part of chapter 7 was published as an article in *Critique of Anthropology* and as a paper in *Feminists Theorize the Political* (Alonso 1988b; Alonso 1992b). Part of the preface to part II was published in *Annual Review of Anthropology* (Alonso 1994), and parts of chapter 8 are planned for publication in *Identities*.

Many people at the University of Arizona Press contributed their talents to the publication of this book. In particular, I would like to thank my editor, Joanne O'Hare, who has been extraordinarily patient and helpful. Finally, I am deeply grateful to the Clara Lee Tanner Foundation for a grant that made publication of this book possible.

Thread of Blood

INTRODUCTION

> The Revolution of 1910, initiated and sustained in Chihuahua, is one of the last links in a historical chain that the Apache played a key role in forging. In order to demonstrate this point, it is enough to examine the list of names of the rural people who rose up in 1910 in San Isidro, Bachíniva, Santo Tomás, Namiquipa, Temósachi, Pachera, and Ranchos de Santiago. The majority of them have the same first and last names as their fathers, grandfathers, and great-grandfathers, names that appear in old documents attesting to the campaigns against the Apache organized in these communities. All that these rural people did was to turn their weapons against the new invaders of their communities and lands. And also against despotism and privilege. A good part of this tradition of rebelliousness and antiauthoritarianism was forged in the secular struggle against the Apache. There is, then, a thread of blood that links the Indian wars to the revolution.
>
> Orozco 1992:31; my translation

In April of 1917 the Mexican revolutionary Pancho Villa attacked the *pueblo* of Namiquipa, Chihuahua, from whence had come many of his strongest supporters, including members of his elite fighting corps, the Dorados, or Golden Ones. According to oral tradition, Villa and his men burned the town and raped many women. They also stole food, fodder, and horses and sacrificed cattle to eat. Many Namiquipans attribute Villa's actions to his *higados de apache* (Apache guts), that is, to what they construe as his cruel, bloodthirsty, and barbaric nature. He had even planned to burn many of the women alive with green wood (an Apache vengeance), but they were rescued at the last minute by one of his officers. In the face of Villa's savagery, oral tradition adds, the men of the community founded the *defensas sociales*, local militias whose task was to defend the town against the incursions of the Villista "hordes."

I arrived in Namiquipa in June 1983, intending to do anthropological and historical research on the town's involvement in the Mexican revolution of 1910–20. During the course of my stay, I heard this narrative many times, from many people, including those who had been alive in April 1917. Significantly, eyewitnesses initially gave the version of events provided by oral tradition and had to be closely questioned before they divulged what they had actually "seen"; by and large, it was the houses of the members of the local militia that were burned, and their unmarried female relatives who were raped. Villa's actions, some of them explained, were motivated by a logic of vengeance, prompted by the betrayal of the *confianza* (intimacy and trust) he had earlier enjoyed with the men of the pueblo, who had subsequently cooperated with Villa's enemies, including the Americans of Pershing's Punitive Expedition. When the members of the militia, the *sociales*, heard that Villa was coming, they fled to the mountains, leaving the town undefended.

An opposite view of the events of April 1917 is provided by Alberto Calzadíaz Barrera, a local historian notorious for his Villista sympathies, who interviewed many Namiquipan revolutionaries, as well as survivors of the attack on the pueblo:

> For some reason, during the first week of the month of April 1917, the sociales . . . led by the Colmenero brothers and their allies . . . had concentrated themselves in Namiquipa . . . . One night when no one was expecting anything to happen, the leaders of the sociales were having a good time dancing to gay local music. Those Namiquipans who did not participate in this gaiety were in their homes as usual. They had shut their animals in their corrals very early. Everything was tranquil. Just before dawn the Villistas fell upon the pueblo. Like Apaches, they galloped wildly through the town on their runaway horses. The majority of the men of the place barely had time to mount their horses—many of them bareback—and race for the plain en route to the mountains. The first shots were heard in the neighborhood of La Plaza, where the sociales' leaders had been celebrating. None of these leaders made even the slightest comment, as they immediately understood the significance of those gunshots. Rapidly, like meteors, they took to their horses and abandoned the town at all speed.
>
> It was not quite light . . . four in the morning . . . what a sad dawn. The majority of the attackers were concentrated on the north side of the pueblo, precisely where the leaders of the sociales had been dancing. They exchanged bullets, and the Colmenero brothers fell dead . . . about a block from the town square. There were other deaths in La Plaza, as well as in the neighborhood of El Molino, which is in the extreme south of the pueblo. Everything fell to the Villistas without much effort. Shouts of *"Viva Villa!"* were heard near and far.
>
> Twenty percent of the houses of Namiquipa were burned by the Villista leader Miguel García, and crimes followed in abundance, committed by some officers who pompously called themselves Dorados, even though in reality they were nothing but dirt. . . .

Some Villistas had seized my Uncle Gregorio, and as they were walking down a street, they met Colonel Carmen Delgado, an acquaintance of my uncle's, who asked where they were taking him. Colonel Delgado ordered my uncle set free and then told him, "Look, Goyito, go to Don Pedro Barrera's house and tell him that I need a bedroom and look after this girl there for me." On his horse was a beautiful *señorita*, sister of the Colmenero brothers. She was going to pay with her honor for the excesses that her brothers had committed against people whose only crime was to have been Villista sympathizers, as everyone was when Villa was winning.

All the women were told to present themselves to General Villa in the headquarters established in the neighborhood of El Molino, and as these unfortunates were walking to see Villa, they were met by a leader who asked if Doña Guillermina, wife of Don Luis Bustillos, was among them; out of fear, they dared not answer, but finally things became clear; the Villista leader was Colonel Belisario Ruiz—a member of the Dorados—and Luis Bustillos and his wife, Guillermina, were his godparents.

When all those women heard Colonel Ruiz say that Villa had not ordered them to present themselves, they almost cried with joy, and they continued to follow the road to Villa's headquarters. The guard asked them to halt and did not let them approach. General Villa came out and asked them why they were there. "They ordered us to present ourselves," the women explained. "I gave no such order. What would I do with so many old ladies? Go back to your homes, that's the best thing you can do," Villa answered.

By then Colonel Ruiz had already ordered that all the single women from decent families be assembled in the house of Doña Francisquita Barrera, where a special guard would watch over them. (Villa's enemies would later say that these women had been burned alive.)

Meanwhile, houses that were found locked and abandoned were plundered and burned. . . .

The truth is that not a single woman was burned, let alone women who were in their homes. Many excesses were committed by the so-called indispensables, who still boast of having been Dorados. But the Dorados were others.

They burned houses, but not all of those that belonged to

Villa's real enemies; people who were not involved, who had not taken sides, did not have anything to lament. My family's house was not harmed, and neither were many other houses. There were women whom the soldiers forced, as happens elsewhere; but there were also girls and women who voluntarily gave themselves to the soldiers. That is very human. (Calzadíaz Barrera 1980:90–92; my translation)

Calzadíaz Barrera's narrative at once foregrounds and makes light of the rape of Namiquipan women, representing them as victims of forcible violation as well as agents of their own pleasure, whose dishonor was a product of their own will. A contradictory construction of this collective rape is also part of Namiquipan oral tradition. Men sometimes conclude their narrative of the attack on the pueblo with the following joke:

When the Villistas attacked the pueblo, they rounded up all the young women in the town square and they were going to rape them. When she heard what was happening, one ugly old hag who lived alone said to the other older women, "What a terrible thing! But if they're going to take one of us, they're going to have to take all of us!"

In this introduction my goal is to show how some of the central questions posed in this book emerged from the stories Namiquipans tell about their past: What are the political stakes in constructing the past? How does memory become a key site for the negotiation of identities and the making of community? What effects of meaning and power are secured by likening Villa to an Apache? How are ethnicity, class, and gender articulated? Why are women the medium through which men negotiate their own honor, and what does this entail for relations between and among men and women? How is the female body, with its coded vulnerability to rape, used as a trope for other "bodies" — for the nation, for the corporate community, for ethnic categories — whose boundaries, always in danger of being breached, are purportedly in need of male protection?

These and other questions led me to rethink the temporal frame of a project originally defined as a study of Namiquipans' involvement in the Revolution of 1910–20. What became clear in my initial weeks in the town was that Namiquipans' participation in and discourse about the Mexican Revolution could not be understood without an analysis of their prior involvement in frontier colonization and in protracted warfare against indigenous peoples, particularly the Apache. Through nearly three centuries of combat between indigenes and colonists, the Chihuahuan frontier of Mexico became a society organized for warfare, with specialists in violence, and a distinct discursive regime predicated upon a militarized construction of honor. In order to advance projects of territorial conquest and subjugation of indigenes, the state mobilized members of subaltern groups for warfare from the eighteenth through the nineteenth century. Many of these peasant warriors were *serranos*, or "people of the mountains," non-Indian inhabitants of Chihuahua's Sierra Madre. They included the men of Namiquipa, a rural pueblo that functioned as a military settlement colony from 1778 to 1886.

This book provides an account of the making of serrano communities on the northern frontier of Mexico from the colonial period to 1920. It explores the formation of the frontier, the development of Apache raiding there, the establishment of military settlement colonies in the region, the fate of the lands given to the colonists by the state in exchange for fighting the Apache, and the ideology of frontier warfare. To the end of encouraging a "warrior spirit" among serrano men, the state promoted a construction of gender and ethnic honor that predicated masculine reputation, access to land, and membership in a corporate community on valor and performance in warfare against "barbarians." In this ideology, "civilized" women became symbols of an ethnic and sexual purity that was purportedly threatened by the "onslaughts of the savages," and hence were held to be in need of male protection and defense.

From the late 1850s to 1910, interlinked processes of state formation and capitalist development transformed Mexican society. The one-time agents of "civilization," the militarized serrano peasants, subsequently became redefined by the state and elites as obstacles to "order" and "progress." The extensive corporate land grants and the relative political autonomy of serrano communities came under attack. In response, serranos constructed an ideology of resistance based on a social memory of the frontier past and on the notions of gender, ethnicity, and class. This ideology motivated their repeated confrontations with the state in the late nineteenth and early twentieth centuries and also shaped their participation, as part of Madero's and Villa's armies, in the 1910 Revolution.

This book traces the "thread of blood that links the Indian wars to the revolution," marking the continuities as well as the breaks that characterize it. Although the book focuses on Namiquipa, it is not a "community study" predicated on an assumed isomorphism between analytical, sociocultural, and spatial boundaries. Serrano communities were the product not only of local but also of regional, state, and global projects. Hence, rather than segregating local practices from regional to global processes, I demonstrate how the formation of serrano communities is affected by and effects broader negotiations of culture and power. Likewise, although I am concerned, above all, with telling the story of a particular time and place, I use this story as a point of departure for reflecting about more general theoretical concerns. Thus, this book is also about the articulation of power and identity in the processes of subjection, which entail constructions of subjectivity—in short, it is about hegemony.

Although hegemony has largely been theorized in relation to class, I argue that ethnicity and gender are also central to the practices of ruling, to the making of subaltern culture, and to the formation of subjects. Although I focus on the role of the state in the construction of hegemony, I also stress regional and local specificity in the processes of domination and subordination and examine the different ways in which subaltern peoples engage these processes, contesting and reformulating as well as accepting and reproducing them.

By paying attention to the articulation of gender, ethnicity, and class, and to the divergences and convergences of local and state projects over a long time span, I show the utility of integrating anthropological and historical forms of analysis. Such an anthropological history is centered on the complex negotiations of meaning and power that link as well divide dominant and subaltern, colonists and indigenous people, men and women, revolutionaries and elites, putting into question easy dichotimizations of powerful and powerless, of popular and official culture, of accommodation and resistance, of self and other.

The colonialist politics of a supposed contrast between the Western self and the non-Western other have been evident in my own experience as a Cuban living in the United States. My family history involves a link not only to the Cuban but also to the Mexican Revolution. My great-great uncle, Manuel Márquez Sterling, was the Cuban ambassador to Mexico at the time. He supported the revolution and tried to prevent the assassination of President Francisco Indalecio Madero. After Madero was assassinated, my great-great uncle took Madero's family to Cuba in a Cuban warship; my mother recently gave me a locket featuring a quetzal, which Madero's family had given to my great-great uncle. His book on the events he witnessed, *Los Ultimos Días del Presidente Madero*, is one of the classics of Mexican historiography.

In 1983, when I discussed my decision to do research on the revolution in Namiquipa with other anthropologists, some of them questioned why I would choose to work with peasant "Indian killers." The ethnic and class position of Namiquipans, in the eyes of these anthropologists, made them "people without culture," "rational," and hence "too transparent for study" (Rosaldo 1989:199). Peasants were boring. Why not "learn Nahuatl and study Aztec kingship?" suggested one distinguished professor.

One of my goals in working with non-Indian northern Mexicans has been to disrupt this opposition between "zones of cultural visibility and invisibility" on the ethnographic map and call into question the equation of culture and exoticized difference it presumes (Rosaldo 1989:198). My interest in anthropology is not motivated by "imperialist nostalgia" (Rosaldo 1989:69) but instead by a curiosity about the emancipatory visions of marginal people and the possibilities and limitations they articulate. Although the standpoints of the subaltern, as Haraway cautions, are not "innocent positions" (1991:191), there is scholarly and human value in "seeing from below." I prefer to communicate my own critical positioning vis-à-vis such local visions through irony and paradox rather than through totalizing monologue.

Popular emancipatory visions have rarely received the attention they merit in the historiography of resistance and revolution. With the exception of certain works (Alonso 1988a, 1988b; Scott 1976, 1977a, 1977b, 1985; Friedrich 1977, 1986; J. Comaroff 1985; Koreck 1988; Taussig 1980; Guha 1983; Mallon 1988; Nugent 1988, 1993; G. Smith 1989; Stern 1987; Joseph and Nugent, eds. 1994), an analysis of resistance as cultural struggle has been absent from much of the literature on peasant movements. In the wake of the Vietnam War, an inordinate amount of research was devoted to determining which peasants rebel, when, and why—a why concerned with generalizable, "objective" triggers rather than the "subjective" meanings given to protest by rebels (e.g., Paige 1975; Deal 1975; Waterbury 1975; Tutino 1986). What has been missing from the plethora of studies of peasant rebellion generated during the 1970s and 1980s is an understanding of how resistance is organized, rendered significant, and legitimated by those who rebel; the dominant tendency in the scholarship on peasant movements has been to portray the subjects of resistance as "people without culture."

The same opposition between the rational and the cultural motivates another influential approach to peasant resistance, derived in large part from the writings of Eric Hobsbawm. His distinction between "pre-political" and "political" forms of protest (1959) is informed by a teleological and essentialist notion of class struggle, which privileges the proletariat (and their party leaders) as the perfect subject-object of history while delegating the peasantry, characterized in this instance by too much "culture," to the backwaters of the past. In this book I write against the grain of the opposition between the symbolic and the utilitarian by paying attention to the reasons of culture and the culture of reason, arguing that subaltern discourses of protest implicitly recognize that power circulates throughout the social body and is not simply concentrated in government structures. Contesting the quotidian effects of power through discourses that are often rich in somatic metaphors, subaltern forms of resistance often focus on the constitution of social subjectivities, redefining the ways in which power is embodied. As such, they challenge hegemonic state projects and articulate a politics of social and cultural struggle.

The revolutionary potential of frontier peasants in particular was stressed by Wolf more than two decades ago (1969:270). He argued for the importance of understanding the "traditional" values and meanings that have motivated peasant resistance to the social and ideological dislocations engendered by processes that have revolutionized social life on a global level, namely, modern state formation and capitalist development. Paradoxically, Wolf concluded that "it is the very attempt of the middle and free peasant to remain traditional which makes him revolutionary" (1969:270). Insightful though it is, Wolf's thesis begs the question, for as more recent work suggests, the "traditional" itself needs to be redefined (Hall 1981; Hobsbawm and Ranger 1984). What I demonstrate in this book is that the "traditional" is a form of understanding and legitimating the present in relation to a past that is never passively reproduced but always actively produced in relation to the "modern" (Alonso 1988). Traditions are often articulated through what Bakhtin calls "epic genres," whose "constitutive feature is the transferral of the represented world into the past," a past that is presented as given and absolute (1981:30).

The frontier past the serranos fought to recover was not unmediated or given but idealized, revalued, and authorized in the conjunctures of resistance. Yet this utopian past was not wholly "invented" either. The investigation of frontier society and ideology I present here demonstrates how serrano resistance was shaped by historical experience, albeit an experience whose memory was not static but living, not unquestioned but contested, and hence responsive to changing circumstances and emergent struggles. What interests me is how the "traditional," as an interpretive mode, constructs its persuasiveness by effacing its own re-workings of memory. Drawing on Bakhtin's insights, I show that there is a correlation among the types of domination, ideologies, and genres of history, and the location in time of utopias.

The book is divided into two parts. Part 1 analyzes the making of serrano communities, the social organization of violence, and the ideology of warfare on the frontier in the eighteenth and nineteenth centuries. Chapter 1 develops a historical sociology of frontier violence, and chapters 2, 3, and 4 analyze the ideology of honor entailed in warfare, showing its centrality to serrano life and to the colonization of the frontier. I argue that without an analysis of the social relations, mode of organization, and ideology of frontier warfare, it is impossible to understand the mobilization, discourses, and leadership styles of the insurgent Chihuahuan peasantry.

Part 2 focuses on the macro-level processes of state formation and capitalist development that promoted the integration of the frontier into the nation and the world market in the nineteenth and twentieth centuries. I analyze the transformations in frontier society and specify the new forms of subjection-subjectivity they entailed for subaltern groups. I show that for the serranos, centralization and development resulted in reversals in status position and class situation, as well as in unacceptable redefinitions of forms of social identity. I delineate the modes of serrano resistance to these changes, focusing on violent and nonviolent, extraordinary and everyday forms of protest and insurgency, and demonstrate how serrano discourses of resistance were informed by a frontier ideology of honor and a utopian memory of the past.

The Frontier
Civilization and Barbarism

What Is the Frontier?

The inhabitants [of Chihuahua], principally those of the countryside, are more developed and stronger than those of the South of the Republic. Their ancestors were warriors who fought the barbaric Indians and the inclemencies [of the climate]; [the people of the countryside's] predilection for the use of arms and for horseback riding is a result of this heritage. They are excellent shots and gallant horsemen. The character of the population is of an uncommon and even rebellious independence.   Creel 1928:45–46; my translation

In the New World the frontier is conceived as a liminal space, betwixt and between savagery and civilization, a place where the struggle of human beings against the wilderness assumes a particularly harsh form, where society's domestication of nature is always contingent and threatened. As an outpost of the civilized polis, the frontier is viewed as lying at the margins of state power, between the laws of society and the freedoms of nature, between the imperatives of obedience and the refusals of defiance. The liminality of the frontier, its location on the creative margin between the wild and the social, makes it the locus of liberty and possibility. Frontier societies are viewed as less routinized and law abiding and more open to individual advancement and self-mastery. Hence the fascination of the frontier and the charismatic qualities frequently attributed to its settlers.

This New World construction of the periphery underlies both academic and native visions of the Mexican frontier. The "peculiarities" that distinguish the North and Northerners from the Center and its inhabitants are commonplaces in scholarly and folk discourses and are generally attributed to the region's frontier past.[1] For Chihuahuans these "peculiarities" are metonyms of an irreducible difference, one that makes the North "another country" (*otro país*) and Northerners a distinct people. Constantly contrasted with the "brownness" of Southerners, the "whiteness" of *norteños* is the visible index of what is viewed as a distinct, northern "nature." Relative to other Mexicans, *norteños* were and are considered to be brave, independent, rebellious, self-sufficient, and hardworking. Northern society was and is more democratic, egalitarian, and open to individual achievement.

Examples of this typification of norteño society and identity abound (e.g., Jones 1979; León-Portilla 1972; Zavala 1957; Weber 1982; Lister and Lister 1979). Significantly, Jordán entitles his history of Chihuahua *Chronicle of a Barbarian Country*, making plain that "barbarian is a synonym of force and will . . . of a supreme and invincible thirst for liberty" (1981:21; my translation). Norteño jokes about *chilangos* articulate the same vision.[2] And the National Action Party (PAN) has galvanized support among Northerners through the rhetorical manipulation of this construction of self and society.

Clearly, at one level this vision of the North as the limen between the natural and the social articulates the frontier's peripheral location vis-à-vis the center of state power. As such, it has been key to the political project of the state as well as to frontier people's resistance to central domination. Such stereotypes were integral to an expansionist ideology of conquest that legitimated the colonization of frontier territories and of the indigenous groups that lived there by defining these zones as "untamed" space. Moreover, subsequent attempts by the central state to integrate the frontier into the nation relied on a negative valuation of the "wildness" of the periphery. Ironically, frontier resistance to centralization was motivated by a positive valuation of the "wildness" of the periphery, which made the North the locus of liberty.

But ideology is not "false consciousness." These typifications of the North resonate with people's experience. As Eric Wolf has observed: "Frontier North and Indian South are two different worlds, with different color, smell, texture. The Mexican Republic straddles both, but the cultural gap between them continues to divide them to this day" (1959:9). What is needed is an analysis of frontier society and ideology that accounts for northern "peculiarity" in social and historical terms.[3]

By and large, frontier studies have been disappointing because of the weight given to environmental factors as the deus ex machina of society and history (e.g., Lattimore 1968; Wyman and Kroeber 1957; Miller and Steffen 1977). Analysis often proceeds by creating an elaborate metaphor that assimilates the social to the natural. For example, the democratic character of frontier society and the importance of personal autonomy as an ideal in the construction of social identity are attributed by Jordán (and others) to the openness and vastness of the landscape: "The mountain, the desert, or the sea forges independent wills. . . . That liberty of space and medium have consequences for personality itself. The climate puts its stamp on northern man—that of its force—and endows him with an equally concrete characteristic: his will. They are exigencies of the land and of the medium" (1981:10; my translation).[4] This metaphor is widely used to "explain" the development of a distinct frontier "ethos" and "mentality." Yet this very trope calls out for analysis. As Harvey notes, space is often treated "as a fact of nature, 'naturalized' through the assignment of common-sense everyday meanings" (1989: 203) that need to be questioned rather than reproduced uncritically.

What is required is a processual analysis that uncovers the formation of frontier peculiarities and reveals their embeddedness in a regionally specific set of social relations, discourses, and bodily practices, centrally motivated by the Spanish and Mexican states' projects of territorial conquest. A specific conception of space underwrote those projects; conflict between colonists and indigenes on the frontier was in part "over the proper sense of space that should be used to regulate social life and give meaning to concepts such as territorial rights" (Harvey 1989:203). This conception of space was key to the construction of subjectivity and subjection on the frontier.

A number of writers have emphasized that the distinctive process of conquest of indigenous groups on the frontier was the key factor in the shaping of norteño society (Wolf 1959; Jones 1979; León Portilla 1972; Zavala 1957; Carr 1973; Holden 1984; Orozco 1992). Indeed, this is the crux of the matter. But as Holden points out, little attention has been given to a precise identification of the consequences of endemic warfare for the structure of northern society (1984:2). And as Jones observes, the role of subaltern groups in frontier settlement and warfare has largely been ignored (1979:3-4, passim). Moreover, there has been almost no analysis of the effects of three centuries of warfare on the development of norteño ideology. In addition, the relationship between the social organization and the ideology of frontier warfare, and the subsequent resistance of frontier specialists in violence to the transformations engendered by processes of state formation and capitalist development still need to be investigated.

The Northern Frontier: Resistance and Revolution

Pancho Villa surges from another phenomenon, one which has not been very clearly understood. Which phenomenon? The frontier. (Aguilar Mora in Campbell 1985:8)

In an article on political dissent in Chihuahua during the 1980s, Enrique Krauze remarks, "Exactly one century ago, the war [with the Apache] ended [in Chihuahua]; but not the culture of warfare" (1986: 34). Krauze argues that centuries of frontier conflict shaped northern society in fundamental ways, producing a distinct regional identity, social vision, and culture of warfare that have persisted to the present and continue to underwrite resistance to the Center.

Several writers have suggested that the involvement of the northern provinces in the Revolution of 1910–20 was motivated and shaped by a frontier past that made norteño society distinct from the rest of Mexico (Zavala 1957; León-Portilla 1972; Carr 1973; Holden 1984; Aguilar Camín 1979; Orozco 1992). For example, Jones states that the North's frontier past predisposed it to become "the guardian of liberty and promoter of the democratic way of life." He adds that

> individualism, regional isolation, village orientation, resistance to outside control, innovations and a reliance upon themselves . . . all set the colonists of northern New Spain apart from people elsewhere. The . . . intermarriage among classes and races, and dependence on one another also contributed to the homogeneity and feeling of separateness of frontier people. It is, therefore, understandable that certain communities and provinces in the northern region stood in opposition to what their citizens thought was an unfair, tyrannical influence from outside sources, an effort to regulate their affairs and lifestyle. The North became the bulwark of resistance . . . this region played an enormous role, furnishing leaders, arms, and ideas in the initiation, continuation and achievement of the Mexican Revolution in the twentieth century. (Jones 1979:253)

In the case of the popular movement based in Chihuahua, however, some scholars have begun to systematically investigate this connection. Early on, Katz hypothesized that the revolutionary mobilization of peasants from Chihuahuan "military settlement colonies" [5] such as Namiquipa was an outcome of the transformation of the frontier into the border at the end of the nineteenth century. These peasant-warriors had played a key role in the conquest of the frontier and had "acquired military skills, arms as well as the consciousness of constituting a special elite fighting against the 'barbarians' " (Katz 1976b:67–68). Knight also pointed out the importance of the frontier military tradition of this revolutionary peasantry, noting that serrano resistance displayed many of the characteristics of frontier society (1986:I:115–27). Until recently there was a lack of research at the regional and local levels, which was needed to develop these insights; despite their key role in the conquest of the frontier and in the revolution, the peasant military colonists of Chihuahua were largely ignored by historians and anthropologists alike. That situation has changed in the wake of the publication of recent studies following Katz (1981), including Alonso 1988a, 1988b, 1988c, 1992a, 1992b; González 1988; Lloyd 1983, 1988; Koreck 1988; Nugent 1988, 1989, 1990, 1991, 1993; Nugent and Alonso 1994; Osorio 1988, 1990. The voluminous writings of Calzadíaz Barrera provide information that is corroborated by this more recent research at local and regional levels.

As Carr observes, "macro-level analysis of national politics, including studies of formal institutions," long eclipsed regional- and local-level studies of the Mexican Revolution (Carr 1980:3). Beginning in the 1970s and 1980s, however, there has been a burgeoning of local and regional studies of the revolution, reflecting a general trend in Mexican historiography (see Fowler-Salamini 1993), heralded, in part, by Luis González's invitation to "microhistory" (1974). Key anthologies and book-length regional and local studies of the revolution include Aguilar Camín 1979; Brading 1980; Falcón 1984; Fowler-Salamini 1978; Friedrich 1977, 1986; Jacobs 1983; Joseph 1982; Joseph and Nugent (eds.) 1994; Katz 1981, 1988; Nugent 1988, 1993; Osorio 1990; Schryer 1980; Benjamin and Wasserman 1990; and Wasserman 1984. Womack 1968, Cockcroft 1968, and Meyer 1967 were exceptions to the earlier trend toward national-level studies, and Gilly 1971 was an important departure from the predominant "political" and "diplomatic" historiography of the revolution.

The results of regional- and local-level studies have challenged the earlier characterization of the revolution as a unified national event, lending strength instead to the argument that it is best viewed as a concatenation of complex sociocultural and historical processes with specific regional and local modalities. Concerned above all with the articulation of popular culture, revolution, and state formation, such studies have generated "revisionist" and even "postrevisionist" interpretative trends in the historiography of the revolution (Joseph and Nugent, eds., 1994:3–23). Revisionists (see Bailey 1978; Carr 1980; Fowler-Salamini 1993; Joseph and Nugent, eds., 1994; Miller 1988) have critiqued the earlier populist vision of the revolution, arguing that instead of vindicating popular agrarian grievances, it led to the cooptation and defeat of popular movements by elites and the postrevolutionary state. Yet despite the value of their critique of modern state formation in Mexico, by "centering their analyses on the relationship between the national state and regional leaders and movements (without extending the analysis down to the local level) . . . [revisionists] have . . . 'brought the state back in,' but left the people out" (Joseph and Nugent, eds., 1994:11). In contrast to revisionists, postrevisionists (see essays in Joseph and Nugent, eds., 1994) make popular social memory and discourses of resistance central to their analyses while eschewing the romanticism of the populists. Postrevisionists recognize the real setbacks experienced by popular movements in Mexico without depriving these of all agency; they trace the complexities entailed by the articulation of popular struggles and the state, identifying the forms of negotiation deployed by the subaltern. This book is part of the postrevisionist trend, but it is distinguished from most postrevisionist works by its focus on gender, as well as by its integration of anthropological and historical perspectives and by its long *durée* temporal framework.

CHAPTER ONE

The Social Organization of Warfare

Known as the land of war (*tierra de guerra*), the Chihuahuan frontier was the locus of endemic warfare between colonists and indigenes from the seventeenth through the late nineteenth century. Perhaps more than other frontiers in Latin America, Chihuahua attracted, produced, and supported specialists in violence. The social organization and ideological construction of violence became key to the reproduction of frontier society.

As Baretta and Markoff point out, violence is often naturalized as "brute force" and thus is seen to require little or no analytical elaboration. Hence,

> sufficient consideration is not usually given to the varied and subtle effects of the ways in which the capacity for violence is structured in social life. But consequences follow for any society from the presence or absence of full-time military specialists, from the forms of their organization, from the regional distribution of control of organized violence, from the advantages and disadvantages associated with the use of force, and from the norms associated with such use. (1978:587)

Clearly, an analysis of the social and ideological structuring of violence is a prerequisite for an understanding of frontier society and history.[1]

For more than two centuries the North was a society organized for warfare. Violent conflict between invaders and indigenes was one of the fundamental factors in the formation of norteño society and ideology (Holden 1984; Florescano 1969; Zavala 1957; Jordán 1981; Orozco 1992).

Geographical, Social, and Historical Background

Frontier North and Indian South are not physically separated by any major geographical barrier, although an increasing aridity divides the two regions: "A great dry land stretches from the Twenty-second Parallel to the borders of the United States and beyond" (Wolf 1959:8). Straddling the desert are two great mountain chains, the Sierra Madre Occidental and the Sierra Madre Oriental, which sweep down from the north to meet at the isthmus of Tehuantepec (Thomas 1941:3). In the valleys and on the margins of the mountains, as well as along the rivers and streams that cross the plateau, there is a limited amount of land suitable for agriculture. No exception to the general topography of the North, Chihuahua is 45 percent desert, 30 percent dry grassland and oak savanna, and 25 percent pine forest and subtropical deciduous forest. Only 5 percent of its land area is suitable for crops (Wasserman 1980:28).

At the time of the Spanish conquest, the arid and mountainous North was peopled by numerous seminomadic groups of hunters and gatherers whom the Aztec collectively labeled Chichimec, or "Sons of the Dog" (Wolf 1959:9). For the Spaniards the conquest of these indigenous peoples was to present far more serious difficulties than those posed by the sedentary agricultural groups of the Central Valley, who were already subjects of a state. The northern expansion of the Hispanic frontier[2] generated centuries of warfare with indigenes whose expertise in violence presented a serious obstacle to Spanish and Mexican colonization. Although the Spaniards had extensive experience in frontier warfare, obtained in the Moorish Reconquest, and the Mexicans were heirs to centuries of frontier violence, the Apache continued to raid Chihuahuan settlements and haciendas for livestock and captives until 1886, when they were officially "pacified" and confined to prisons and reservations in the United States.

The Hispanic colonization of what is today Chihuahua[3] began in the second half of the sixteenth century (Almada 1955:26-27). For the first one hundred years, however, settlement was largely confined to the mining region of Santa Barbara and to the adjoining agricultural and stock ranching valley of San Bartolomé, located in the south near the border with Durango (Jones 1979:83-84; Lister and Lister 1979:22-29). In the seventeenth century the efforts of the state, the church, and the colonists to "reduce" the Indians to religion, vassalage, and civilization triggered decades of Indian uprisings. By the turn of the century the indigenous peoples of Chihuahua and their Apache allies had succeeded in destroying most of the missions and settlements beyond the southern part of the state (Lister and Lister 1979:44–50, 58–59; Almada 1955: 54–88; Jordán 1981:97–114, 125–53; Hughes 1935:334–63). Thus what is now Chihuahua was largely colonized in the eighteenth and nineteenth centuries (Jones 1979:89). The exposition and analysis that follow will be restricted to this time frame.

The colonization of Chihuahua was spurred by the same collective projects and personal ambitions that motivated the conquest of the Central Valley. The promise of new sources of wealth, and of the Indian laborers that its production required, initially attracted entrepreneurs to the north. That "disease of the heart" for which Cortés maintained gold was "the specific remedy" drove elite adventurers to spearhead the northward advance in search of precious metals and the wealth and honor that their discovery conferred (Wolf 1959:161; Zavala 1957:40; Almada 1955:26–27; Lister and Lister 1979:19–22).

As deposits of silver and gold were located, *haciendas*, large estates, and *ranchos*, smaller properties, sprang up. On the frontier, title to haciendas or ranchos could easily be obtained by purchase from the Crown at relatively low rates (Myres 1979; Zavala 1957:41–43). The vast arid plains of the North provided excellent pasture and spurred the immigration to Chihuahua of cattle ranchers who had to compete with farmers in the Central Valley for land.

Cattle haciendas were particularly suited to northern conditions. These extensive productive enterprises required little capital investment or economic infrastructure. Moreover, they could operate with a small labor force because the hardy, half-wild stock did not require much care (Myres 1979). Established to supply the mining communities, these landed properties combined the large-scale production of beef and hides with the raising of agricultural crops. Thus a distinct regional economy founded on mining, stock raising, and agriculture quickly developed on the frontier (Florescano:1969:67; Lister and Lister 1979:37; Carr 1973:323; West 1949). The economic interests of the elite usually combined investments in these complementary spheres of production.

For the Spanish state the colonization of the frontier represented a key source of precious metals for the metropole and of revenues for the royal treasury (Wolf 1959:162, 187). After independence the mineral wealth of Chihuahua continued to be of interest to the new Mexican state. Moreover, Chihuahua acquired an important strategic value. Located on the new border between Mexico and the "Colossus of the North," which had taken half the national territory, Chihuahua was now a frontier in both senses of the term.

For the church the frontier promised a new harvest of souls to be "reduced" to religion and the Christian life, as well as the chance to acquire property, which made it one of the biggest landowners in the country until the application of the liberal laws of *desamortización* in the 1860s (Wolf 1959:165). During the colonial period Franciscan and Jesuit missionaries flocked to the North, ready to become martyrs and re-enact the sacrifice of Christ in order to wrest heathen souls from the devil, so glorifying the one true faith. For the Spanish state the church promised to serve as an important instrument in the pacification of indigenes and their transformation into subjects.

Yet the implementation of these diverse projects of church, state, and entrepreneurs was to be limited by the resistance of indigenous groups to conquest. The distinctiveness of frontier society is largely due to the fact that the Indians of the North fought tenaciously and with some success against the imposition of colonial projects. Constant warfare with indigenes was to result in the redefinition of these projects and in the development of a society different from what the conquerors had envisioned.

Civilization, the Mother of Barbarism

[Their] rapacity toward the whites has continued to be the same: because it is the effect of a war of extermination that a barbarous policy undertook with more valor than success. (Humboldt 1966:187, my translation)

In a sense the Apaches held the Spanish frontiersmen in tributary vassalage, extracting from the settlers and their subject Indians a never-ending subsidy. (Moorhead 1968:15)

To cite Lattimore's celebrated phrase, on the Chihuahuan frontier "civilization was the mother of barbarism." First, the conquest of indigenous peoples and their "reduction" to "civilization" was legitimated by constructing them as "barbarians." Second, although indigenes such as the Apache had engaged in warfare and raiding prior to the conquest, it was the disruption of native society and the displacement of native groups caught between the expansion of the Anglo-American and His-

panic frontiers that turned them into specialists in violence. Conflict between colonists and indigenes was spurred by their different conceptions
of space and the notions of property they underwrote. The Apache and
the Comanche fought to preserve a way of life that was based on transhumancy and, eventually, on raiding. The notion of the polis deployed by
the Spanish and Mexican states presumed the existence of fixed boundaries that differentiated what was inside—the sovereign property of the
Crown and later the nation—from what was outside. Moreover, the
state and the frontier colonists could not conceive of a form of living,
working, and governing that was not tied to settled life in pueblos, cities,
and haciendas (Orozco 1992:17). Third, Hispanic and Anglo-American
colonists furnished the Apache with more efficient means of warfare,
as well as with markets for the livestock, captives, and booty obtained
from raiding.

Throughout the seventeenth century the indigenous peoples of Chihuahua, such as the Toboso, the Manso, the Conchos, and the Tarahumara, were in a nearly constant state of "rebellion" engendered by the
advance of the colonial frontier and by the processes of subjection that
the colonists, the church, and the state tried to impose on them (Lister
and Lister 1979:44–50, 58–9; Almada 1955:54–88; Jordán 1981:97–114,
125–53; Hughes 1935:334–63). Although by the end of the seventeenth
century these groups had been "pacified," their potential for renewed
rebellion and for an alliance with the Apache made them a constant
threat to society in the colonists' eyes. Moreover, they were never successfully transformed into docile subjects who could be integrated into
the dominant society and economy. The Conchos and the Toboso were
exterminated, and the Tarahumara began a process of "passive rebellion" that continues to this day, a flight into the inaccessible reaches of
the Sierra Madre Occidental, where they have been able to maintain a
relative autonomy and live a life apart (Nugent 1982).

For the Spaniards and the Mexicans, the "pacification" of the Apache
and the Comanche proved a much more difficult, long-term enterprise
than the "reduction" of the indigenous groups of Chihuahua. In the
eighteenth century the Apache ranged over a huge expanse of territory
extending mostly to the north of the current U.S.–Mexican border, from
the upper reaches of the Colorado River in Texas to the headwaters of
the Santa Cruz River in Arizona (Moorhead 1968:3). From this heart-
land the Apache attacked the frontier provinces to the south of the current border, establishing *rancherías* in the mountains that they used as

temporary bases for raiding haciendas, pueblos, and convoys of travelers and merchants, obtaining captives, livestock, weapons, and booty (Smith 1962, 1963, 1965).

Spanish and Mexican military forces and settlers were at a great disadvantage in warfare with the Apache.[4] The frontier was too extensive and settlements were too scattered to be efficiently patroled and defended by soldiers and colonists (Worcester 1951:1, 5), and after 1848 the Apache could use the border to their advantage, eluding Mexican pursuit by interning themselves in the United States and vice versa. Fighting skills and bravery became critical dimensions of masculine prestige in Apache society. Resistance to conquest, plus the means of warfare obtained from the enemy, produced some of the most formidable warriors in the New World, fighters who knew how to use the tactics of terror and guerrilla warfare to paralyze their enemies (Ball 1970, 1980; Smith 1963:41; Faulk 1979:42). Until frontier soldiers and settlers learned to fight like Apaches, their strategies were ineffective against these indigenous guerrillas, who moved silently over familiar terrain and were able to surprise frontier outposts, settlements, and haciendas before dispersing quickly into the shelter of the mountains.

Although Apache raids on Chihuahua began in the late seventeenth century, they were sporadic until 1748, when they intensified to the point of posing a serious threat to frontier colonization.[5] A form of resistance to colonialism, raiding was seen as a means of taking vengeance against the invaders (Ball 1970, 1980; Terrazas Sánchez 1973:112, 134–37). Also, by the middle of the eighteenth century, the products of raiding had become critical to the reproduction of Apache society. Through this form of primitive accumulation, the Apache were able to meet their subsistence needs as well as obtain the horses and weapons that warfare required.

From 1748 to 1790 the Apache did indeed hold the colonists in "tributary vassalage." In Nueva Vizcaya alone, between 1748 and the early 1770s, the Apache killed more than four thousand people; losses in livestock exceeded twelve million pesos in value (Worcester 1951:10).

Contemporary accounts of the damages and devastation caused by Apache raids present a bleak picture of frontier economy and society. O'Conor's report of 1776 devotes fourteen pages to a "narrative of the destruction, thefts, deaths and other types of damages" inflicted by the "barbarians" on the province of Nueva Vizcaya (cited in González Flores and Almada, eds., 1952:20–34). Thousands of deaths; the abandonment of settlements, haciendas, and ranchos; huge losses in livestock; paralysis of the mining industry; and the decline of commerce were the results of only three decades of Apache attacks. And the situation did not improve. In 1783 the "most prominent" settlers—*hacendados* and *rancheros*—of the Basúchil Valley, the breadbasket of western Chihuahua, complained of "the unhappy state in which the Indian enemies have placed those who inhabit this frontier . . . with their continual insults—deaths and thefts of horses, mules, cattle, and the rest . . . and the growing insolvency in which we find ourselves."[6] These landed proprietors calculated that in Basúchil the Apache had killed thirty people, taken fourteen captives, and "stolen" 1,516 head of livestock in an eighteen-month period.

During the eighteenth century colonial policy toward the "barbarians" oscillated between a war of extermination and an attempt to obtain a relative if temporary truce in hostilities by supplying the Apache with daily rations of food and liquor, as well as horses and arms, and settling them in reservations near military outposts.[7] Deploying a utilitarian logic, the colonial state tried to turn the Apache into subjects by fostering their "private interests," taking advantage of existing needs and creating new ones that could be satisfied only through dependency on the Spaniards (Gálvez in Worcester 1951:100–3). By the turn of the century, a combination of warfare and inducements to peace had worked; from 1790 to 1831 the majority of Apache groups stopped raiding in Chihuahua (Escudero 1834:249; Almada 1939:8–9; Faulk 1979:74; Moorhead 1968:283–90).

Three factors motivated the renewal of Apache and Comanche raids on Chihuahua in 1831. First, the newly independent Mexican state could not support the professional military establishment maintained by the Spanish Crown on the frontier; moreover, four decades of peace had led to a decline in the settler population's fighting skills and "warrior spirit" (Escudero 1834:249–50). Second, neither the national nor the local treasuries could afford the cost of maintaining the Apache in their reservations: rations were cut and colonial peace pacts were broken (Escudero 1834:249–50). Third, the colonial peace policy of fostering new "needs" among the Apache backfired after independence. Beginning in the 1830s, the Apache found a ready market among American traders for the captives, livestock, and booty taken on raids in Mexico. Through barter with American merchants, the Apache could satisfy these needs and interests while conserving their freedom from Mexican domination (Weber 1982:95-100; Smith 1962:32; Smith 1963:34; Martínez Caraza 1983:128-29).

For these reasons Apache raids on Chihuahua were more intense after independence than during the colonial period. Beginning in the 1840s, Apache attacks on Chihuahua became so frequent that American mercenary George Evans was prompted to remark, "The whole country seems to be governed by the Apache Nation, and those pretending to rule dare not say that they are masters" (cited in Smith 1965:134). Mexican authorities blamed the U.S. government and military, whom they believed were aiding the Apache in their war against the Mexicans to the end of annexing the frontier provinces (Martínez Caraza 1983:130-31). The Apache managed to gain territory and were able to maintain permanent camps in the mountains of Chihuahua (Terrazas 1905:101-4).

In the mid-1860s settlers succeeded in driving the Apache from their permanent camps, and raiding in Chihuahua diminished (Terrazas 1905: 99, 105). Yet the Apache continued to raid in Mexico, sweeping down from the United States to attack Chihuahuan settlements and haciendas until 1886, when they were finally defeated by the combined military actions of Mexicans and Americans (Terrazas 1905; Almada 1939; Chávez 1939; Martínez Caraza 1983).

The Transformation of Colonial Projects

The projects of the cattle ranchers and miners who came to Chihuahua in search of sources of wealth and Indian labor became redefined on the frontier. Indian resistance successfully prevented implantation of the servile forms of labor that prevailed in the Central Valley (Florescano 1969:63; Wolf 1959:193-94; Zavala 1957:37; Jones 1979:31; Jordán 1981:93; Orozco 1992:28). "Free" wage labor in New Spain originated in the northern mines, where it predominated by the seventeenth century (West 1949:47-52). Indian rebellions, but above all the depredations of the Apache, limited the expansion of landed properties and curtailed the growth of the cattle and mining industries until the latter part of the nineteenth century. Although indigenous groups did lose their best lands to the colonists, massive encroachments by hacendados on the lands of Hispanic peasants were postponed until the 1860s. The social organization and ideological construction of warfare empowered armed peasants and hacienda workers, who resisted what they perceived as abuses or denials of their right to honor. As a result, until the end of the Apache wars, relations of production in the North assumed a less exploitative form than elsewhere in Mexico, and the worst abuses of debt peonage were mitigated (Carr 1973:323; Orozco 1992:28).

The church's harvest of Indian souls proved relatively meager on the Chihuahuan frontier. Efforts to reduce the indigenes to the Christian life were largely a failure. Moreover, the scarcity of priests on the frontier fostered the emergence of a folk Catholicism among the Hispanic peasantry that held the potential for conflict with church orthodoxy and its representatives. As a result, the church never became as strong a political force in the North as it was in the Center (Carr 1973:323). Moreover, it came to play only a secondary economic role in the North. Lands were almost exclusively in secular hands, and there were no great ecclesiastical properties as in the rest of Mexico (Carr 1973:322).

Although the Spanish state's ambitions for extracting wealth from the Chihuahuan mines were not wholly disappointed, the Crown paid a high price for the maintenance of a military establishment capable of providing a minimum of security on the frontier (Moorhead 1968, 1975; Faulk 1979; Gálvez in Worcester 1951:97; Croix in Thomas 1941). Moreover, the indigenes did not become the docile subjects that figured in the absolutist state's vision of a planned New World utopia. As a result, the Crown was forced to offer generous terms to settlers of any race or class who were willing to "populate" frontier regions and serve as models of "civilization" for the "barbarous Indians" (Jones 1979). After independence the Mexican state continued to honor these privileged terms of settlement until the diminishing of hostilities with the Apache. As we shall see, these settlers' relatively privileged access to the means of production, their ideology of ethnic and military honor, and their role in the social organization of warfare hardly made them docile subjects. The armed peasants of the Chihuahuan frontier were always potential rebels.

In short, neither the elite nor the church nor the state managed to secure the same dominance on the Chihuahuan frontier that they exercised in the rest of the society. To a great extent, this was the result of the Indian wars and the forms of organization and ideological constructions they generated.

Barbarism, the Mother of Civilization: The Social Organization of Warfare

A reciprocal specialization in violence developed among indigenes and invaders on the Chihuahuan frontier. Warfare between Indians and colonists involved not only an exchange of weapons but also of techniques, disciplines, forms of organization, and values. "Barbarism" was the mother of "civilization" in several respects.

As in Apache society, the line between warfare and everyday life became blurred: settlers became part-time military specialists, and upon retirement soldiers received land grants and became settlers. The colonists learned to fight like the indigenes. The colonial and Mexican states' attempts to impose conventional military disciplines on frontier warriors were a failure because such strategies were ineffective against the guerrilla tactics deployed by the Apache. Instead, frontier fighting skills were learned from the Apache, as well as from day-to-day activities such as hunting, livestock tracking, roping, and herding.

Even during the colonial period, when the state bore the main responsibility for warfare, violence developed a charismatic form of organization that was never fully brought under state control. Career officers with no experience in frontier warfare were poor commanders. Like the Apache and the Comanche they fought, frontiersmen became military leaders because of their extraordinary valor and fighting skills, not because of state-conferred mandates. Moreover, both full- and part-time specialists in violence gained a great measure of autonomy in the conduct of warfare. No fully bureaucraticized army emerged on the Chihuahuan frontier. Neither the colonial nor the Mexican state secured a true monopoly of force. Fighting skills and valor became central to the construction of masculine honor within frontier society; ironically, the "indomitable independence" and the "love of liberty" for which the colonists castigated the Indians came to be prized by the invaders themselves.

Frontier Warfare in the Colonial Period

The support of full-time military specialists was integral to the colonial state's attempt to secure control over warfare between colonists and indigenes on the frontier. During the eighteenth century the colonial state augmented the number of presidial soldiers in the northern provinces; whereas in 1729 frontier forces comprised only 734 men, by 1789 the number had increased to more than 3,000 (Moorhead 1968:88-90). Like the regular Spanish army, the frontier forces that garrisoned fortified outposts known as *presidios* were paid by the Crown. However, the frontier military differed from the regular army in several respects.

Full-time military specialists were not career soldiers but men recruited from the frontier provinces: they "were neither elite troops nor raw recruits but hard-bitten, home-grown *vaqueros* who were at ease in the saddle . . . and accustomed to the cruel and unconventional tactics of Indian warfare" (Moorhead 1975:178) Moreover, whereas recruitment to the Spanish army was limited to men of "honorable" origins, those of "infamous" racial descent—*mestizos* and *mulatos*—were admitted to the frontier forces, and Indian auxiliaries were used by presidial troops (Moorhead 1975:182-84; Tjarks 1979).

Membership in the presidial forces furnished access to social honor. In the words of Captain Zebulon M. Pike, an American military spy who was in Chihuahua in 1807, a frontier soldier "considers himself upon an equality with most of the citizens and infinitely superior to the lower class, and not unfrequently you see men of considerable fortune marrying the daughters of sergeants and corporals" (Pike in Coues 1895:796). By fighting the Apache, subaltern groups were able to achieve military honor on the frontier and to improve their status position. Furthermore, upon retirement soldiers became eligible for land grants in the communities where they served; they were able to acquire small properties and improve their class situation. For example, Francisco Vásquez, who was the *alférez* of the Segunda Compañía Volante (Second Flying Company) of Namiquipa, received the Rancho de Aranzazú upon retirement in 1785.[8]

In principle, frontier forces operated under a special body of military law prescribed by the state, which differed from that of the regular army (Moorhead 1968:87; Moorhead 1975:27-95; Gálvez in Worcester 1951; Faulk 1979:67-78; Croix in Thomas 1941). Nevertheless, in practice, legal regulation of warfare was largely ignored on the frontier. While contemporary observers praised the extraordinary valor and horsemanship of frontier troops, they continually lamented the irregularity, the disorganization, the lack of discipline, and the poor subordination of these forces.[9] As Bernardo de Gálvez, the Mexican viceroy, noted in the late 1780s, frontier fighters did not evince the "subordination" of regular soldiers. Instead, they demonstrated "a contempt for [royal] regulations . . . insofar as these bind and subject. The laws, the pragmatics, the prohibitions have no force or are lukewarmly observed. . . . This is an evil difficult to remedy today because these people, reared in liberty and used to independence, are no longer in a state to suffer with resignation the rigor of the laws." [10]

Not only legal regulations but also conventional military disciplines and strategies were ignored by frontier forces (Pike in Coues 1895: 796–97). Frontier warriors learned to fight like their enemies, attacking "without regularity or concert, shouting, halloing and firing their carbines" (Pike in Coues 1895:797). [11] In short, state attempts at legal-rational regulation of the frontier military were largely a failure.

Officers achieved their position through military charisma, [12] and although the state ratified their leadership, it was not the primary source of legitimacy. Moreover, the military leaders were relatively egalitarian in their exercise of authority and respectful of their subordinates' rights to pride and honor. As Gálvez noted, frontier soldiers, "like all men of spirit," were "extremely punctilious" about their honor: officers were obliged "to address soldiers as equals in all conversations." [13] Any "insulting threat" issued by a superior provoked the "defiance" of subalterns, and officers lacked the means of punishing such insubordination. The camaraderie of members of a charismatic military community, of equals before death, prevailed over the formal inequalities of a state-imposed military hierarchy.

Outnumbered by the Apache and the Comanche, the permanent military forces maintained by the Crown were never adequate to the task of frontier defense; whereas in the 1770s it was estimated that the Apache had a fighting strength of 5,000 men, the presidial forces did not reach 3,000 (Worcester 1951:18; Moorhead 1975:73, 91). Moreover, the Apache's hit-and-run guerrilla tactics required that all points on the frontier be defended. To this end, the state took measures to militarize the population and to transform subaltern groups and classes— above all, the free peasants—into part-time specialists in violence.

Evidence of the importance of the role played by civilians in warfare is provided by Pike's computation of the total military strength of Nueva Vizcaya in 1807. Pike estimated that there were only 1,100 "regular troops" in the province (in Coues 1895:793). However, of a population of approximately 200,000 civilians, 13,000 were armed men, 5,000 of whom possessed firearms and 8,000 of whom had only bows, arrows, and lances (Pike in Coues 1895:764, 793). [14] Nueva Vizcaya had more armed citizens than any other Mexican province, and most of these were probably concentrated in Chihuahua, since according to contemporary sources, Durango was relatively free of Apache attacks.

If the colonial state's ability to impose a legal-rational form of systematization on the frontier army was minimal, its capacity to regulate the organization of part-time military specialists was even more limited. The role of free peasants in the settlement and conquest of the frontier has been neglected in the historiography of the North (Jones 1979; Nugent 1994). As part-time military specialists, these peasants played an important—if understudied—part in frontier warfare (Jones 1979; Holden 1984; Nugent 1994). Under the administration of Teodoro de Croix, military governor of the Provincias Internas (1776–83), the role of peasants in frontier defense was expanded. In order to reinforce the line of presidial garrisons with an inner cordon of military outposts, Croix established a series of "military settlements" populated by peasants (Croix in Thomas 1941:127–30; DePalo 1973:224–25).

Through a decree issued in November of 1778, five peasant military colonies—Janos, Casas Grandes, Galeana, Cruces, and Namiquipa—were established in northwestern Chihuahua, one of the areas most subject to Apache raids.[15] Located in a high valley of the Sierra Madre Occidental that is watered by the Santa María River (see map 1), Namiquipa was the site of an abandoned Franciscan mission to the Conchos Indians; in 1778 it was populated by a few Indian families.[16] Local church records indicate that these families, many of them Tarahumara, lived in a *pueblo de indios*, which continued to have a separate existence even after the establishment of the new military colony. In order to attract "civilized" settlers, extremely generous terms were offered to prospective colonists by the colonial state.

Like the Indian pueblos of the Center, these peasant military colonies were "closed corporate communities."[17] Corporate property rights to more than 112,000 hectares were accorded to each pueblo by the state. "Sons of the pueblo" had joint rights to the land grant as a whole and to common pasture and woodlands. *Jefes de familia*, male nuclear family and household heads vested with traditional patriarchal authority, had rights over individual agricultural and house plots. Local authorities had jurisdiction over the pueblo's land. They were responsible for the distribution of agricultural and house lots, as well as water rights, and for the regulation of collective uses of *ejido*, or common land. Equal rights to land were to be given to all settlers, regardless of status or class.

Birth was a key criterion for access to land and for membership in

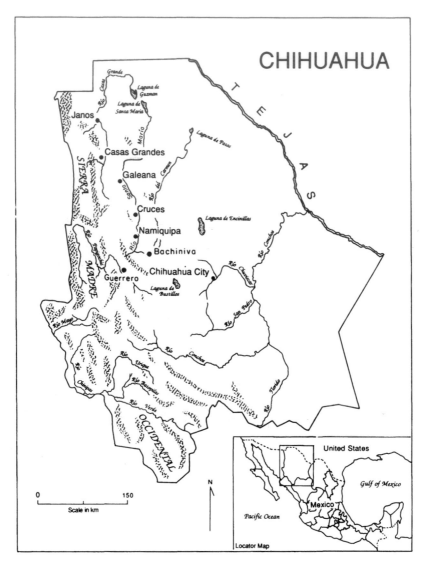

Map 1. Namiquipa is in a high valley of the Sierra Madre Occidental that is watered by the Santa María River. Map reprinted with permission from Daniel Nugent, *Spent Cartridges of Revolution: An Anthropological History of Nami-quipa, Chihuahua*, p. 10 (University of Chicago Press, 1995).

the community; kinship was one of the principles for establishing land rights, which were transmissible by inheritance. Locality also defined access to the means of production, since *originarios*, original colonists and their descendants, were to be preferred over *foraneos*, or outsiders, in the internal distribution and sale of lands.

After the first ten years colonists were free to buy or sell lands. Hence, land rights could also be obtained by purchase. However, the devasta tions of the Apache wars left settlers with few opportunities for accumulation. The internal market in land was highly limited until the late 1850s, and economic differentiation within the community was minimized. On the whole, differences in wealth were linked to the life and economic cycles of peasant households. Young married males who were just starting out as independent producers and who had no adult sons to share agricultural tasks had fewer animals and probably less land than their elders, who had a lifetime of productive activity behind them.

The state endowed these peasants with other privileges, including financial subsidies, loans of agricultural tools and work animals, and tax exemptions. In return for these honors, settlers had to fulfill military obligations to the state. Membership in these peasant military colonies and corporate as well as individual rights to land were contingent on fighting against the Apache and in defense of the state.

Although according to the founding charter, peasants were to be given title to their individual holdings, in practice this was not done.[18] Rather, family heads had *derechos de posesión* (rights of possession) to specific plots, usufruct rights to common pasture and woodlands, and property rights only as members of a corporate community. For these militarized peasants, rights to land did not emanate from legal titles but instead from membership in a community, from the uninterrupted possession and continuous working of the land, and from the fulfillment of military obligations.

Frontier army forces were assigned to some of these military settlements; for example, the Second Flying Company was stationed at Namiquipa. Peasant settlers were obliged by the terms of their land grants to cooperate with the presidial forces and came to play an important role in frontier defense as they became integrated into a charismatic military community. Local parish records indicate that the line between soldiers and settlers became blurred: peasants became militarized and soldiers developed strong links with civilians by marrying into peasant families and by becoming settlers upon retirement.

In short, during the colonial period civilians, largely members of subaltern groups and classes, came to play an important role in frontier defense. By linking military obligations to land rights, the state was able to militarize the peasants of communities such as Namiquipa and to transform them into part-time specialists in violence. These peasant-warriors became both producers and destroyers, life givers and life takers. Settler participation in warfare was either self-organized and financed or supervised and regulated by presidial captains who enjoyed a great deal of autonomy from the state in the conduct of warfare. The charismatic organization of violence evident in the regular frontier army also characterized civilian forms of participation in warfare.

In contrast to subaltern groups and classes, the economic elite played a limited role in fighting the indigenes, although some of the well-to-do did join the frontier army or the militia corps. The dominant classes' main contribution to warfare was financial. Subsidies from rich merchants, miners, and hacendados to the state or to self-organized groups of frontier settlers helped to defray the costs of warfare (DePalo 1973: 231, 234). In addition, hacendados sometimes armed certain of their workers, particularly the cowboys, and maintained small nuclei of part-time military specialists on their estates. In 1769 the government of Nueva Vizcaya had authorized landed proprietors to arm a minimum of ten workers who could act as a security force to protect livestock from Apache raids (Almada 1955:121). The correspondence of the Hacienda de Encinillas suggests that some workers on this estate were armed at least part of the time. Access to arms empowered the workers and enabled them to resist abuses by administrators.[19]

Nevertheless, Chihuahuan hacendados did not maintain large private armies, as some have assumed.[20] On the one hand, the economic resources of the landed elite had been decimated by the Indian wars. On the other hand, the general scarcity of labor, as well as the reluctance of many workers to undertake the risks of service on those haciendas that bore the brunt of Apache and Comanche raids, militated against the recruitment of large private armies. On the whole, available evidence indicates that landed proprietors were largely dependent on the state and the frontier army for protection.[21] Not until after independence, when permanent military forces were no longer maintained on the frontier, did armed hacienda cowboys play a more important role in warfare.

Prisoners of War During the Colonial Period

The colonial state defined *gente de razón* who were captured by the Apache as *cautivos* (captives) and Apaches captured by presidial forces as *prisioneros* (prisoners of war).[22] The majority of Apache prisoners of war were women and children rather than adult men: for example, from May 1786 to May 1789, 610 Indian women and children but only 55 men were taken prisoner by the forces of the Provincias Internas (excluding Coahuila and Texas).[23] Apache prisoners of war met a number of different fates. They were sometimes exchanged for Hispanic captives,[24] used as incentives in peace negotiations with the Apache,[25] or forced to play a role in military strategy.[26] They could also be allocated as booty to reward presidial troops and settlers. In 1763, Manuel Muñoz, captain of the presidio of Junta de los Ríos Norte y Conchos in Nueva Vizcaya, was given permission to distribute prisoners of war on condition that "those Subjects in whose power the Indians have been put are to be told that they are not to be enslaved and that they are to be given a good education"; this "boon," however, was granted only for his most recent campaign.[27]

Although Indian slavery had been outlawed by the Crown in 1542 (Gutiérrez 1991:150), historical records indicate that at least some Indians, probably prisoners of war, were bought and sold in Nueva Vizcaya. The parish records of Namiquipa, site of the Second Flying Company, document the baptism of an "Indian" baby girl who had been bought by her mistress for a cow in 1803; that of an Apache baby girl who was purchased by her mistress for a mare in 1804; and that of an "Apachita" who was given to the lieutenant of the company in 1805.[28] These children were probably destined to become domestic servants; a colonial edict of 1728 ordered that Indian servants had to be Christianized.[29]

Because of Nueva Vizcaya's proximity to Apache bases, the local exploitation of the labor of Apache prisoners of war presented serious problems. Not only was the rescue of prisoners of war one motive for Apache attacks, but Apaches pressed into service who managed to escape could provide warriors with intelligence that would make their raiding more effective. Hence, by the 1770s Apaches taken prisoner by the forces of the Provincias Internas began to be relocated to Mexico City, Veracruz, and Havana.[30]

Initially, men, women, and children, sometimes together and sometimes separately, were transported to their destinations in chain gangs (*colleras*) escorted by presidial troops. Plague, smallpox, and tuberculosis killed many of them along the way; the sick were hospitalized or given to citizens en route, the dying were baptized, and the dead given Christian burial.[31] The mortality rate of children was so high that the state ordered that colleras be restricted to adults, an order that does not seem to have been heeded.[32] Apache prisoners of war sometimes committed suicide.[33] Still others tried to escape; one group of prisoners managed to shoot at their guards, who in turn opened fire and then cut the ears off the dead Indians[34] (presidial troops removed the heads or ears of dead Apaches and used them to substantiate tallies of enemies killed). A royal order dated April 11, 1799, directed that all Apache prisoners of war be sent to Havana to prevent their escape and return to Chihuahua;[35] the relocation of Apache prisoners of war continued through the end of the colonial period.

Relocated Apache men, women, and children met different fates. Children were adopted by "civilized" families either en route or at their destinations.[36] Since Apaches under seven years of age were considered "educable," those who adopted them had to Christianize them and provide them with schooling.[37] Apache women, considered hard workers by the colonists, were allocated to households in Veracruz and Havana and probably used as domestic servants.[38] More research is needed on the fate of adult men. Although I did find a discussion of the exploitation of the labor of male prisoners in the harvesting of tobacco,[39] the widespread use of the epithet *gandules* (idlers) for Apache men suggests that the colonists had low expectations for their use as labor, one reason that adult males were usually killed rather than taken prisoner.

Overall, my research on the fate of prisoners of war in Nueva Vizcaya suggests that the local consumption of Apache labor was limited by the risks it entailed and that the market in Apache prisoners may have been largely confined to children. This differs from the general picture of a developed market in Indian slavery painted for colonial New Mexico by Ramón Gutiérrez (1991), one of the few historians to have done research on the fate of indigenous prisoners of war. Yet even Gutiérrez's data indicate that the enslavement of Apache prisoners in New Mexico was confined to a relatively short period, from 1700 to 1759, before the height of the Apache wars (1991:153–54). Sources indicate that Apache prisoners were sold not only to *gente de razón* but also to other indigenous people; in 1732 the governor of New Mexico issued an edict prohibiting the sale of "Apachuelos" by settlers to Pueblo Indians.[40]

What about the fate of the Hispanic captives of the Apache? My primary sources contain little information about them during the colonial period. Published sources indicate that the Apache, like the colonists, killed adult men and took women and children prisoner (Stanley 1962; Terrell 1972; Namias 1993). Captives could be sold, traded, ransomed, or used as inducements in negotiating treaties with the colonial government. Apache men could marry female captives, and the progeny of these unions would be considered Apache (Terrell 1972:101-2). Young boys could be trained as warriors. The institution of "adoption" (Terrell 1972:101-2) served to supplement the losses of warfare and the high infant mortality among the Apache. Yet adoption seems to have entailed varying forms of incorporating captives into Apache social life; more research is needed on this point.

Frontier Warfare after Independence

During much of the century after independence, the central government was extremely weak, as well as poor in fiscal resources. To a great extent, the responsibility for frontier defense became displaced onto provincial governments (Almada 1955:205, 210; Weber 1982:107-21; Martínez Caraza 1983:122-24). Lacking the resources to sustain a professional army, provincial governments were not able to contribute to the maintenance of the presidial forces, which soon declined. By 1833 the permanent military force of Chihuahua, paid by the central government, numbered only six hundred men who were badly equipped.[41] In subsequent decades federal support for frontier forces remained at the same level or declined. As a result, the main burden of defense fell on the civilian population (Holden 1984:15; Almada 1955:195, 201-2, 205, 209-11; Weber 1982:107-21). Members of subaltern groups and classes—particularly free peasants and hacienda cowboys—were to bear the brunt of the fighting, while members of dominant groups and classes contributed to subsidizing the costs. Part-time specialists in violence operated with a considerable degree of autonomy. Since the struggle against the indigenes was largely waged by civilians, the Mexican state had less control over the organization of warfare than the colonial state, which had maintained an army on the frontier. However, the Mexican state retained control over important aspects of frontier warfare, including the distribution of the means of force and the cultural construction of organized and socially sanctioned violence.

In order to mobilize and organize civilians for warfare, the Chihuahuan government took military censuses of the population: from the 1830s to the 1870s, "able-bodied" men between the ages of eighteen and fifty were counted and registered (Almada 1955:195, 201–2, 211, 220). Those suitable for military service were incorporated into militia units that were organized by locality and stratified by conventional military hierarchies of command. Primarily destined for localized warfare with indigenes, these militias could also be mobilized against "internal and external enemies" of the state; moreover, the oldest civilians often served as a local police force.[42] Since the well-to-do could exempt themselves from militia service through financial contributions, the brunt of military obligations came to be borne by free peasants and hacienda cowboys.[43]

Through a decree issued by the central government, dated March 21, 1826, the "flying companies" of the frontier army, including the one stationed at Namiquipa, were disbanded (Escudero 1834:56). However, rural pueblos such as Namiquipa, which were located in districts that were the key targets of Apache attacks, such as Galeana and Guerrero, persisted as peasant military colonies. Both the state and the settlers continued to define membership and rights to land in these communities in terms of the fulfillment of military obligations imposed by the Chihuahuan government.[44] Until the end of the Apache wars, the colonial charter of Namiquipa continued to be used in local administration by the municipal functionaries who replaced the presidial captains as local authorities after independence.

The state's registration and incorporation of "able-bodied" men into militia corps was more important as a technology of power through which military obligations became defined as part of the duties of citizenship than as a means of organizing warfare. Although local- and district-level state functionaries carried out their instructions and organized these militia, they existed mostly on paper. In practice, the military organization of the peasants of such communities as Namiquipa did not correspond to the legal-rational prescriptions of the militia regulations. Instead, as in the colonial period, military organization assumed a charismatic form. By 1852 the state had recognized and legitimated the existence of alternative modes of organization; the Chihuahuan government passed legislation that allowed settlers to organize themselves for defense as they saw fit when circumstances required it (Almada 1955:238).

Four types of leaders were in charge of organizing and waging frontier warfare.[45] First, in peasant military colonies such as Namiquipa, men who possessed extraordinary fighting skills and bravery gained a local following within their pueblos. When necessary, local leaders such as Isidro Lazo and Benigno Arvizo of Namiquipa mobilized "sons of the pueblo" into loosely organized groups to repel attacking indigenes; they also solicited permission and resources from the state to wage minor "campaigns."[46] Locality was a key principle of social relatedness both in warfare and in everyday life.

Second, major offensive campaigns that incorporated fighters from several pueblos were organized by charismatic leaders with a regional following. Such leaders as Santana Pérez, Mauricio Corredor, Blas and Hermenegildo Quintana, and Joaquín Terrazas had their authority ratified by the Chihuahuan government, which gave them an official military rank and provided them with permission and resources for major campaigns.[47] Although these leaders usually sought state authorization, at times they campaigned without official knowledge or sanction. For example, in 1883, Santana Pérez and Mauricio Corredor, the famous Guerrero District Apache fighters, led 268 settlers from their own municipalities and pueblos on an expedition into the neighboring province of Sonora without the prior knowledge of the Chihuahuan government. At the junction of the Gila and Sauceda Rivers, one of the most important battles of the Apache wars was fought without state sanction. After heavy fighting, the settlers defeated a large force of indigenes on July 2, killing 457 Apaches and taking 313 prisoner.[48]

Third, state functionaries played an important part in the discursive construction, financing, and organization of violence against indigenes. Through decades of constant warfare, the line between civil and military authority became blurred. During much of the nineteenth century, Chihuahua had both a governor and a military commandant; at times both roles were filled by the same individual (Almada 1955:passim). Military skills and valor became requirements for political office. The legitimacy of authority hinged on the ability to deploy force against "others" as well as on the capacity to secure the "consent" of subjects. The Chihuahuan governor García Conde, a one-time presidial cadet, enjoyed great popularity and legitimacy because of his effective handling of the military situation. When he was removed from office by the dictator Santa Anna, Chihuahuan settlers of all social classes and groups protested (Almada 1955:214; Almada 1980:90–97). By contrast, popular dissatisfaction with Governor Antonio Ochoa's management of warfare compromised his legitimacy; in 1859, Ignacio Orozco, the demoted *jefe político* of Guerrero, was able to mobilize popular support for a rebellion against Ochoa's administration. The allegation that Ochoa had not "managed the War with the Apaches well" was central to Orozco's ability to gain support among the peasant warriors of Guerrero District municipalities such as Namiquipa and Bachíniva.[49]

Municipal and district authorities were key to the conduct of warfare. During the first three decades of independence, these functionaries were either appointed by higher-level government officials or voted in by the adult males of their constituency, depending on whether the national regime was centralist or federalist; after the Mexican constitution of 1856 was passed, their ascendence to office was through popular elections (Almada 1955:passim). The legitimacy of municipal and district authorities depended both on the support of the state and on the backing of local constituencies. Since the members of the communities they administered were armed, these functionaries' power rested almost entirely on the "consent" of their constituencies. The legitimate exercise of authority became subject to the norms and values of a frontier code of honor and was substantially dependent on the possession of masculine military charisma.

Simultaneously "sons of the pueblo" and government functionaries, municipal and district authorities were military brokers who mediated between the state and the local warriors and charismatic military leaders of communities such as Namiquipa. On the one hand, they supplied peasant warriors and their leaders with the authorization and the resources to conduct campaigns. On the other hand, they regulated the social use of violence and kept higher-level functionaries informed about who was waging war, when, and how.[50] On the whole, in the conduct of warfare, municipal and district authorities were a source of organization, leadership, and resources. It was through them that the state managed to gain knowledge about and a measure of control over the use of violence against indigenes.

By regulating the supply of arms and munitions and by providing warriors with needed resources, the state was able to gain a measure of control over the management of warfare. Peasants were often too poor to buy the arms and ammunition, the horses and mules they needed for community defense. Even though the peasant-warriors of Namiquipa were unusually well armed, in 1849 about 50 percent of them lacked their own weapons, and all were dependent on the state for ammunition.[51] Peasant fighters generally were unable to equip themselves fully and relied on the state to supply them with some of the means of warfare. These arms were doled out to volunteers when they went on campaigns and subsequently retrieved by municipal and district authorities, who kept them on deposit. Not only was the state usually informed about campaigns, but by controlling the supply of arms and munitions, it had the power to determine which campaigns would be waged and thus regulate and legitimate the use of violence.

The state also exercised control over warfare by acting as a fount of honor, as the source of the prizes and privileges given to subjects who fulfilled their military duties and who embodied the values of the frontier code of honor. These rewards included rights to land, tax exemptions, rights to booty captured from defeated indigenes, and "prizes of honor," which were cash payments given to warriors for Apache scalps and prisoners. Through such "material and moral incentives," the state was able to arbitrate the use of force in society by fostering, legitimating, and rewarding only certain forms of violence, namely, those that advanced its goals of territorial conquest and domination. Through secular rituals that conferred or denied honor, the state was able to produce and reproduce a cultural construction of warfare and to regulate the militarization of subjects in peasant military colonies such as Namiquipa.

Whereas subaltern groups and classes bore the brunt of fighting, the elite contributed to the financing of warfare through voluntary and forced contributions exacted by the state.[52] Moreover, as state functionaries, members of the elite played a leadership and organizational role in warfare. Landed proprietors also contributed to the war effort by arming hacienda workers, particularly cowboys. Legislation passed by the Chihuahuan government required haciendas to maintain a small armed force, which could be mobilized by estate administrators for the protection of the haciendas as well as the defense of neighboring settlements and properties.[53] In addition, hacienda cowboys were recruited for major offensive campaigns waged by charismatic regional leaders or district authorities (Terrazas 1905:passim). Empowered by their military role, hacienda cowboys were able to achieve a better class situation and status position than the peons who labored on the estates of the Center and South. Access to military honor improved the social status of hacienda workers, while their military skills and possession of firearms allowed them to exact better treatment from administrators and to enforce their right to pride and social respect. As a result, the worst abuses of debt peonage were mitigated on the Chihuahuan estates.

Prisoners of War after Independence

The information provided by Mexican archives on Apache prisoners of war after independence is quite sparse. For example, my research in the Archivo Municipal de Ciudad Guerrero (AMCG) uncovered a wealth of information about the Apache wars in the nineteenth
century, but only one reference to the fate of prisoners. A letter from the
secretaría de estado in Chihuahua to the *jefe político* of the Guerrero District, dated March 2, 1857, ordered that prisoners taken in campaigns
be given to those officers who distinguished themselves in action, with
the stipulation that the officers "civilize, educate and inspire them with
horror of the savage life."[54] One oral source[55] indicates that captive
children were taken in by Mexican households. Manuel Romero relates
that after the death of Victorio, the famous Apache chief, at the battle
of Tres Castillos in October 1880, two of his children, a fourteen-year-
old girl and a four-year-old boy, were taken prisoner; the girl was taken
in by Enrique Creel, and the boy, by the Romero household. Baptized
Victor Castellanos, he was educated at a private Catholic school and ap-
parently raised as a member of the family; indeed, his godmother was
Manuel Romero's mother.

Apache oral sources paint a less benign picture of the fate of Indian
captives of the Mexicans. As in the colonial period, Mexican forces
killed adult males and old women and took young women and children prisoner (Ball 1970:20, 101–2; Ball 1980:4, 79). After the battle of
Tres Castillos, about one hundred prisoners—young women, children,
and half-grown boys—were taken to Chihuahua City and sold into
"slavery" (Ball 1970:101–2, 169–70; Ball 1980:45–47). Apache women
preferred to die of starvation than remain as slaves of their captors (Ball
1980:80n) and did their best to escape, returning to their own territory
from places as distant as Mexico City (Ball 1970:169–70; Ball 1980:
45–46). Women were put to work in gold mines, in maguey fields, and
in households (Ball 1970:169–70; Ball 1980:5, 45–46). The treatment
of children seems to have been better than that of adults; as Gutiérrez
comments, "When a slave was obtained in infancy, close emotional at-
tachments developed with the master" (1991:184). Such was the case of
Martine, a Nednhi Apache who was captured by Mexicans as a small
boy and sold to a childless, well-to-do, elderly couple who lived on a
rancho near Casas Grandes, Chihuahua. The couple had him baptized
Martín and became "deeply attached to him"; when Martine's "foster

father and owner" fell ill, he gave him "a good mount and a pack horse, food, blankets, and a paper saying that he was no longer a slave" and made arrangements for him to rejoin the Nednhi (Ball 1980:109).

What happened to Mexican captives of the Apache? From the Mexican point of view, their fate was dire indeed. Writing in 1842, one Chihuahuan lamented:

> Unfortunately, our fellow citizens have sensed and continue to sense that those human beasts [the Apaches and Comanches] have no other guide than the power of their passions; they raze our fields, steal our fortunes, convert our innocent children into miserable and stupid slaves, brutally satiate themselves with our daughters and wives, and when their deadly arrows have turned us into victims, mutilated while alive, we suffer a horrible series of torments. . . . This is savage man![56]

Apache oral sources indicate that

> the Indians preferred to let the cooperative Mexicans live in order to provide them with future supplies of horses. If the Mexicans were uncooperative or too poor to cooperate, the Indians stole their women and children. If the boys were young enough, they could make good warriors of them. The little girls were also important because Apaches usually spaced their children from four to five years apart and the tribe did not increase rapidly. (Ball 1980:213)

The variability that characterized the fate of Hispanic captives of the Apache during the colonial period seems to have persisted after independence. Some adult women became "slaves" of Apache women (Ball 1980:3). Other oral sources state that captives who were loyal to the tribe were not mistreated and that many of them refused to return to their former way of life (Ball 1970: 105, 132–33). James Kaywaykla comments that captive boys were trained to be warriors if they had the capacity and that they did the same work as Apache boys, taking care of the horses and doing other tasks about the camp: "In a sense they were slaves, but they were treated as well as I" (cited in Ball 1970: 113–14).

More research is needed on the fate of captives of both Indians and Hispanics, as well as on captivity narratives. The paucity of information for the northern Mexican frontier, and indeed for Latin America in general (see Socolow 1992), contrasts with the plethora of scholarship on the topic for the Anglo-American frontier (see Namias 1993). What is obvious is that the capture of women and children was a key strategy of warfare for both sides, one whose meaning is not exhausted by the demographics of attrition and increase nor by the utility of captive labor but also extends to the dishonor of the enemy other.

Conclusions

[Civilian military obligations and a militarized settlement pattern] were instruments of conquest, much like *encomienda, repartimiento,* or *congregacion* were in southern and central Mexico. Unlike the latter, however, those of the North were imposed [by the state] not on the indigenes but on the invaders. (Holden 1984:3)

Through more than two centuries of endemic warfare between indigenes and invaders, the distribution and legitimation of power within frontier society was conditioned by the social organization of the uses of force. Relations between the state and its subjects and between dominant and subordinate groups and classes were inflected by the social organization of violence and the distribution of the means of force.

The state's achievement of a monopoly of the uses of force in society is a long-term process. While the state can effectively manage certain aspects of the social deployment of violence, it can lack control over others. Clearly, neither the colonial nor the Mexican state had a true monopoly of force on the frontier. First, and most obviously, the state did not control the Apache's use of violence. Second, the state's control over settlers' use of force against indigenes was not total.

By permitting and prescribing only certain forms of violence—those that advanced projects of territorial conquest and consolidation—both the Spanish and the Mexican states retained the power to regulate the colonists' use of force. To this end, they fostered the militarization of frontier subjects—particularly members of subaltern groups and classes. Not only did the state legitimate the use of violence against indigenes, it made warfare against the Apache a source of personal prestige and status honor for the peasants of Namiquipa and other military colonies.

However, frontier warfare was never fully brought under state control. No truly bureaucraticized and disciplined army emerged on the frontier, even during the colonial period, when full-time military specialists were maintained by the Crown. In part, this was due to the character of warfare itself. Conventional military disciplines and strategies were ineffective against the guerrilla tactics favored by the Apache. Ironically, in the late nineteenth century, when the Mexican state sent a bureaucraticized army against the peasant-warriors of sierra pueblos such as Tomochi, Temósachi, and Namiquipa, the Apache fighting skills of the serranos enabled them to successively defeat several divisions before they were finally subdued.

On the whole, state attempts to impose legal-rational organization and conventional military discipline on full- and part-time frontier military specialists were a failure. "Barbarism" became the mother of "civilization." Invaders fought like indigenes, and frontier warfare developed a charismatic form of organization. In the frontier army, as well as in military colonies such as Namiquipa, qualification for military leadership was principally based on extraordinary valor and military skills rather than bureaucratic appointment or social privilege. No rigid military hierarchies prevailed, and relations among military leaders and followers were characterized by the camaraderie of equals before death. In addition, the forms of rewarding specialists in violence were not legal-rational but patrimonial and charismatic.[57] Although during the colonial period presidial soldiers received wages, like civilians, they were also compensated with rights to land. After independence, the members of subaltern groups and classes who bore the brunt of warfare were rewarded with rights to booty, a charismatic form of remuneration.

Although part- and full-time military specialists possessed considerable autonomy in the organization and conduct of warfare, they remained dependent on the state for arms and ammunition. By restricting the supply of arms and ammunition, the state was able to regulate and to retain a certain control over the use of force on the frontier. The state also retained control over the deployment of force by making peasants' rights to land contingent on the fulfillment of military obligations. Although these rights, vested in male household heads, were transmissible through inheritance, they had to be constantly revalidated by fighting for the state whenever necessary. Through founding charters such as Namiquipa's, relations between the state and militarized peasants became constituted as a reciprocal flow of obligations and rights through which the state as patron bestowed subaltern military colonists with honors and privileges, theirs only by virtue of fulfilling military obligations. Established during the colonial period, this particular relationship between the state and militarized peasants continued after independence.

Members of dominant groups and classes did not become military overlords on the frontier. Unlike the peasantry, the state did not endow hacienda owners with rights to land in return for military obligations; it is in this sense that Jones remarks that on the frontier "the [peasant] municipality . . . replaced the feudal lord" (1979:6).

Relations between dominant and subordinate groups and classes, and between subjects and the state, were substantially modified by the social distribution of the means of force. The militarization of members of subaltern groups and classes such as the peasants of Namiquipa was simultaneously a form of subjection and a form of empowerment. In return for the fulfillment of military obligations, peasants were rewarded by the state with rights to land and diminished claims on their economic surplus. Moreover, state rule of such armed peasants relied more on consent than on coercion.

The peasants' role in warfare also mitigated their exploitation at the hands of the hacendados. Not only were militarized peasants such as the Namiquipans well able to defend communal lands from encroachment by haciendas, but hacendados were dependent on these peasant warriors for defense. In addition, continual warfare checked the expansion of landed estates: many haciendas remained abandoned until the 1860s. As a result, the propertied class's encroachment on peasant lands did not begin until the 1860s and did not gain momentum until the 1880s. Like the peasants, hacienda workers also benefited from their military role and were able to achieve a better class situation and status position than the peons of the Center and South. On the Chihuahuan frontier, relations of production were less exploitative than elsewhere.

Not only did militarization result in the improvement of the class situation and status position of peasant warriors and hacienda cowboys; it also made them potential rebels. On the frontier the domination of subaltern groups and classes by the state and by the elite was always more tenuous and conditional than elsewhere. Domination depended more on the legitimate exercise of authority according to the norms and values of a code of honor than on the threat of force. The state's subjection of militarized peasants such as the Namiquipans relied on a perceived reciprocity between community and state whereby military obligations were fulfilled in exchange for officially conferred honors and privileges such as rights to the means of production. When the flow of reciprocity was broken by the state, the Namiquipans had both the "just" grievances and the military skills that were conducive to rebellion.

The distribution of control over organized violence also had an important impact on center-periphery relations. On the frontier the legitimacy of authority became linked to the waging of warfare. Allegiance to the Center was crucially dependent on its support or neglect of the struggle of frontier colonists against indigenes. The Center's financing of frontier warfare during the colonial period gained it the loyalty of the periphery: significantly, the northern provinces, including Chihuahua, fought against the independence movement.

After independence the central government was weak and the national treasury was poor. Control over frontier warfare passed to provincial governments, fostering a resentment of the Center, which had left the frontier in a state of "orphanhood."[58] At the same time, regional control of warfare empowered the provincial elite. Although the Chihuahuan government continued to be subject to the central government in important ways and remained a part of the administrative apparatus of the Mexican state, it gained a measure of autonomy from the Center. As a result, members of dominant classes and groups in Chihuahua tended to favor the liberal party, which envisioned the nation as a federation of states and in principle conceded more autonomy to provincial governments than did the conservative party (Krauze 1986:33ff).

Provincial control of warfare also fostered the development of a regional imagination of community, of a consciousness of being Chihuahuans first and Mexicans second (cf. Krauze 1986:40). In addition, the organization of warfare itself fostered a parochial consciousness among the Namiquipans and other armed peasants, since their primary military responsibility was the defense of the local community. When peasants' loyalties to their *patria chica*—their "little motherland"—conflicted with obligations to the region or the nation, it was the former that took precedence over the latter.

The state's hegemony does not simply rest on its control over the means of warfare or on its capacity to legitimate only restricted uses of violence, but also on its ability to make the very identity and status of subjects hinge upon only certain uses of force. On the frontier a settler who appropriated the property of another "civilized" man was dishonored and punished as a "thief," whereas one who took women, horses, and other booty from the "barbarians" was honored and rewarded as the epitome of heroic masculinity and ethnic superiority. By according or denying honor to its subjects, the state was able to regulate the uses of force. In 1836, for example, the peasant warriors of northwestern Chihuahua authorized themselves to confiscate the private property of the well-to-do in order to obtain the resources to wage warfare against indigenes (Almada 1955:207). By defining the appropriation of private property as a form of theft—an illegitimate use of violence and a source of dishonor—the Chihuahuan government was quickly able to make them desist.

Significantly, "civilized" settlers who turned to theft redefined their ethnic identity; by "posing in dress, speech, and manners as Apaches, they functioned in such ways as to enjoy the protection of the law," profiting from raiding while conserving their status as honorable subjects (Smith 1962:39). That settlers had to create an alternative identity in order to elude state sanctions against the illegitimate uses of violence suggests that the construction of subjectivity was of great importance to the state's hegemony and regulation of the social uses of force.

In the eighteenth and nineteenth centuries, an ideology of ethnic, gender, and class honor was central to the construction of subjectivity on the frontier. The meanings, values, and norms of honor oriented the production and reproduction of relations of domination, the distribution of social prestige and status, and the location of agents in the social organization of warfare. The dissemination of this ideology became key to the state's militarization of subaltern groups and classes, such as the peasants of Namiquipa, and to its management of the deployment of violence on the frontier. This ideology was an instrument of conquest in two senses: the state deployed it to manage the militarization of its own subjects and to restrict the social uses of force, as well as to prescribe the conquest of the indigenes by the invaders.

CHAPTER TWO

Honor and Ethnicity

Along with class, gender, age, and sexual orientation, ethnicity is one of the dimensions of identity key to the construction and negotiation of status (Weber 1978:305) and, hence, of power in state societies (B. Williams 1989:70-71). More specifically, ethnicity entails "a subjective belief in . . . common descent because of [subjectively perceived] similarities of physical type or of customs or both, or because of memories of colonization and migration" (Weber 1978:389). Ethnic affiliation is calculated contextually, through the concatenation of ethnic "boundary markers" (Barth 1969), that is, culturally constructed indices of categorical identies endowed with differential worth and purpose.

Despite its lack of scientific validity and the widespread rumors of its demise, the belief in biological races, what Appiah calls racialism (1990:5) is by no means dead in scholarship (on this point see Shanklin 1994:16ff). The false precept underlying racialism is that ethnic groups are genetically pure breeding populations with distinct, homogeneous, and bounded cultures. As Barth argued more than twenty years ago, this primordialist notion of ethnicity "begs all the critical questions" (1969:11).

Weber, sometimes cited as one of the ancestors of primordialism (e.g., Comaroff 1992:50), recognized that "ethnic fictions" were the product of the diverse economic and political conditions of social groups and that phenotype or cultural differences did not lead to the production of these fictions or to group formation (Weber 1978:389-95; see Smith 1993). Indeed, as R. T. Smith's reading of Weber stresses, even when

categorical identities become one of the bases for status group formation, group boundaries are not fixed but shift in relation to struggles for
power, prestige and privilege. Moreover, differences in style of life are
the historical product of groups' distinct social and economic locations,
everyday practices, and differential interpretations of an idiom of distinction (Smith 1993).

Ideologies of ethnicity have two closely related dimensions: one refers
to subjective classifications of collective identity, and the other involves
"the stereotypic assignment of these groupings . . . to niches within
the social division of labor" (Comaroff 1992:52). Through the fusion of
these two dimensions, ethnicity becomes a "protectionist" ideology that
legitimates the control of dominant groups over economy and society
and denies similar entitlements to subaltern groups, calling into doubt
their shared humanity (Comaroff 1992:52–53).

The bipolarity of ethnicity is paralleled by the duality of honor.
As Pitt-Rivers observes, honor has two interrelated dimensions: virtue
and precedence (1965:passim). While honor-virtue defines the ethically
valued aspects of social being, honor-precedence determines the right
to privileged social status and to power. The unity of these two dimensions, which can and do conflict, is the basis for the legitimation of
authority and the reification of social inequalities; the right to precedence becomes the corollary of virtue. The parallel dualisms of honor
and ethnicity define the intersection of these two ideologies of difference
in concrete social and historical circumstances. Social actors endow collective identities with differential virtue while negotiating their claims
to precedence (cf. Weber 1978:385–93, 933–35).

Honor and Ethnicity in the Center: Colonial Period

After traveling through Mexico in 1803, Humboldt concluded:

It is clear that in a country governed by whites, the families that
are believed to have the smallest proportion of black or mulatto
blood are naturally the most honorable. In Spain it is a sort of title
of nobility not to descend either from Jews or Moors; in America
the skin, more or less white, decides the rank a man occupies
in society. A white man, even if he rides on horseback barefoot,
imagines himself to be of the nobility of the country. . . . There is,
then, a great interest, motivated by vanity and concern for pub-

lic esteem, in calculating exactly the fractions of European blood that characterize each of the diverse castes. (1966:90; my translation)

In fifteenth-century Spain a concern with protecting the "purity of blood" from Jewish and Moorish "contamination" was incorporated into the code of honor (Gutiérrez 1980:89-99). Brought to the New World by the Spanish conquerors, an ideology of honor, in which the purity-impurity of blood was central, became the basis for racial distinctions, which evoked the dichotomy of associations between Christian and heathen and differentiated the conquerors from the conquered (Gutiérrez 1980:96-98; McAlister 1963:353).

A hierarchical ideology of honor, based above all on color, underpinned the organization of colonial society into ideally closed, endogamous status groups of differential rank with divergent roles in the division of labor and unequal access to the means of production. As the bishop of Michoacán reported to the king of Spain in 1799:

> [The population is] composed of three classes of men. . . of whites or Spaniards, of Indians and of castes. I consider that the Spaniards comprise the tenth part of the total mass. Almost all the properties and riches of the realm are in their hands. The Indians and the castes cultivate the soil; they serve the wealthy and live solely from their physical labor. From this there results between Indians and whites that opposition of interests, that reciprocal hatred, that so easily arises between those who possess everything and those who have nothing, between the masters and the slaves; . . . one is rich or miserable, noble or infamous by right and by deed. (Cited in Humboldt 1966:70; my translation)

In this pigmentocratic "regime of castes" (*régimen de castas*), somatic distinctions in skin color, eye shape, hair quality, and the like became the visible indexes of what were construed as natural inequalities of social being. Ontological differences, constructed in terms of a series of homologous oppositions in which pure-impure was a core distinction, underpinned the honor of Spanish conquerors and the infamy of conquered Indians and enslaved blacks. A hermeneutics of descent, based on a calculus of types and mixtures of pure and impure blood, specified the quality (*calidad*) of social subjects and endowed them with a differential value that defined their place in society. Religion, color, blood, and descent became fused in the calculation of status and in the determination of class membership.

Relations of production and relations of power became reciprocally defined in the racial investment of bodies. Virtue, constructed through race, determined the right to precedence. Subordinated groups were incorporated into society and economy as members of an "impure" tributary labor force, destined by their "infamous nature" to perform the manual tasks which were defined as dishonorable and polluting by the Spanish elite. Through this logic of racial difference, power was personified and embodied; relations of domination and exploitation were produced, naturalized, and legitimated in the construction of social subjectivity.[1] The colonial state played a key role in the genesis and reproduction of this system of stratification, drafting and enforcing legislation which established and maintained status and class inequalities, and which promoted marital endogamy (McAlister 1963:365; Gutiérrez 1980:250–65; Nash 1980:142–45).

The Ideology of Honor on the Frontier: Eighteenth and Nineteenth Centuries

On the Chihuahuan frontier the ideology of honor that was dominant in colonial society was revalued in a number of ways. First, the hierarchical idiom of color and descent that made somatic distinctions the ground for differential access to virtue and precedence was transformed into a more fluid logic in which cultural differences became the primary criteria for determining ethnic affiliation and hence the value and status of subjects. Second, personal valor and fighting skills became salient to the construction of male honor; the broad social distribution of military-gender honor provided a basis for frontier egalitarianism. Third, opportunities to accumulate economic capital were not as determined by color and descent on the frontier as they were in the Center. Used to obtain the symbols of civilization or redistributed to clients so it became a sign of patriarchal beneficence, economic capital could be transformed into symbolic capital and deployed in the acquisition of prestige and status.

Relative to the Center, frontier society was more egalitarian because the subaltern groups that distinguished themselves in warfare and led a "civilized" existence could achieve prestige and status despite "impurities of blood." Moreover, entrepreneurs of "infamous" racial origin could acquire wealth and transform it into honor. This revaluation of the ideology of honor on the frontier was the result both of distinct sociohistorical conditions and of efforts by members of subaltern groups to gain access to the signs of prestige and status, to contest their place in the social hierarchy, and to redefine the inscription of relations of domination by exploiting the relative openness of the frontier.

Honor and Ethnicity on the Frontier: Eighteenth and Nineteenth Centuries

Radically different sociohistorical conditions defined the intersection of honor and ethnicity on the frontier, as compared to the Center. Known as the land of war (*tierra de guerra*), the Chihuahuan frontier was the scene of endemic warfare between seminomadic indigenes and Hispanic colonists from the seventeenth to the nineteenth century. Warfare with Indians, more violent and continuous in Chihuahua than elsewhere, shaped the structure and consciousness of frontier society.

Ethnicity, Warfare, and Conquest

Ethnicity did not become the *primary* basis for the construction of the social division of labor (Jones 1979:70, 248; Weber 1982:214). Ethnic affiliation continued to be one of several factors determining access to the means of production.[2] But it was more a determinant of status position, that is, of the subject's location in a hierarchy of social honor and of the positive-negative value accorded to this location, than of class situation, that is, of the subject's positioning vis-à-vis the means of production and the market (cf. Weber 1978).

On the Chihuahuan frontier ethnicity was not grounded in the subjection of Indians as economically useful bodies but instead in the conquest of "savage" bodies whose "wildness" was seen as so socially destructive that it precluded their utility as a force of production (cf. Taussig 1987). Intractably and irredeemably "savage," the "barbarians" could not be incorporated into the civil polity or the spiritual community of the redeemed. As the viceroy affirmed in 1786: "I positively believe that the vanquishing of the heathen consists in obliging them to destroy one another. They are not capable . . . of being reduced to the true religion or to vassalage without a miracle of the Almighty (Gálvez in Worcester 1951:98; my translation). Or as General Emilio Lamberg, inspector of

Chihuahua's military colonies, wrote in 1851: "One should make peace with the Indian, as Napoleon used to say, with an army in front of one; and while they do not see a section of troops on top of them, they will always conserve themselves as rapacious wild beasts, destroying the state [of Chihuahua] as they continue to do to date" (in Lozano 1949:281; my translation). In short, during the eighteenth and nineteenth centuries, a logic of territorial conquest rather than economic exploitation underpinned the subjection of frontier indigenes and posited their social exclusion, that is, their extermination or segregation (León-Portilla 1972:110–11; cf. Taussig 1987).

Civilization, Barbarism, and Progress

Ideologically, the opposition between civilization and barbarism prevailed, and this concept was already understood in terms of the philosophy of progress. (Zavala 1957:39)

By the eighteenth century the opposition between "civilization," construed as a cultured way of life and form of being at the acme of human and social progress, and "barbarism," viewed as a wild, natural, and primitive condition of existence, had acquired a greater saliency on the frontier than the contrast between sacred and profane.[3] This opposition was key to the construction of ethnicity and to the social distribution of ethnic virtue and precedence.

In European languages, *culture* in "all its early uses was a noun of process: the tending of something, basically crops or animals" (Williams 1983:87). From the early sixteenth century, "the tending of natural growth was extended to a process of human development" (Williams 1983:87). This reinscription of *culture* was based on "an elaborate metaphor, which [drew] upon the terminology of crop breeding and improvement to create an image of man's control, refinement and 'domestication' of himself" through the transformation of nature (Wagner 1981:21).

Closely related to and often used as a synonym for culture, *civilization* as "a state of social order and refinement" had its roots in the Latin *civilis*, "of or belonging to citizens," and *civilitas*, "community" (Williams 1983:57–60). As the etymology of the term makes evident, the notion of civilization presumed that cultural refinement and social order were interdependent. The civil subject was a member of a *social* community, a subject of a well-ordered polity.

Inflected by an Enlightenment philosophy of progress, the concept of civilization on the Chihuahuan frontier was motivated by a notion of culture as a process of transforming wild nature and simultaneously domesticating the natural self. Plow agriculture, mining, and stock rearing were privileged as instances of civilized production, considered to be one of the preconditions for the creation of social community and of civil subjects. In addition, as a state of human development and cultural refinement, civilization was thought to be predicated upon the existence of the polity, construed as the foundation of a fully social life. Effects of power were embedded in ethnic identities: the civilized subject was a political subject. Sedentary life in settlements established by the state, subjection to authority, and conformity to the norms and values of the well-ordered polity were integral to the definition of the civilized subject on the frontier. Power and civility were inscribed not only in subjects' productive activities, way of life, and relationship to authority but also in their being. As the human capacity to domesticate both the "natural" self and the "natural" world, as the quality that allowed civil subjects to control the brutish instincts and passions of nature and to shape themselves as social beings in accordance with the norms and values of *civilitas*, reason (*razón*) was seen to be the ontological foundation of civilized existence. But what "civilization" signified is best educed by examining what it was opposed to—"barbarism," life in a state of nature.

The Incivility of the State of Nature: The Apache as the Barbaric Other

The Apache who harass these lands are extremely ferocious by condition, bloodthirsty by nature, barbarians in their way of life, of an indomitable temperament; they are a great rabble of thieves who live like wild beasts in the countryside, on cliffs and on crags. They are so pertinacious in warfare that they never lay down their arms, so vigilant that in putting up a defense they sell their lives at the price of many deaths, so rude in their comprehension that neither the cold nor the clouds nor the burning sun can vanquish them, so indomitable that neither affection nor favors can domesticate them, neither punishment nor death can reduce them. They go around in packs like wild beasts, moving around on all thoroughfares, where their ferocity pardons neither gender nor age. They live from robbery and maintain themselves by thefts. (Father Miguel Xavier Almanza, 1740, cited in Terrazas 1973:39–40; my translation)

Upon its formation as a free and sovereign nation, our country received as a sad legacy from the Spanish government a portion of Mexicans born in a state of barbarism, ignorant of all the principles of civilization, their customs reduced to the satisfaction of their animal needs by means of force and destruction. (Mexican secretary of war, 1835, cited in Weber 1982:83)

Through symbolic inversion, seminomadic "Indians," and especially the Apache, became defined by the state and by the colonists as barbarians who lived in a state of nature—construed as the antithesis of civilization and its virtue, of society and its beneficial order. Situated on the frontier between the human and the animal, the cultural and the natural, the Apache were imbued with the disorderly and destructive power of those located on the margins of sociocultural categories, of those who transgressed the boundaries and separations, and confused the distinctions, of sociocultural order (cf. Taussig 1987).

Although for the colonists the Apache were nominally human, their life in "a state of nature" placed them closer to the animal than the human pole. Thought to be wanting in reason, the "barbaric Indians" were constructed as beings of "ferocious condition" and "animal" instincts, creatures who, like the "wild beasts," lacked the capacity to domesticate their natural selves and the natural world. In the state's and the colonists' eyes, the Apache were the quintessence of wild nature and of its destructive force. And this wildness was also a sign of unrestrained liberty, of nature's freedom from the strictures of the social, of the indomitable quality of the savage—a perpetual threat to the hierarchies of dominance of the well-ordered polity.

Both the colonial and the Mexican states produced a knowledge of Apache nature so as to generate strategies and techniques for destroying, if not taming, it. The hermeneutics of official texts were motivated by the imperatives of conquest and its legitimation; it is significant that many of these accounts of the Apache were produced by frontier military officers. Since the frontier continued to be tierra de guerra, no rupture in the construction of these indigenes marks the transition from colony to nation, for the relationship of state and colonists to the Apache remained substantially unchanged by independence. No less than their colonial predecessors, the authorities of the Mexican state were concerned with determining the quality (*calidad*) of these Indians so that they could subjugate or exterminate them.

Quality (*calidad*), as much a classificatory as a valorizing term, was used to denote ethnic status and identity. Gutiérrez characterizes calidad as racial status defined by legal color (1980:100), but McCaa argues that calidad on the frontier was "an inclusive impression reflecting one's reputation as a whole. Color, occupation, and wealth might influence one's calidad, as did purity of blood, honor, integrity, and even place of origin" (1984:477–78). In the three examples of official discourse we will examine here,[4] the calidad of the Apache was configured not so much by the somatic signs of color but more by the cultural indexes and icons of a civilized versus barbaric condition and style of life. What were the features of Apache lifeways that representatives of the colonial and Mexican states, as well as frontier colonists, identified as the privileged emblems of barbarism?

In colonial and postcolonial society, configurations of space were forms of dominance that fixed identities by inscribing them in the topography of day-to-day life and also localized the practices of subjects, allowing for their documentation and regulation by the state. The well-ordered polity was one in which all types of subjects had their defined and particular "places" (*lugares*). Place was both an icon and an index of social being.

The frontier, relative to the Center, was conceived of as a liminal zone, characterized by a greater degree of motion and fluidity, ambiguity and disorder. Thus, the regulation of frontier subjects' location in and movement across space was a priority for the state. Planned and orderly settlement was central to the colonization (*colonización*) of the wilderness and to the reduction (*reducción*) of its savage inhabitants.[5] Indeed, *reducción* was a Spanish term for the concentration of dispersed populations into the urban units of a proper polity.

Transforming unbounded nature into bounded social space was integral to colonización, since such boundaries were signs of the sociocultural domains and distinctions that ordered the civilized polity. To "leave one's place" (*salirse de su lugar*) is a phrase that continues to be used today to signify a breach of the sociocultural order and an abrogation of the norms, values, and meanings that configure and regulate identities. Significantly, displacement or exile was one of the gravest punishments conferred on transgressors of order during the colonial period (1728 edict in Hernández Rodríguez 1939).

As Father Almanza's remarks indicate (see quotation at beginning of this section), the transhumancy of the Apache was one of the privileged signs of their barbaric condition and quality. In the colonists' eyes, the Apache were always "leaving their places." *Andan siempre errantes* (they are always wandering) is a figure of speech repeatedly used to characterize the Apache (e.g., Lamberg in Lozano 1949:273). Place for them was a place to stop, not a place to stay. In O'Conor's words, "These barbarians inhabit, according to the Seasons of the year, those stopping places which offer them the best opportunity for their maintenance . . . but without the necessity of maintaining or conserving these Lands because they have others which are the same wherever" (in González Flores and Almada 1952:78). Nature, brute instinct, and animal need were seen to dictate the Apache's perpetual movements. For the colonists this continual motion was an index of the Apache's barbarism—of their wild animality, of their natural condition and style of life, of their lack of the reason and sentiments of civilized persons, in short, of their location outside the society of the *gente política* (political people).[6]

In the colonists' eyes, perpetual motion also made Apache men enemies to be reckoned with. It was a source and a sign of animal strength and vigor. As Cordero noted, "The continuous movement in which he lives . . . makes him agile and nimble in such a degree that he is not inferior in speed and endurance to horses, and certainly he is superior to them when in rugged and rocky territory" (in Matson and Schroeder 1957:338). Moreover, the Apache's freedom from place meant that they had no territory to safeguard and could conduct war anywhere; as O'Conor remarked, "They are not obliged to defend, protect, nor maintain any Stopping Place, Site or Population" (in González Flores and Almada 1952:79).

In official discourse the Apache's lack of fixity in space was a rhetorical figure that condensed diverse significations. Placelessness was a privileged sign of the barbarians' "quality"—of their animality and incivility, of their wild potency and indomitableness, of their location outside the social in the unbounded space of nature.

Significantly, the characterization of the Apache as in constant motion is frequently juxtaposed with their construction as thieves who lived by appropriating that which belonged to others. Indeed, this metaphor occurs twice in Father Almanza's remarks: "They are a great rabble of thieves who live like wild beasts in the countryside" and "They go around in packs like wild beasts, moving around on all thoroughfares.

. . . They live from robbery." Civilized production presumed a socialization of productive space and an attachment to place as property, as that which was proper to male selves, as the patrimony of heads of family, households, and communities. Property rights in land, including *derechos de posesión*, were a sign of work, of the activity that transformed nature, and as such were indexes of civilization. In the colonists' eyes, not only did Apache men have no property in land, but they also did not work.

Unlike civilized men, who actively transformed nature, the Apache, like "wild beasts," used force to prey on what belonged to others or passively appropriated what nature produced. In Cordero's words, "Besides the meat which is supplied by his continuous hunting and cattle stealing in the territories of his enemy, his regular food consists of the wild fruits *which his territories produce*" (in Matson and Schroeder 1957:339; my emphasis). For the colonists, even the domestic crops that the Apache raised were produced by nature and not by work. As Cordero went on to add, the Apache "raise some little corn, squash, beans, and tobacco, *which the land produces more on account of its fertility than for the work which is expended in its cultivation*" (in Matson and Schroeder 1957:339; my emphasis).

In the Apache world, as imagined by the colonists, the law of brute force characterized even relations of consanguinity, those bonds that, above all others, should have been regulated by the community of "shared substance" (Schneider 1968). In this vein Cordero commented: "It is worth telling about the peculiar distrust of one another in which they live, even though they are related, and the precautions they take on approaching when they have not seen each other for a long time. *The Apache does not even approach his own brother without weapons in hand, always on guard against an attack or always ready to commit one*" (in Matson and Schroeder 1957:349; my emphasis). Lacking all sentiments of fraternity, Apaches had no polity or society and they related to each other like wild beasts who had no consciousness of community: "Their propensity for stealing and for doing damage to others is not limited particularly to those whom they know for outright enemies . . . but it extends itself also to not pardoning each other, since with the greatest facility the weaker see themselves despoiled by the stronger; and bloody battles are stirred up amongst the different groups" (Cordero in Matson and Schroeder 1957:349).

In official discourse this asocial condition, this state of nature, was

represented as one of wild liberty. Construed as a quality of temperament, this savage freedom was inscribed in the Apache's very being.
"Their peevish temperaments," Cordero wrote, "cause those of this
nation to have a character which is astute, distrustful, bold, proud, and
jealous of their liberty and independence" (in Matson and Schroeder
1957:339). For the colonists, however, the free savage was not noble but
bestial. Absolute liberty from the constraints and control of the well-
ordered polity was a sign of a deficiency of reason, the quality that allowed human beings to transcend the imperatives of brute instinct and to
civilize their natural selves. Hence, the asocial liberty of the Apache was
not truly freedom but the tyranny of the strong over the weak. In official
discourse the Apache's "jealousness of liberty and independence," their
resistance to colonial domination, became construed as an emblem of
barbarity. Rebellion and barbarism were rendered synonymous. Indeed,
for the colonists, *Apache* signified *rebel*. Significantly, General Emilio
Lamberg located the etymology of Apache in an ur-instance of opposition to colonial domination: "The name of Apaches remained with them
from those times when they rose up and rebelled against those apos-
tolic ministers [who had tried to Christianize them], because in their
language, rebels are called Apaches" (in Lozano 1949:273).

Not surprisingly, the colonists' dehumanization of the Apache was
extended to the Apache's discourse, for the contradictions of turning
human beings into wild beasts were mediated by "naturalizing" their
language. Although as a specifically human faculty, language was an
index of the Apache's quality as human beings, for the colonists, the
asociality of the Apache was such as to make even their discourse uncivil: "They never greet each other, nor take leave of each other, and
the most polite action of their society consists in looking at each other
and considering each other a short space of time before speaking on any
business" (Cordero in Matson and Schroeder 1957:349). Uncivil discourse was an acultural and hence natural form of speech; thus, "the
most polite action" of the Apache's entailed silence. According to Cordero, the Apache language was "deficient in expressions and words, and
this gives rise to a boresome repetition which makes conversation extremely diffuse" (in Matson and Schroeder 1957:337). Hence, even the
faculty of speech did not culturalize the Apache in the colonists' eyes. Indeed, their language—like the names of their tribes, which, according to
Cordero, were taken "now from the mountains and rivers of the region,
now from the fruits and animals which are most abundant" (in Matson
and Schroeder 1957:336)—was naturalized and rendered improper.

What an analysis of official representations of the Apache as barbarians makes evident is that effects of power were naturalized and embedded in the construction of ethnicity: opposition to the state and refusal to embody the hegemonic meanings and values that configured civility and kept subjects in their places became a sign of ethnic otherness. Those who resisted effects of power were defined as barbarians, as natural beings to be conquered and tamed by their betters, the bearers of reason and civility who represented the apogee of human development and refinement.

Defined as wild, both the landscape and the indigenes of the frontier became the objects of a "civilizing" process construed as the domestication of the wilderness.[7] The barbarians had to be tamed or the progressive achievements of civilized production and colonization would be eradicated. Distinctions of place and property would be obliterated, and bounded social space would degenerate into unbounded nature. Only the sterile desert wilderness would remain.[8] These imperatives were clearly articulated by one Chihuahuan hacendado:

> Chihuahua has always been open and is so today—more than ever—[the war] having acquired a decidedly malign character that threatens interests,[9] the most essential organs of social life itself: we speak of the cruel war that for centuries has been carried on by the barbaric Indians found on the northern frontiers and which they wage today with even more rapacity.[10] For the Chihuahuans it is . . . a question of . . . existing or perishing without glory at the hands of barbarians . . . [who wish] to recreate the desert in which the eye of the Apache finds its pleasure."
> (Escudero 1839:9; my translation)

If the colonists did not conquer, they and the civilization they represented would perish.

That the official construction of the Apache as barbarians was a product of the imperatives of conquest should by now be evident. The subjection or extermination of rebellious frontier indigenes and the appropriation of their territory by the state were inscribed in and legitimated by the logic of ethnicity. The "barbarism" of the Indians necessitated and justified their subjection, and their purported placelessness deprived them of any autonomous right to a frontier territory defined as an "unpopulated" wilderness, free to be claimed by the Spanish Crown and later by the Mexican state.[11] Ethnic virtue determined ethnic precedence in this logic of conquest and territorial domination. The frontier belonged by right to the agents of "civilization," who would reclaim the "wilderness" and make it bear the fruits of "progress."

The Gente de Razón: Reason, Civility, and Ethnicity

As the preceding reading of official discourse demonstrates, a homology between two oppositions, civilization-barbarism and reason-animal instinct, motivated the logic of ethnicity on the Chihuahuan frontier in the eighteenth and nineteenth centuries.[12] The overarching distinction became *gente de razón* (civilized people possessing reason) versus *indios bárbaros* (barbaric Indians lacking in reason).

The terminology of ethnicity underscored the rationality of the civilized and the animality of the savage. On this cattle frontier, the idiom of animal husbandry became a metaphor for human subjection. "Barbaric Indians" were characterized as *broncos*, a term used to designate wild or unbroken animals. Indians who had been "reduced" or placed under the "yoke" of Christianity and colonial authority were labeled *mansos*, a term used to refer to animals that had been castrated and domesticated (Gutiérrez 1980:35). In the limen between "savage" and "civilized" beings, construed as having lost the wild animality of the former without acquiring the human reason of the latter, these *indios mansos* had the status of children. Segregated in closed corporate communities, under the patrimonial tutelage of church and state, they were denied the prerogatives of a fully social being.[13]

As the foregoing discussion of the notions of civilization and barbarism made evident, the key emblems that differentiated the civilized from the barbaric were: sedentariness versus transhumancy; alienable property rights in plots of land (including derechos de posesión) accorded to male "family chiefs" versus nonalienable, communal usufruct rights awarded to indios mansos versus the perceived indifference to property of the indios bárbaros; agriculture, mining, and stock breeding versus hunting and gathering; work versus raiding; Catholicism versus Indian religions; Christian marriage versus indigenous rites; the Spanish language and literacy versus Indian languages and illiteracy. The multiple and polysemous signs of a civilized as opposed to barbaric existence condensed a vision that made civilized production the precondition for civil subjects and the foundation for an ordered society. Those who actively domesticated nature were construed as the only ones capable of "civilizing" their "natural" selves.

These signs of civilization could be achieved by Hispanicized social actors. Legal and customary prohibitions that hindered the access of mixed bloods to the signs of prestige and status, as well as to the means of production, were attenuated on the Chihuahuan frontier so as to attract settlers who could become agents of the state's civilizing project (Jones 1979:passim). Jones argues that "conditions on the frontier tended to erase differences between whites and mixed bloods. Although separate counts were taken in statistical data, it became common to classify people according to two generic categories: *indios* and *no indios*" (Jones 1979:95). Many of the *no indios* had Indian and black ancestors, but they were classified as gente de razón because they upheld a "civilized" style of life (Griffen 1979:107; Tjarks 1979).[14]

Based on his statistical analysis of census and parish records for Parral, Chihuahua, from 1788 to 1790, McCaa (1984), in contrast to Jones, concludes that distinctions between whites and mixed bloods were locally viable, although he maintains that ethnic affiliation was based not just on somatic features but also on the signs of a civilized style of life. During the colonial period military rosters, population censuses, and ecclesiastical records of baptisms, marriages, and burials used categories that differentiated between whites and mixed bloods; the principal categories were *español, mestizo, mulato,* and *indio.* The continued use of these categories in military rosters, population censuses, and church records reflects royal and ecclesiastical policies designed to shore up the *régimen de castas* in New Spain as a whole. Moreover, it is difficult, if not impossible, to determine whether the ethnic affiliations inscribed in parish records were determined by the priests, who were often outsiders, or by the inhabitants of the communities themselves and hence to ascertain whether these records reflect locally viable distinctions.

My own examination of the parish records of Namiquipa—Archivo de la Iglesia de Namiquipa (AIN)—for the years 1780–85 and 1789–91 (which are incomplete and inconsistent and hence not very suitable for statistical analysis) suggests that distinctions between Spaniards and mixed bloods were blurred in practice (although they were more or less maintained in the records). Even a superficial examination of these records educes a number of cases of "racial drift" among the categories español, mestizo, and mulatto, that is, of unstable and changing affiliation, which suggests that these boundaries were fluid and blurred. Racial drift, particularly for mulattos, seems to have been upward in the cases I did trace (this is consistent with the local oral tradition of origins, which does not recognize any descent from mulattos). The diminished saliency of racial distinctions among the gente de razón on the frontier is also suggested by the fact that racial affiliation is not consistently specified from year to year in the Namiquipa parish records and, when it is, appears to reflect the judgment of the priest and not the self-identifications of local individuals. For example, in 1790 (one of the years for which records are most complete), the racial affiliation of the child is omitted in twenty-one of twenty-seven baptisms, and of the six for which race is specified, only two are mixed bloods (one mestizo and one mulatto); in thirteen of sixteen marriages, race is specified but mixed blood categories are not used, and the only distinctions are español or indio (these marriages are homogamous); race is specified in only four of twelve deaths and all four are indios. Thus, in all of the entries for 1790, mixed blood categories appear only twice. Distinctions between whites and mixed bloods, however, are made in subsequent years *by a different priest* (1802–1805) and racial affiliation is once again provided for the majority of cases. Such inconsistencies make the use of these records highly problematical.

The one document I found that does contain information about how ethnic identity was determined supports Jones's rather than McCaa's conclusions. In response to the viceroy's request for information about the ethnic affiliation of officers and soldiers, Manuel Muñoz, captain of the presidio of Junta de los Ríos Norte y Conchos in Nueva Vizcaya, himself a peninsular Spaniard, wrote in 1764:

> Most of them are Spaniards of this country [*de este Pais españoles*], with some insertion of mestizos, coyotes and mulatos; there is little difference among them, since these are usually the most appropriate persons for service in these presidios because they are used to work and accustomed to maintaining themselves in the occasions and cases that the exercise of their service entails, consuming the ordinary rations that the country offers . . . which the delicate Spaniards of the realm could not tolerate; in addition, the little valor and spirit for fighting with the Indians is to be expected of the majority of these Spaniards. In this respect, I report all those in service who have straight hair and who are almost white as Spaniards of the land [*españoles de la Tierra*].[15]

Of the fifty men in the company, Muñoz categorized thirty as Spaniards, four as coyotes (which he explains are the offspring of a Spaniard and

an Indian), four as mestizos (which he states are the offspring of a Spaniard and a coyote), seven as mulattos, one as an Indian, and four he did
not identify. These categories are further subdivided using adjectives re-
ferring to phenotype or descent. Español has the most subdivisions; in
addition to *español de la tierra* and *español del reino*, used exclusively in
his letter, in the roster Muñoz introduces *español, español oscuro* (dark
Spaniard), *español crespo* (curly-haired Spaniard), *español limpio* (clean
Spaniard), *español blanco* (white Spaniard), and *español legitimo* (legitimate Spaniard). Coyote is broken down into *coiote, coiote rosado* (pink
coyote) and *coiote oscuro* (dark coyote); mestizo into *mestizo* and *mestizo
oscuro* (dark mestizo); and mulatto into *mulato* and *mulato blanco* (white
mulatto).

Muñoz's letter and roster indicate that differences between *españoles*
and the *castas* had become blurred and that a process of "whitening" was
taking place, enabled by the subdivision of the categories, which per-
mitted the inclusion of a wider range of phenotypes. Although Muñoz
considered somatic characteristics in determining calidad, the honor attached to military service and the valor and fitness of his men for frontier fighting were his most important criteria. Interestingly, although
an español del reino himself, Muñoz negates the peninsular prejudice
against frontier, creole Spaniards, arguing instead that the latter were
hardier, braver, and better suited for presidial service than the former.

The blurring of distinctions between españoles and the castas is consistent with the progressive whitening of the "civilized" population at-
tested to by oral tradition (cf. Taussig 1987). Since reason, or the capacity
for civilization, was identified with Spanish blood, many Hispanicized
mestizos and mulattos were able to "bleach" themselves (*blanquearse*)
and, as "civilized people," become de facto whites. According to Humboldt: "All the inhabitants [of Nueva Vizcaya] are white or at least they
consider themselves as such. All believe they have the right to take the
title of *don* [an honorific index usually reserved for the Spanish elite],
although they may not be anything other than . . . *petits blancs* or *mes-
sieurs passables*" (1966:188; my translation).

The preference for white wheat flour in the diet of the gente de razón,
rather than cornmeal, which was associated with Indianness, was one
index of this transformation. By the end of the eighteenth century,
Northerners consumed more than one-third of the entire wheat harvest,
even though they comprised only one-fourth of the total population
(Humboldt 1966:261–62).[16]

A "whitened" history of origins accompanied and naturalized the "bleaching" of the population. According to this invented tradition, the conquest and settlement of the frontier had been carried out by Spaniards, that is, whites, and miscegenation with Indians had been negligible, and with blacks, impossible.[17] On the frontier Indians became radically the other; they were an enemy to be exterminated or segregated in enclaves rather than incorporated into colonial society. As the origins of the "civilized" frontier population were reconstructed, the proportion of Indian blood held to run in norteño veins became minimized, if not totally expunged.

Chihuahuans today boast of their collective "whiteness." For example, although in ethnic terms the people of Namiquipa descend from mulattos, mestizos, and Indians as well as whites, they affirm that as a group they are "mostly Spanish" and refuse to recognize any admixture of "tame" Indian blood; that they should have black blood is unthinkable. As ethnic affiliation became redefined in Chihuahua and in the North as a whole, whiteness became central to the creation of a regional sense of community and personhood. This invented tradition of origins is very much alive today and is regularly evoked in the construction of a distinct norteño identity, opposed to that of the Mexicans of the Center, who are subjectively apprehended as "less white" and disparagingly referred to as chilangos.

Indianization: Juh's Gold Nuggets

The redefinition of ethnicity on the frontier entailed not only a process of whitening and Hispanicization but also a process of Indianization. One of my good friends in Namiquipa, Doña Aurora, told me she was a descendant of Juh, "the ablest of the militant Apaches after Victorio" (Thrapp in Ball 1980:xi), chief of the Nednhi Apache (known as the Chiricahua by Mexicans and Americans) (Kaywaykla in Ball 1970:xiv). She explained that Juh was born in Namiquipa during the nineteenth century; the son of a Spaniard, Leonardo Leyba, and an Apache, Benigna Arvizo, he was baptized Lino Leyba.[18] According to Doña Aurora, Lino Leyba chose to leave Namiquipa and join the Apache. He would return to the pueblo every so often to visit his mother, bringing her gifts of gold nuggets. Although Juh's stronghold was the Sierra Madre on the border of Sonora and Chihuahua, relatively close to Namiquipa, he never attacked the pueblo.[19]

Not only Hispanicized Apaches but also gente de razón opted to live with the Indians, redefining their culture and ethnicity. Juan Domingo Ochoa, a fourteen-year-old youth who had been captured by the Apache, chose to escape and return to Coahuila. But in his declaration to the military authorities in 1776, he told of many other captives who had remained with the Apache:

> Once he arrived in the Apaches' *ranchería*, they flogged him and cut off his left ear, putting him to work taking care of his master's horses. There were many families in the *ranchería*, and among them a group that had just arrived, fleeing the Comanches, which was headed by a Spaniard called Andres, who had been a prisoner in the Durango jail. . . . He saw several boys and women captives who were from . . . this province and Nueva Vizcaya. He also saw a mulatto man whose upper lip had been cut off . . . who, of his own free will, had gone to join the Indians, with whom he is now very happy, harming the settlers, and that he is married to an Apache woman. That this mulatto, like the aforementioned Captain Andres, tried to persuade him not to escape, painting a picture of the free and lazy life he would enjoy if he remained with the Indians.[20]

More broadly, these processes of Hispanicization and Indianization indicate that the frontier was a zone of intercultural exchange and transformation; the fluidity of ethnicity suggests that not only the boundaries of color but also those of culture and way of life were blurred and subject to redefinition in practice. This is precisely why official rhetoric was so rigid; the binary opposition of civilization and barbarism asserted the existence of an absolute difference that could never be sustained in practice.

Conclusions

On the Chihuahuan frontier in the eighteenth and nineteenth centuries, ethnicity did not become the primary basis for the division of labor; rather, the logic that opposed the "civilized" to the "savage" was a product of the imperatives of territorial conquest and domination. The discourse of ethnicity was central to an ideology of frontier warfare that legitimated civilization's use of force and delegitimated barbarism's use of violence. The Apache's use of violence became construed as atrocity in the service of theft, as brute force without any legitimate end, as one more sign of a barbaric nature. As Jordán points out, for the colonists' and the state, cruelty was one of the salient characteristics of Apache barbarism (1981:180).[21] Although the colonists' warfare against the Apache reveals a parallel use of terror, it was defined as honorable because it represented the defense of civilization and all that it stood for.

Relative to the Center, the calculation of ethnic affiliation assumed a more fluid form. Culture and status were more important than color in the determination of ethnic identity. Inequalities between whites and mixed bloods were attenuated as the castas acquired access to the signs of honor that were denied them elsewhere.

The construction of ethnicity not only inscribed effects of power in Indian identities but also in those of the gente de razón. The logic of civility empowered the gente de razón vis-à-vis the Indians while it also subjected them to the state, equating rebellion with barbarism. Ethnic virtue entailed conformity to the hegemonic meanings, norms, and values promulgated by the state and was contingent on the transformation of nature, on work.

The revaluation of ethnicity on the frontier was an outcome of a particular set of historical conditions, of the actions of social agents and of the policy of the colonial and Mexican states. In order to advance and legitimate territorial domination, the colonial and Mexican states fostered the construction of Indians as barbarians, as subhuman beings who were a part of a raw nature that had to be tamed so that society and economy would not be destroyed by the threatening disorder of the wilderness. At the same time, the colonial state relaxed the application of the legal strictures that separated whites and mixed bloods elsewhere until after independence. Gente de razón, such as the peasants of Namiquipa, who worked and fought to consolidate the state's dominion over the frontier, were rewarded with the honors and privileges consonant with their role as agents of civilization. But access to ethnic virtue entailed a construction of identity that enjoined submission to the state and participation in the project of conquest. The official discourse of ethnicity was as much about subjecting the civilized as it was about taming the savage; the colonizers had to be colonized before they could become agents of the state's project of territorial conquest and domination.

The construction of ethnicity and the definition of state policy were also products of the actions of social groups on the frontier. The efforts of mixed bloods and Hispanicized "Indians" to exploit opportunities for access to honor and to "bleach" themselves contributed to the re-definition of the inscription of ethnicity. Tragically, the resistance of indigenous groups, such as the Tarahumara and the Apache, to domination and exploitation shaped a "barbarous" state policy that posited the social exclusion of Indians through their destruction or containment in social enclaves and made Indianness ideologically other.

The otherness of the "barbarians," their assimilation to an untamed nature, endowed them with the potency of the wild and with the hyper-masculinity of the undomesticated. The frontier concept of nature was not unitary: nature had different aspects, and these distinct facets were differentially gendered. Wild nature—symbolized by the desert and the sierra—was harsh, threatening, sterile, hostile, unnurturing, and as masculine as the power to bestow death. Domesticated nature—symbolized by the agricultural field—was nurturing and as feminine as the power to bestow life. In the colonists' eyes, the Apache became the epitome of an untamed masculinity construed as the "natural" basis of power and authority. If, for the colonists, the domestication of the wilderness, the transformation of nature into the patrimony of men, was its feminization, then the subjection of the wild Indians was their emasculation. Gender and ethnicity became complexly interpenetrated in the colonial construction of other and self.

CHAPTER THREE

Honor and Gender
Purity and Valor

Remembered today as one of Namiquipa's honorable patriarchs and courageous Indian fighters, Don Jesús was initiated into manhood on his first campaign against the "barbarians." Still very much a boy, he rode out of the pueblo with the adult male warriors. Full of pride atop his horse, he passed a group of señoritas, young virgin women of marriageable age, who laughed when they saw this boy going off to do a man's duty. Piqued in his budding sense of honor, Jesús boasted to the señoritas, who had gently mocked his presumptions of manhood, that he was *tan hombre*—so much of a man—that he would bring back the testicles of an Apache. When the campaign returned, Jesús rode into town, proudly displaying this proof of manhood and of valor in warfare to the señoritas, who instead of laughing at him, reacted with fear and shame.[1]

Like the sons of the English landed aristocracy, who are smeared with the blood of their "first fox" as a sign of the passage from boyhood to manhood, Jesús had been blooded. But the multivocal emblem of his transformed subjectivity, of his valor and his value, of his power to emasculate others while enhancing his own virility, was the sex of an "other" man. Official discourse had so successfully obliterated the humanity of the Apache that they could be maimed and hunted with the same impunity as the fox.

The story of Don Jesús's initiation into manhood exemplifies the concatenation of gender and ethnicity in the construction of subjectivity, honor, and warfare on the Chihuahuan frontier. Indeed, this interlinkage is embedded in and indexed by the terminology of ethnicity itself. As discussed earlier, the adjective *manso*, used to characterize both "pacified" Indians and castrated domestic animals, connotes tameness, subjection, and loss of masculinity. Conversely, the adjective *bronco*, used to characterize "untamed" Indians and animals, connotes virility—an undomesticated masculine potency and force.

For the colonists, the conquest of the frontier indigenes was a metaphoric and at times literal castration, a castration that enhanced the masculinity of the vanquisher and diminished that of the vanquished. In their attempts to subject the "barbarians," the colonists deployed a multiplicity of practices that feminized the ethnic other and stripped him of his masculine potency and power.

One example was the colonists' taking of Indian, particularly Apache, scalps. As Pitt-Rivers has pointed out, the head is a principal site for actions that confer or deny honor (1965:25, 74). Scalping was a symbolic castration that stripped the enemy other of honor and potency by devirilizing him and conferred prestige on the victorious self by enhancing his masculinity.[2] Ironically, it was the famous Apache fighter Santana Pérez who in 1888 demanded that the Chihuahuan government investigate the castration of a Tarahumara Indian by the settlers of Bocoyna.[3]

Considering all this, what becomes evident is that although gender and ethnicity are analytically distinct domains of subjectivity-subjection, in social action the boundaries between them are blurred. As Brittan and Maynard remark, "The practice of domination in one sphere is never insulated from its practice in another sphere" (1984:180). But more generally, the pervasiveness of tropes of masculinity and femininity in discourses of domination points to the centrality of gender in the configuration of power and powerlessness.

In northern Mexico gender imagery pervades power-laden contexts and informs the construction of other forms of domination. Not only do tropes of gender configure relations between and among men and women, but they also image relations between civilized and savage, rich and poor, powerful and powerless, encompassing and encompassed, penetrating and penetrated—bodies, selves, spaces, categories, domains, and so on. Masculinity is a sign of power, independence, autonomy, closure, control over bodily boundaries, and the capacity to penetrate the bodies, selves, and spaces of others. Femininity is a sign of powerlessness, dependency, openness, lack of control over bodily boundaries, and the capacity to be penetrated and encompassed by others (cf. Paz 1985).

How and why did gender become a key site for the production of relations and effects of power on the Chihuahuan frontier? How was gender concatenated with those other forms of oppression, ethnicity, and class? How were gender and honor interlinked?

What Is Gender?

> In order to begin to specify this other kind of subject ["a subject en-gendered in the experiencing of race and class, as well as sexual, relations; a subject, therefore, not unified but rather multiple"[4]] we need a notion of gender that is not so bound up with sexual difference as to be virtually coterminous with it. . . . A starting point may be to think of gender along the lines of Michel Foucault's theory of sexuality as a "technology of sex" and to propose that gender, too, both as representation and as self-representation, is the product of various social technologies . . . and of institutionalized discourses, epistemologies, and critical practices, as well as practices of daily life. Like sexuality, we might then say, gender is not a property of bodies or something originally existent in human beings, but "the set of effects produced in bodies, behaviors, and social relations" . . . by the deployment of "a complex political technology." (de Lauretis 1987:2–3)

Absent from the major bodies of social theory articulated from the eighteenth to the early twentieth century, gender has only emerged as an analytical category in recent times (Scott 1986:1,066). What, then, is gender? The question is worth posing because, like other theoretical concepts that are simultaneously part of the cultural repertoire of daily life, "gender" is fraught with multiple significations.

Widely used to signify the cultural as opposed to the natural basis of sexual difference, *gender* denotes the social construction of masculinity as well as femininity. Nevertheless, the word has most frequently been used in a descriptive sense as a synonym for women and as a term that designates an analytical domain configured by the relations between the sexes, narrowly conceived and delimited by the domestic sphere (Scott 1986:1057). Quite often gender has been held "not to apply" in those areas of social life where women have been rendered invisible.

This descriptive sense of gender reproduces Western cultural distinctions and in particular such contrasts as feminine and masculine, domestic and public, civil society and the state. As such, it has obscured the complex concatenation of gender and power and allowed scholarship on warfare, the state, and "the masculine domain" to exclude considerations of gender (Scott 1986:1,057).

For feminist scholars the insight that "the personal is political" has always made gender a site of oppression. However, the restriction of gender to women and the domestic domain has made it difficult to relate constructions of sexual difference to the broader dialectics of domination and subordination (Scott 1986, 1987; essays in de Lauretis 1986; de Lauretis 1987; Dubisch 1986). As such, the analysis of patriarchy—of men's control over the sexuality, reproductive capacities, and labor power of women—has often had to rely on essentialist and ahistorical explanations which posit a universal masculine need to exploit women rather than examining how forms and technologies of power have produced historically situated effects of gender (cf. Scott 1986:1,057–61).

Marxist-feminist scholarship has been an exception to this ahistorical trend. However, by collapsing gender and class, by seeing gender as a function of the requirements of modes of production or as solely based on male control of female labor-power (e.g., Hartmann 1983), Marxist-feminism has deprived gender of its specificity (much in the same way that economistic accounts have emptied race of its particularity) (cf. Brittan and Maynard 1984:35–70; cf. MacKinnon 1983).

As Dubisch and others suggest, in order to understand gender we must recuperate the specificity of sexual difference while simultaneously moving beyond it, "seeking out its relationships to other aspects of social life" (Dubisch 1986:35; Scott 1986, 1987; essays in de Lauretis 1986; de Lauretis 1987). Likewise, in order to understand social life we must include gender as a central category of analysis (ibid.). The approach taken here seeks to do that by analyzing domination in relation to the construction of subjectivities—forms of personhood, power, and social positioning. Gender is viewed as a dimension of subjectivity that is both an effect of power and a technology of rule. The dialectic between processes of gender construction and state formation becomes a central analytical issue.

From this point of view, gender is not only the social construction of sexual difference, that is, of distinctions between male and female, but also a primary site for the production and inscription of more general effects of power and meaning, a source of tropes that are key to the configuring of domination and subjection. Gender, as Scott notes, is "a primary way of signifying relations of power" (1986:1,067). As such, it is implicated in the construction of power itself and in the configuration of other dimensions of subjectivity, such as ethnicity and class (Scott 1986, 1987; essays in de Lauretis 1986; de Lauretis 1987).[5]

If gender configures class and ethnicity, so also do class and ethnicity configure gender. Not all men obtain access to the privileges of patriarchy, and not all women secure its "protections" (Davis 1981; Brittan and Maynard 1984; Mullings 1984, 1986). As qualities inscribed in fixed and naturalized bodily contrasts, masculinity and femininity are ascribed states. But gender identities are also achieved statuses that have to be constantly negotiated and validated and are contingent upon other dimensions of subjectivity. What this indicates is that gender cannot be viewed as wholly bound up with sexual difference but must be understood in relation to the totality of the effects of power inscribed in selves and bodies.

The importance of the body in mediating between sociocultural order and subjective experience has long been recognized by anthropologists. The classic works of Mauss (1973), Van Gennep (1960), Douglas (1966), and Turner (1967, 1969) attest to the role of the human body as a "presocial 'base' upon which collective categories and values are engraved" (Comaroff 1983:4). However, many anthropological studies of the symbolic construction of the body have been framed by a Durkheimean problematic concerned above all with the reproduction of sociocultural order. What has been missing from much of the anthropological literature on the body is a consideration of power, an understanding that the embedding of meanings in bodies is simultaneously the inscription of power in subjects. The body, which Terry Turner (1980) has aptly called "the social skin," provides power with an "alibi" and with a site where it can be displayed and rendered exemplary.

The alibi is a concept developed by Roland Barthes to characterize the cultural process whereby history is transformed into nature (1972:127–31). Alibis imply an "elsewhere." Embedded in the body personal, the effects of meaning-power of the body politic are given an alibi in nature:

> Through modes of socialization (both implicit and explicit) the "person" is constituted in the social image, tuned, in practice, to the . . . system of meanings that lies silently within the objects and conventions of a given world. . . . once they have taken root in the body, acquired a "natural" alibi, such meanings assume the appearance of transcendent truth. The physical contours of

> experience thus appear to resonate with the external forms of an "objective" reality. (Comaroff 1983:4–5)

What allows the body to become an alibi for power is an ontology that situates the social skin in the "elsewhere" of a nature outside society and history and hence beyond the scope of human transformation. An epistemology that enables certain signs to be interpreted as natural, objective givens rather than as social and semiotic products is also implicated in this erasure of history.

Like myth, the body is not "read" as a "semiological system but as an inductive one. Where there is only an equivalence, he [the social actor] sees a kind of causal process: the signifier and the signified have, in his eyes, a natural relationship" (Barthes 1972:131). The iconic and indexical character of many somatic signs facilitates their apprehension as facts of nature rather than culture.[6] Inscribed in bodies, effects of power-meaning are interpreted as natural truths or causes.

Godelier has observed that "It is not sexuality which haunts society, but society which haunts the body's sexuality" (cited in Scott 1986: 1069). As a form of oppression that privileges the somatic, gender provides a particularly apt alibi for power—hence the tenacity with which society haunts the body's sexuality. Moreover, because such tropes are alibied, they are often deployed in the construction of other forms of oppression. Thus, concepts of power frequently "build on gender," although they are not always literally about sexual difference (Scott 1986:1,069). Godelier adds: "Sex-related differences between bodies are continually summoned as testimony to social relations and phenomena that have nothing to do with sexuality. Not only as testimony to, but also as testimony for—in other words, as 'legitimation'" (cited in Scott 1986:1,069). The tropes of sexual difference in turn haunt society, albeit in a different sense from that which Godelier intended.

Feminist writers have been at the forefront of disseminating the insight that bodies are sites of power (e.g., essays in Suleiman 1986). Much of the feminist literature, however, has focused exclusively on the construction of female bodiliness. Male bodies are largely absent from analyses, located on the fringes of a discourse that neglects to fully scrutinize how "men" are constituted. This marginalization of the masculine has been motivated by a politics that argues that feminist scholarship must provide a corrective to dominant perspectives that have rendered women invisible. Yet gender, by definition, is relational; analysis must begin to focus on masculinity as well as femininity.[7]

An analysis of gender as an effect of power and a technology of rule must recognize that the meanings that configure subjectivities are valorized and valorizing constructs (Collier and Yanagisako 1987). In northern Mexico gender is a key dimension of honor, of the positive-negative value accorded to distinct forms and facets of personhood. As such, gender is critical to the positioning of subjects in a hierarchy of status and power (Ortner and Whitehead 1981).

Nature, Culture, and Gender Honor

In an important article Sherry Ortner argues that women's subjection to men is motivated by a universal homology between the structural contrasts nature-culture and female-male (1974). In elaborating this thesis, Ortner draws on Lévi-Strauss's structuralist method as well as his notion that the exchange of women by men is the model for communication and hence the grounding for culture (Lévi-Strauss 1963).[8]

Ortner's position has been criticized on both theoretical and ethnographic grounds (e.g., essays in MacCormack and Strathern 1980). One of the most insightful comments on Ortner's thesis has been made by Donna Haraway:

> Nature-culture and feminine-masculine lace into networks with each other; the terms do not relate as isomorphisms or unidirectional parallels. That is, the paired distinctions feminine-masculine, body-mind, nature-culture, animal-human, and so on are systematically related to each other, but in many ways. Feminist analysis has frequently erred in assuming that the equation of woman with nature, animal, dark, etc., is the only relationship built into the series of dual terms. These dualist axes are story operators, ways of structuring relationships. They are not static ascriptions. (1986:84–85)

Haraway's remarks are pertinent to an analysis of gender in Latin America. *Pace* Ortner, in Hispanic ideology, both masculine and feminine honor are construed as having "natural" and cultural dimensions (Pitt-Rivers 1965:43–45; Gutiérrez 1980:38). Moreover, the natural and cultural aspects of gender are not rigidly opposed as absolute and mutually exclusive contraries. Although separable analytically, these aspects of gender are conjoined and blurred in practice as well as opposed and contrasted.

As a "story operator," nature-culture is deployed in the construction

of stereotyped personae that are models of and for positively and nega-
tively sanctioned forms of being and doing. Masculine personae include
the *macho*, the *chingón*, the *hombre*, the *tímido*, and the *cabrón*. Feminine
personae include the *virgen*, the *madre*, the *puta*, and the *chingada*.

Machos, Hombres, and Tímidos

> The timid man [*hombre tímido*], the shrunken man [*hombre en-
> cogido*], he who excuses himself from appearing in the world, he
> who never dares to act independently but instead waits for some-
> one to give him some impulse or help, never does anything useful
> in the world. Modesty is an estimable trait, but a man who is
> more than modest, who always tries to place himself out of sight
> and who excuses himself, is a man whom all despise and whom
> none respect. The world admires a man who dares to look at it
> face to face [*frente a frente*] and who raises himself up proudly
> and erectly [*erguido*] and defies obstacles. (Article in *El Correo
> de Chihuahua*, July 2, 1903; my translation)

The natural aspect of male honor is *machismo*, demonstrated
above all in valor, virility, autonomy, and mastery.[9] In Chihuahua the
testicles (*huevos*) are viewed as the physical source of natural masculinity.[10] The signifier (*huevos*) is apprehended as a *cause* of the signified
(natural male qualities).

Macho qualities are seen as the prerequisites for action in "the world,"
that is, in the secular, public sphere. Construed as the basis of physical force, these masculine attributes are considered to be the natural
foundation for power and for honor-precedence. The capacity to dominate without being dominated is a sign of having huevos. A macho is a
man who can say, "*A mi no me manda nadie*," that is, "Nobody orders
me about." Far from being timid, such a man faces the world (*le hace
frente al mundo*) and defends the autonomy of his self, the integrity of
his patriarchal domain, and the inviolability of his rights to women and
to property in the face of other men's challenges.

By contrast, the timid man (*hombre tímido*) who is overly dependent
on and dominated by others is an emasculated, denatured, and therefore feminized male. Hiding himself from the world, avoiding the public
sphere as if he were a woman, the tímido is "shrunken" (*encogido*).

In Mexico sexual intercourse is a source of tropes and images of domination and subordination. A verb that always connotes the sexual act, *chingar* is a polysemous term whose semantic range is close to that of the English word *rape*—" 'the act of taking anything by force, violent seizure (of goods), robbery, and, after 1481, the violation of a woman' " (Vickers 1986:214)—as well as to that of the English *fuck*. As Octavio Paz glosses it, *chingar* "denotes violence, an emergence from oneself to penetrate another by force. It also means to injure, to lacerate, to violate—bodies, souls, objects—and to destroy" (1985:76–77). The masculinization of power and the feminization of powerlessness are seen to be grounded in corporality and in the sexual act.

In Namiquipa a macho is a *chingón*, that is, a man who can *chingar* but who cannot be *chingado* by others. The potent male body is endowed with physical closure, with nonpermeable margins, as well as with the capacity to open, penetrate and rupture other selves, bodies, and domains. Although macho attributes are valued as the basis for honor as precedence, they are also viewed as the "cause" of actions that violate the norms and meanings of honor as virtue. Prey to the force of natural passions (*pasiones*) and instincts (*instintos*) that he cannot fully control, the macho can "lose all sense of reason" (*perder la razón*) or enter an infrasocial state where he is "out of his senses" (*fuera de su sentido*), engaging in acts of destruction and aggression that are construed as conduct that is "out of order" (*fuera de orden*).

The cultural dimension of male honor represents the socialization of the qualities of masculine "nature," the ordering and control of instincts and passions by reason (*razón*) and morality (*moral*). An hombre is a man who demonstrates *verguenza* (shame) and *respeto* (respect) in his actions. *Verguenza* and *respeto* entail the recognition of social obligations and encompass numerous qualities of the self, including honesty, generosity, the ability to reciprocate, the capacity to respect others' rights to honor, the dedication to work, and the fulfillment of responsibilities to one's family and community. To act with respeto and verguenza is a sign of proper socialization and of honor-virtue.

Being an hombre presumes possessing and demonstrating not only the cultural attributes of honor-virtue but also the natural qualities of honor-precedence. If a man has respeto and verguenza but lacks huevos, he is not an hombre but a tímido. Virtue without precedence is no longer virtue; for example, modesty is revalued as timidity. Conversely, if a man has huevos but lacks respeto and verguenza, he is not an hombre but a macho. Precedence without virtue is no longer a legitimate claim to status and authority but instead is an illegitimate abuse of force: *machismo* becomes *fuera de orden*, that is, threatening to social and cultural order. Hence, neither denatured nor undomesticated masculinity are really honorable or manly. True masculine honor presupposes both virtue and precedence, both natural and cultural qualities and attributes (cf. Pitt-Rivers 1965).

Clearly, in Chihuahua masculinity is dual, construed as simultaneously reproductive and destructive, at once regenerative of and threatening to social and cultural order. The precedence and virtue dimensions of honor and the natural and cultural dimensions of masculinity are concatenated in a contradictory unity. There is a perpetual tension between these dimensions of gender honor, a tension that has to be maintained and managed if a man is to be an hombre rather than a macho or a tímido.[11]

Masculinity and Legitimate Authority

> The father figure is two-pronged, the duality of patriarch and *macho*. The patriarch protects, is good, powerful, wise. The *macho* is the terrible man, the *chingón*, the father who has left, who has abandoned a wife and children. The image of Mexican authority is inspired by these two extremes. (Paz 1985:336)

> Authority as political power claims always to be moral authority, and the word therefore enjoys the same duality as honour [e.g., as virtue and as precedence]. (Pitt-Rivers 1965:37)

In Chihuahua the dualities, contradictions, and tensions of honor and of masculinity inflect constructions of authority and obedience. Legitimate authority is seen as predicated on the ability to secure consent as well as on the capacity to exercise force. In order for a man's authority to be apprehended as legitimate, he must possess and demonstrate the natural as well as the cultural qualities of masculinity, the precedence as well as the virtue dimensions of honor.

For the Namiquipans the ideal leader is an *hombre de respeto* who knows how to *fajarse los pantalones* (keep his pants on and tightly belted) as well as how to act with verguenza and respeto, according others the honor that is their just due and fulfilling his obligations to the community. Such a leader knows how to *hacerse valer* (make himself valued by others) and *darse a respetar* (make himself respected by others).

Leaders who embody only one of the polarities of masculine honor have no legitimacy. A leader who is a tímido lacks the basis for precedence and the ability to exercise force. A leader who is only a macho, who abuses his power and denies respect to others, lacks the basis for virtue and the capacity to secure consent. Such a leader is a *sinverguenza* (one without shame) and an *abusón* (abuser) who fails to treat others with the *consideración* (consideration) they deserve. Unlike the hombre de respeto who is *el padre de su pueblo* (the father of his community), he is a *padrastro* (a stepfather, a bad father), a *cacique*, one who rules by force alone.[12]

The contradictory unity of precedence and virtue, natural and cultural male attributes, is the foundation for the traditional authority of the patriarch in the household domain as well as of the patrimonial leader in the political sphere. Patriarchal and patrimonial authority are iconically related. Indeed, the term *jefe* (chief) is used to address both fathers and leaders. A father has authority by virtue of his traditional role, but whether his sphere of power is the household or the public domain, he must exercise his mandate in accordance with the norms and values of honor, for the well-being of the group rather than for his own interests.

The charismatic authority of military chiefs and of leaders of resistance movements is also founded on the contradictory unity of masculine honor. In serrano communities, charismatic authority is always somewhat routinized and fused with traditional authority. As Weber points out:

> The two basically antagonistic forces of charisma and tradition regularly merge with one another. This stands to reason, for their power does not derive from purposive-rational regulations and their observance, but from the belief in the sanctity of an individual's authority. . . . The external forms of the two structures of domination are also often similar to the point of being identical. It is not directly visible whether the companionage of a war leader with his followers has a patrimonial or charismatic character; this depends upon the spirit which imbues the community, and that means upon the basis of the ruler's claim to legitimacy: authority sanctified by tradition or faith in the person of the hero. The transition is fluid. (1978:1,122)

This slippage between traditional and charismatic authority has a historical basis. Through centuries of conflict with indigenes and through subsequent decades of struggle against the state, the contrast between the extraordinary and the ordinary, between warfare or rebellion and everyday life, lost its sharpness. Nevertheless, despite this slippage, the tension between tradition and charisma is not altogether diffused.

Authority, like masculine honor, is a contradictory unity that is always in danger of disintegrating into its component poles and losing its legitimacy. Not surprisingly, obedience is also fraught with paradoxes, tensions, and ambiguities. To pay just deference to those with *legitimate* authority is a sign of verguenza and respeto, of the proper socialization of natural masculinity. At the same time, as we have seen, to be dominated by another is to be emasculated.

These contradictions create a perpetual tension between leaders and followers, fathers and sons. Both the exercise of and the obedience to authority are problematical. On the one hand, the will to dominate and dishonor others inscribed in machismo conflicts with the injunction to respect others prescribed by culturalized masculinity. On the other hand, the "natural" will to be free of others' domination conflicts with the cultural obligation to obey legitimate authorities.

Vírgenes, Madres, and Chingadas

There is a being who can sweeten all of our pain, who can destroy all of our sadness: the mother. God has given her to us so that with her pure kisses she can put a drop of honey on the bitterness of life. God has sent her to us [and placed her] next to the cradle so that when we open our eyes, her wings of love will hide all the obscurity of the horizon, where we are going to fight in order to be conquered by death. God has wanted her hands to fold our hands for the first prayers, and her smile to be the dawn of the infinite [capacity for] hope. She is virtue, charity, the tender part of the heart, the melancholy note of the soul, the immortal fund of innocence that always remains even beneath the folds of the cruelest character. When you feel a good impulse, the desire to wipe away a tear, to succor a disgrace, to break your bread with the hungry one, to launch yourself at death to save the life of your neighbor, look around and you will find by your side, like the guardian angel who inspires you in right thinking, the shadow of your mother. (Emilio Castelar, article in *El Correo de Chihuahua*, February 12, 1899; my translation)

Like masculine honor, feminine honor has both natural and cultural dimensions. The "natural" qualities of femininity are contradictory. On the one hand, women are icons of the Virgin Mary; indeed, from the colonial period to the present, "María" has been a component of most Namiquipan women's names.[13] Hence, women, by "nature," are sexually pure, virtuous, and sacred. The signifier, the intact hymen, is subjectively apprehended as the cause of this signified purity of body and soul. On the other hand, women, by "nature," are capable of being opened by men: they are destined to have their bodily integrity shattered and their sexual purity sullied by intercourse. The signifier, the ruptured hymen, is interpreted as the cause of the signified, female pollution and profanation. Construed as simultaneously pure and polluted, closed and open, sacred and profane, women, unlike men, have no control over the entrances and exits of their bodies.

This construction of femininity is motivated by a dualism of spirit and flesh, by a valuing of the soul over the body that is at the heart of Catholic religion in general and of the doctrine of divine conception in particular. Corporal innocence, transcendence of fleshly impurity, is what made Mary the only human being free of original sin and the only woman to give birth without sex. Conversely, knowledge of the body is what condemned Eve to give birth with pain and, implicitly, to conceive through sexual intercourse.

Like Mary, the ideal woman is the embodiment of a paradox: she is both virgin and mother. Significantly, birth announcements in the 1899 issues of the newspaper *El Correo de Chihuahua* deploy an idiom of divine conception to efface the link between conception and the sexual act: "An angel in the form of a human child is said to have arrived in the home of . . . " (my translation).

As the foregoing quote on motherhood evinces, in Chihuahua women's reproductive capacities are regarded as sacred, and a great deal of social respect is accorded to mothers. *La Madre* embodies the "natural" and divine feminine virtues (*virtudes*) of purity (*pureza*), chastity (*pudor*), and modesty (*modestia*). She is devout (*religiosa*), self-sacrificing (*abnegada*), sweet (*dulce*), timid (*tímida*), submissive (*sumisa*), humble (*humilde*), and tender (*tierna*). Motherhood is the fulfillment of female "nature"; the lack of maternal instincts and qualities is a sign of a "denaturalized woman" (*mujer desnaturalizada*).[14]

The sacralization of virginal maternity is seen to conflict with "the natural facts" of conception—the source of female pollution and shame. As one Namiquipan commented, sex, even with one's wife, is always a "violation" (*violación*) of the woman by the man, a breaching of her bodily boundaries. If intercourse makes a man a *chingón*, it makes a woman a *chingada*. A perpetual index of female dependence and male precedence, intercourse is a mnemonic sign that recalls a paradigmatic wounding:

> The contact with the male body is not a source of temporary infection; . . . it is a source of permanent defeat. . . . Virginity is seen as an invisible armor, and the hymen as a shield designed to protect both the body and the soul of the young girl. Once it has been pierced, once she has succumbed to this first paradigmatic wound, all other wounds become possible. The deflowered female body is irremediably permeable, irreversibly vulnerable. (Huston 1986:129)

The penetrable "nature" of the female body becomes seen as the cause of women's vulnerability, pollution, openness, shame, powerlessness, reduced autonomy, and diminished self-control.

It is tempting to agree with Paz and to see the chingada—the open, violated mother who is steeped in corporality—as an icon of Eve, the source of original sin and hence of female shame (1985:80).[15] Nevertheless, in my archival and field research I have not found any evidence of an overt link between these two representations of femininity. Indeed, in Namiquipa the image of Eve has little public saliency and is vastly overshadowed by that of Mary.

The cultural dimension of women's honor is linked to this *public* denial of the "natural facts" of sexuality and conception. Verguenza for a woman is, above all, sexual modesty and chastity (*pudor, modestía*). Feminine honor entails the recognition that "natural" openness is so shameful that it must be culturally controlled and publicly denied.

In Namiquipa feminine honor is predicated on conformity to a multiplicity of cultural practices that mediate the contradictory "nature" of femininity by imposing a social closure on women. Women are "educated" to evince a *porte recogido*, a collected, withdrawn, and chaste demeanor that is a sign of corporal closure. As in the construction of masculinity, there is an interlacing of place and body: just as women's bodies are closed off, women's lives are enclosed in the *casa* (home, domestic domain). Their passages into the public domain are restricted and contingent on the permission of patriarchal authorities. Fathers, brothers, and husbands oversee the entrances and exits of the casa as zealously as they guard over the orifices of the female body. Women who violate the norms that prescribe bodily closure and domestic enclosure become construed as *mujeres prostituidas* or *putas* (whores).

Conception and parturition index the simultaneously sacred and profane, pure and polluted character of femininity. After childbirth a woman enters a liminal state analogous to illness: the impurity of birth places her in a condition of danger. In Namiquipa and in Chihuahua as a whole, a woman used to be confined to her house for forty days after giving birth, was forbidden to have sexual intercourse, was prevented from going to church, and was not allowed to bathe.[16] After this forty-day period a woman became purified of the profanation of birth, and her sacred status as a mother was socially affirmed. According to the Bible, the Virgin was confined for forty days after giving birth to Jesus.

The contradictory construction of femininity simultaneously subjects and empowers women. On the one hand, women's sacred virtues give them a measure of moral authority over men. As icons of the Virgin, women mediate between the human and the divine, men and God, nature and culture. In Namiquipa women have had a key role in public and domestic religious ritual, in the education (*educación*) of children, in the transformation of raw into cooked food, in the domestication of space, and in the socialization of "natural" masculinity. These "guardian angels" have been a central source of men's honor-virtue, of the good in men's hearts and heads. Moreover, their discourse has arbitrated male (and female) honor and reputation. Although women's discourse is characterized and diminished as gossip (*los chismes, la chirinola*) that takes place off-stage, it has been a powerful political force, one both mocked and feared by men.

On the other hand, the irredeemable permeability of the female body — and all that it signifies — places women under male control. The ideology of gender honor has prevented women from holding political office and from voting in elections and has limited their opportunities to work outside the home and to participate in the public sphere.[17] Vulnerable to all wounds, as well as lacking in the physiological basis for precedence, women have been viewed as "naturally" incapable of wielding power. Realpolitik has been seen to require a hardness of heart and judgment that can only be attained by those who have huevos: power is not an affair of the tenderhearted. Although women are thought to have reason, their minds, like their bodies, are seen as permeable and easily overwhelmed by softer sentiments.

The ideology of gender both enjoins and legitimates the subjection of female generativity to the vigilance and control of patriarchal authority. It prescribes the confinement of women to the safety and sanctity of the casa, the "naturally" and divinely ordained feminine place, the site where women can best fulfill their domestic "natures" and where men can best monopolize and control their reproductive capacities.

In Namiquipa male guardianship of and control over the sexuality and generativity of women are legitimated through a view of conception that affirms that only maternity can be "naturally" established. Except in cases of adoption, a woman is always regarded as both the sociological and physiological mother: the mater is self-evidently the genitrix. By contrast, sociological and physiological paternity do not necessarily coincide: the pater is not always the genitor.

In Namiquipa and in Latin America generally, descent is bilateral, and except in cases of adoption, a child is only a member of a family if he has both his mother's and his father's "blood" (*sangre*). Hence, in social life (if not in myth), the roles of pater and genitor must coincide if honor is to be maintained and if family and society are to be reproduced in orderly ways. Since men are viewed as "naturally" prone to affirming their virility by dishonoring other men's women, proof of physiological paternity is held to rest on male enforcement of the sexual chastity of females. In the eyes of society, a man can only reproduce himself, can only verify his role as both pater and genitor, by successfully monopolizing sexual access to a woman, by maintaining the social closure that functions as an index of chastity. Through this logic of gender, the subordination of women to men and the confinement of women to the domestic sphere is seen as both necessary and legitimate. Otherwise, how could the honor of family and community be preserved?

Although women participate in their own enclosure and confinement, their honor is ultimately in the hands of men. The "masculinization" of women who defend their own honor makes this point evident. In 1894, for example, a Namiquipan woman dressed herself as a man in order to take vengeance on her husband and his brothers; her denaturalization was considered so scandalous to "public morality" that she was sentenced to two months in prison.[18]

Transactions of honor are negotiated through actions or discourses focusing on the body; as Pitt-Rivers observes, "Honor is exalted or desecrated through the physical person" (1965:26). Insults to honor, whether verbal or physical, transgress the boundaries of the body. For women the primary source of dishonor is sexual penetration by men. Even marriage, the legal and divine sanctioning of sexual activity, does not erase the shame of intercourse. For men the sources of dishonor are different. To be shamed as a macho is to permit your valor or your virility to be challenged without riposting; a man who does not defend his honor lacks huevos and thus becomes emasculated. To be dishonored as an hombre includes more than emasculation; it is to allow your possession of the qualities of verguenza and respeto to come into doubt.

For both machos and hombres, attacks on the sexual purity of mothers, sisters, wives, and daughters are insults (*insultos, injurias, ultrajes*) that put valor, virility, and virtue into question and must be avenged if honor is to be restored. Women are a privileged medium through which men can be dishonored; the chastity of women is what ensures the integrity and immunity of the patriarchal domain. If the purity and chastity of a man's mother, sisters, wife, or daughters are sullied, he has to avenge their honor in order to recover his own.

One of the worst *injurias* is to call a man an *hijo de la chingada* (son of the violate-fucked one);[19] the judicial archives of Namiquipa are filled with disputes of honor precipitated by this slur. This epithet implies that a man's mother is open and suggests that she has been fucked by men other than her husband. Such an insult defames not only the mother but also the whole family, challenging its integrity and legitimacy as a social unit. The father becomes a cuckold and the offspring become bastards. The integrity of female bodily boundaries is an icon and index of the integrity of the group (although it is a breaching of these same boundaries that produces the group in the first place).

Since insults that defame (*difamar*) reputations are often responded to with violence, the idiom of gender honor is particularly suited to the construction of warfare. Moreover, the confluence of body and place in the ideology of gender lends itself to the imaging of conflicts over territory.

The maintenance and breaching of bodily and spatial boundaries were integral to the construction and negotiation of domination, subordination, and territorial struggle on the frontier. The cultural construction of gender delineated in the preceding pages shares much with the Iberian logic of honor. However, it was also a product of frontier forms of state regulation and of the dynamic of frontier warfare. As it gave ideological form to warfare between colonists and indigenes, the Iberian idiom of gender honor acquired new resonances on the Chihuahuan frontier.

The Apache wars became the medium for constructing gendered subjectivities, for affirming or denying claims to honor, and for validating or destroying male reputations.

The State and the Construction of Gender Honor on the Frontier

Ten years ago Sherry Ortner argued that there is a link between the ideology of honor (and the values of female purity and male valor that are central to it) and the processes of state formation (1978). Moreover, she suggested that honor had as much to do with the state's subjection of men as it did with the masculinist oppression of women; the patriarchal family, she argued, "domesticated" both males and females.

A colonial edict issued in 1728 by the governor and captain general of Nueva Vizcaya attests to state regulation of subjectivities and reproduction through the deployment and enforcement of constructions of gender honor (in Hernández Rodríguez 1939; my translation). This edict prohibited extramarital unions (*amancebamientos*), declaring them "an abominable sin," and assigned severe penalties to those engaging in illicit sexual practices. Concubines were ordered to "dress chastely" (*honesta y recogidamente*) and were to be punished with "two years of reclusion and service in the hospital" for their second "offense," and with one hundred lashes and exile for their third. Male adulterers were to be declared "infamous" (*infames*) after their third "offense." In addition to being characterized as lacking in honor, panderers were to be completely humiliated and emasculated by being whipped on the public streets by the women whose sexual services they had sold to others.

What this and other texts make evident is that discourses of gender honor that were integral to Iberian ideology became technologies of power deployed by the church and by the colonial and Mexican governments to construct and regulate subjectivity, generativity, and social reproduction. The sacralization of virginity and maternity has long been the basis for state control over the reproduction of domesticated subjects. In addition, the production and reproduction of patriarchal authority at the level of the family-household have been critical to the production and reproduction of patrimonial authority at the level of the polity.

In Mexico the relationships between family and polity, patriarchal and patrimonial authority, have been configured iconically since colonial times. A construction of gender that entails and enforces patriarchal control of female generativity has long been seen as central to the reproduction of family, society, and state.

An article published in *El Correo de Chihuahua*, January 24, 1904, makes the interdependencies of polity and family, patrimonial and patriarchal authority, particularly transparent (my translation). This exhortatory history narrates how the "degradation of woman in her sexual modesty and chastity [*pudor*]" in ancient civilizations provoked divine retribution and created social chaos because "the condition of woman is one of . . . [society's] principal foundations." The text goes on to argue that the "dishonor" of women and the decay of "the family" disrupted and "vilified" ancient society because "the state is nothing but . . . a numerous family, just as the family, in turn, is a small state."

Both the colonial edict and *El Correo de Chihuahua* article exemplify the mutually conditioning and conditioned relationship between patrimonialism and patriarchy, as well as the centrality of gender honor to the production and reproduction of social forms and identities. On the Chihuahuan frontier state regulation of generativity and identity became critical to the production of "civilized" subjects and to the reproduction of an ordered polity whose boundaries and distinctions were seen as perpetually threatened by a deconstructing "barbarism." Moreover, masculine valor and virility and feminine sexual purity acquired particular resonances during the Apache wars. In Chihuahua gender was to attain a distinct import because of ongoing warfare with indigenes.

The State's Militarization of Gender: Valor as Value

Because of their situation, [these provinces] are the ramparts of the whole kingdom of Mexico and are necessarily located on the frontier with the barbarous nations; their inhabitants are obligated to suffer the burdens of militiamen and veterans of the presidios and to all be soldiers. . . . This necessity, otherwise lamentable, has forged in them very recommendable characteristics of honorableness, point of honor, and subordination: they are extraordinarily long-suffering in the hardest travails and very accustomed to the greatest privations, remaining steadfast and impassive even when forced to eat, as they have been many times, the leather of their saddles and haversacks, without deserting or complaining. The result of the union of such excellent qualities . . . is that each settler becomes a tiller of the fields; each peasant, a soldier; and each soldier, a hero who alone is worth a hundred others. (Ramos Arizpe, 1811, in Florescano and Gil Sánchez, eds. 1976:167–68; my translation)

Warfare and violence are not self-evident, natural categories but practices that are culturally constructed and legitimated. In conducting and managing warfare, the state constructs gendered identities that define different domains of value and activity for men and women (Elshtain 1987).

In order to advance projects of territorial conquest and domination, the colonial and Mexican states actively fostered a military investment of male bodies on the Chihuahuan frontier. To this end, the colonial and Mexican states deployed a discourse that privileged masculine virility, valor, and fighting skills and constructed warfare in terms of the idiom of honor. The bearing of arms had long been a source of status honor for the aristocracy in Iberian society (McAlister 1963:350). What was distinct about state deployment of the discourse of gender on the frontier was that military honor was made accessible to subaltern groups and classes. Peasants and not elites became the "Just Warriors" (Elshtain 1987) of the Apache wars. Rather than exploiting the subaltern classes economically, the state used them militarily.[20]

For the state the development of a "warrior spirit" among subaltern groups and classes became a conscious end, especially after independence, when the burden of warfare became shifted onto peasant frontiersmen. The state promoted a construction of warfare in terms of honor in order to develop this spirit because such a logic would make male reputations contingent on military performance. In 1833, for example, the vice-governor of Chihuahua exhorted frontiersmen to fight the Apache in the following terms:

I tell you, fellow citizens, that the fatal hour has arrived for those cruel and irrational[21] beings, and for that very reason it is also time that if their atrocities have instilled in you any terror, you boldly set it aside and of your own accord, each one and all en masse, be ready, at the command of your respective leaders and superiors, to combat and annihilate that despicable enemy, not only because of the obedience and subordination you should pay them, but also as a result of an enthusiasm and a positive ardor to *teach that insolent and perfidious canaille their lesson.* Would it not be a most *shameful degradation*, citizens, if three or four thousand savages should lay waste to the fields, destroy animal husbandry, interfere with agriculture, obstruct commerce, and finally, cause consternation to and *humble the heads*[22] of 1,400 inhabitants[23]? No, Chihuahuans, *let us not permit ourselves to be stained again with such black ignominy*. To arms . . . it is not possible that the ruses and ambushes of the savages should triumph over the resources and perceptions of the enlightened citizen who enjoys the benefits of society.[24]

On the Chihuahuan frontier as a whole and in peasant military colonies such as Namiquipa, male honor became contingent upon performance in warfare. Apache violence was considered a challenge to honor that had to be avenged or the "enlightened citizen" would be dishonored by the "savage." This representation of warfare is prevalent in eighteenth- and nineteenth-century texts and is articulated in such constructions as "punish the insolence of that barbaric enemy" (*castigar la insolencia de ese bárbaro enemigo*)[25] and in ubiquitous references to "the insults of the barbarians" (*los insultos de los bárbaros*) and to their "insolence" (*insolencia*) and "daring" (*osadía*).[26]

To fight and defeat the Apache became a sign of macho valor and virility, as well as the manly virtue that affirmed honor. Not fighting or losing were signs of physical cowardice and of neglect of moral duty. Cowards were stripped of both gender and ethnic honor and likened to Apache women. According to Emilio Elías, the Chihuahuan saying "The Apache Indian women did not fight; they were the ones who poisoned the *jarras*,"[27] continues to be applied to "the cowards who boast of not being men of arms but who cause incalculable harm with their viperous tongues" (1950).

That warfare with the Apache was construed as a struggle for honor between enemies presents an apparent paradox. It is commonly noted that only equals compete with each other for honor (e.g., Pitt-Rivers 1965). However, war is a site of professed inequality and realized congruence. If we examine contemporary representations of Apache character and customs, it is evident that to the colonists and the state the Apache were an anomaly. Ironically, colonists and state functionaries perceived the Apache as "wild animals" whose actions at the same time embodied key values and meanings in the Hispanic code of honor: masculine courage, military prowess, virility, and a concern for the sexual purity of women. For example, describing the Apache in the 1780s, the Spanish viceroy, Bernardo de Gálvez (who fought the British during the American War of Independence), noted that "only the brave man and the faithful woman can aspire to glory in the afterlife; these are the two primary virtues they know, excluding from all happiness those who lack them, condemning to eternal disconsolateness the coward and the adulteress."[28] He might as well have been writing about the Namiquipans or the Chihuahuan frontiersmen as a whole.

Ironically, the perceived similarity between self and other is what allowed warfare to be viewed as a competition for gender honor. The conquest of the "barbarians," however, had to be grounded in a logic of difference that made the colonists ontologically superior to the colonized. This was achieved by constructing Apache identity in terms of *only* the natural dimension of gender honor. The Apache possessed valor and virility, but these "natural" characteristics were not socialized by "reason." As Gálvez asserted, the Apache were "a nation that has not learned philosophy with which to domesticate its natural sentiments."[29] Razón, transmitted in Spanish blood, allowed the culturalization of the self, the taming of "natural" masculinity. Lacking in razón, the Apache had no honor-virtue.

Significantly, the key site for the production of the ideology of conquest was the gender of indigenous men rather than women. Since the colonists viewed power as a "natural" masculine attribute, Indian men rather than women became the primary object of discourses of subjection. In the struggle between colonists and indigenes, Indian women were merely trophies of battle whose capture indexed the defeat and humiliation of the enemy. They were objects or vehicles of value in terms of which men demonstrated their might.

Only humiliation could "punish Apache insolence" and "reduce" their extraordinary masculinity. This was to be accomplished by defeating them in warfare and capturing their women, in short, by dishonoring and emasculating them. Such a strategy required that the colonists themselves become the embodiment of heroic masculinity.

Paradoxically, in order to constitute themselves as paradigms of heroic masculinity, the men of Namiquipa appropriated the Apache's "nature." Ironically, in a colony of peasant Apache fighters, the identification of the self with the other was literalized. The perceived machismo of the Apache became appropriated by the colonists as an emblem of "natural" valor, virility, and power.

According to oral tradition, the Namiquipans are "mostly Spanish";

social memory, however, affirms that some Apache blood runs through their veins. Archival sources indicate that prior to the arrival of the colonists, Namiquipa was the site of a Conchos Indian settlement (Griffen 1979:82). However, the Namiquipans say that their pueblo was originally an Apache ranchería and that Namiquipa means "beautiful valley" in Apache. Today the Namiquipans maintain that their past bravery and indomitableness are a sign of their descent from Apaches. When told what the books claim, they answer that their history of valor and rebellion demonstrates that they have the blood of "barbarians," not of "tame" Indians.

At the same time, the Namiquipans used their Spanish blood to symbolize their difference from and superiority to the barbarians. For it is in Spanish blood that reason, the capacity for civilization, and for "culturalized" masculinity resides.

The distinct resonances that gender acquired through centuries of frontier warfare are clearly evinced in this invented tradition of origins. Namiquipans appropriated the threatening vitality of the other as part of their own substance while simultaneously transforming and domesticating it. Also known as *centauros* (centaurs)[30] and *vaqueros* (cowboys), these peasant-warriors embodied the contradictions of masculinity, honor, and authority already discussed. They were both animal and human, barbaric and civilized, Apache and Spanish, natural and cultural, charismatic and traditional, destructive and regenerative, men of precedence who were life takers and men of virtue who were life givers. In this intersection of gender and ethnicity are inscribed all the dualisms that made the frontier a liminal zone and its subjects interstitial beings, endowed with the creative and destructive power of those located on the margins of the civilized and the wild.

Through this invented tradition, self and other became simultaneously differentiated and interrelated and the struggle between colonists and indigenes became an agon of masculine honor. As Hoch points out, "interracial conquest" is often seen as "an ultimate test of heroic masculinity":

> In such struggle, the most shattering . . . assertion of virility often lay in taking control of the other group's females—most obviously in the institution of slavery—and at all costs excluding them from access to one's own. Defense of manhood demanded above all, the defense of the white goddesses of civilization

against the dark, sex-crazed barbarians at the gates, and such fears provided the most explosive fuel for interracial hatreds, lynching and war. (Cited in Brittan and Maynard 1984:191)

In frontier warfare both the colonists and the Apache captured and enslaved each other's women and children. The capture of "barbaric" women by "civilized" men was represented as the redemption of these beings from a life of savagery.[31] By contrast, the taking of "civilized" women by the "barbarians" was viewed as an insult to the honor of the colonists, one that had to be avenged through violence. In the perception of the colonists, the Apache did not simply steal their women; they also dishonored them by violating their bodily integrity and sexual purity.

Contemporary accounts make reference to the Apache's desecration of the honor of the colonists' women. In 1766, for example, an engineer named Lafora wrote that in Nueva Vizcaya there had been repeated cases in which the Apache "opened up still living pregnant women and taking their babies out, they whipped them with them until both were made to expire."[32] Ten years later O'Conor made almost the same statement about Apache treatment of "civilized" women: "Their tyranny is not satisfied with [robbery and murder] but extends to pregnant women, opening up their wombs with the greatest rigor, inhumanities that cannot even be referred to without offense to sexual modesty and purity [*pudor*]" (in González Flores and Almada 1952:26; my translation). And in 1847 the Chihuahuan government deplored "the outrages and insults that [the Apache] inflict on families, dishonoring the wives and daughters of citizens."[33]

If frontier men were "just warriors," frontier women were "beautiful souls," pure and innocent beings who embodied "values and virtues at odds with war's destructiveness" (Elshtain 1987:xiii). The cultural construction of femininity acquired new meanings in the context of frontier conquest. The "civilized woman" became a complex signifier, one that concatenated the meanings and values of gender and ethnicity. Today in Namiquipa ethnic purity continues to be critical to the social valuation of women; "whiteness" is central to the definition of feminine beauty (Alonso 1992a). Moreover, unlike elsewhere in Mexico, the Virgin Mary, the white goddess of the colonizers, has more cultural saliency than the Virgin of Guadalupe, the brown goddess of the colonized.

As symbols not only of sexual but also of ethnic purity, frontier women had to be protected by "civilized" men from defilement by "barbarians." They were vehicles of male honor and dishonor, representing the most vulnerable point of male identities; men's ability to reproduce themselves hinged on the control of female generativity. Predicated on a monopoly of sexual access to women, this ability was seen to be crucial to the maintenance of social form and cultural order, to the perpetuation of family and polity, to the reproduction of patriarchal and patrimonial authority. And it was precisely this generative capacity, symbolized by women, that the colonists saw the Apache as expropriating when they dishonored "civilized" women, ripped their babies from their wombs, or took them captive. Writing in 1851, General Emilio Lamberg, inspector of military colonies in Chihuahua, lamented that the women and children taken captive by the Apache contributed to their reproduction as a social group (in Lozano 1949).

As that gateway into subsocial being, one particularly pregnant on a frontier that was likewise such a gateway, women needed special enclosure. The sexual closure society imposed on the women *de razón* guaranteed not only the gender honor of the civilized but also their ethnic superiority. Through such discourses and practices, the gender and ethnic honor of the colonists was made to hinge upon masculine performance in warfare. Defeat or victory had consequences for the colonists' very identities, for their personal worth and prestige, and for their status in society.

As Kristeva has noted, the feminine often signifies that which is eternal, that which transcends the changes of history (1982). In Mexico collectivities, imagined as enduring territorial entities, are represented by the feminine (while the masculine symbolizes the group in its active, human, political, and historical aspects). As place and as source of being, pueblo and *patria* are *madres*. Through metaphor, men's defense of the motherland (*patria*) and of the pueblo became equated with their defense of women. The boundaries of pueblo and patria, like the margins of women's bodies, were to be zealously patrolled by men.

After independence frontier violence became glorified as the defense of the patria as the state attempted to weld the imagining of community to the conquest of territory. In 1836, for example, the government of Chihuahua printed and circulated an exhortation from "an inhabitant" to his "fellow citizens" that established a homology between the war against the Apache and the patriotic struggle for independence:

> Is it possible . . . that one part of a pueblo that, not so long ago and with so much heroism, broke the prisons of despotism, triumphing over the potency of a European power . . . should

subject itself today to be the slave of a few tribes of wandering barbarians who have no politics other than robbery and assassination, nor any army other than the caprice of their temerity, nor any moral force other than terror and horror!

A rallying cry, "war to the barbarians so we can be completely free" from "our oppressors" concludes the exhortation.[34]

Such patriotic rhetoric constructed and legitimated the conquest of the Apache as a *defensive* struggle in which civilization, the patria, and liberty were the stakes that defined violence as an honorable pursuit. Men's honor as members of an imagined community became contingent on their willingness and ability to defend it. However, because locality was a key principle in the social organization of warfare, the state's attempt to weld the imagination of community to the defense of territory fostered peasant parochialism as well as nationalism. With serrano peasants the attachment to the local community, the pueblo or patria chica, came first and foremost, and at times conflicted with loyalties to the patria writ large.

Secular Rituals: Moral and Material Incentives

From his balcony [the governor of Chihuahua] also watches the riders file by. They are people of the countryside: herdsmen or tillers of the soil, converted by the land itself into centaurs. They return covered in dust: gray-white in their wide-brimmed sombreros, in their buckskin armor and well-worn moccasins, weapons resting on their legs. They arrive satisfied and proud; their stony glances scan the multitude, toughened by the landscape and by their struggle, a hardness that has since characterized the face of the norteño. As proof of their pride, they raise over their heads, on the point of a stick or of a lance, the macabre raceme. Others, more discreet, carry them on the pommels of their saddles or hang them from the sides . . . Indian scalps! Bloody, nauseating, and semiputrified booty. Magnets for the curious and the flies. (Jordán 1981:246, my translation)

As the secretary of the Chihuahuan government observed in 1856, measures had to be taken so that "the warrior spirit of our inhabitants does not forget its noble origin."[35] Man is moved by "individual interest" and by the "honors" that are his "rewards in the public esteem," the governor of Chihuahua explained to the Congress in 1857.[36] In order to regulate the production of the militarized bodies that warfare required, the state became the fount of honor in the Apache wars, awarding honors—tokens of valor and indexes of masculinity—to those who distinguished themselves in battle.

These honors included, first and foremost, the "prizes of honor" (*premios de honor*), cash rewards given by the Chihuahuan government for the scalps of Apaches killed in warfare.[37] Other honors awarded to frontier fighters by the state were the right to appropriate booty, livestock, and captives taken from defeated Apaches.[38] Moreover, in return for fighting the Apache, the state rewarded frontier settlers with rights to land, tax exemptions, and other privileges.

Cowardice in the face of the Apache brought public ridicule, as well as official contempt, and jeopardized the special rights and privileges that the state accorded to peasant-warriors. Moreover, failure to adhere to the norms of the code of honor led to a revaluation of gender identity. Cowards lost the ideological attributes of masculinity and were symbolically transformed into women. For example, before dismissing them "with ignominy," one eighteenth-century frontier officer forced soldiers who had displayed cowardice in the face of the enemy to parade in public in female attire.[39] Almost one hundred years later the prefect of Chihuahua relayed to the settlers of Namiquipa the governor's contempt for their cowardly retreat from battle with a small group of Apaches. The governor, he emphasized, "cannot comprehend nor explain satisfactorily how fifty armed men, offended by the uninterrupted aggressions of the barbarians and especially by the theft . . . that caused . . . the near ruin of the community of Namiquipa, could back down before five Indians who faced the whole party." The governor, he added, despised citizens who, because of "their lack of patriotism and their cowardice, turn back in horror at the first howls of the barbarians or at the sound of the first shot."[40] By contrast, for their courage and success in other encounters with the Apache, including the battle of Tres Castillos in 1880, the Namiquipans were the object of a very different state response.

The frontier warriors—largely peasants from the districts of Guerrero, Galeana, and Bravos, as well as Tarahumara Indians—who killed the Apache leader Victorio and decimated his band in 1880 were amply rewarded by the state. Apart from a daily wage, the Chihuahuan government paid them a total of 27,450 pesos for scalps and prisoners and allowed them to distribute among themselves the booty taken from the defeated Apaches (Terrazas 1905:71–82; Chávez 1939:362–64). In addition, through a voluntary subscription, 17,000 pesos were raised by civilians throughout the province and distributed among these Apache fighters (Almada 1955:324). Moreover, the frontiersmen were publicly honored in the capital of Chihuahua.

As the returning warriors paraded in front of the palace of government, Manuel de Herrera, the deputy of the Guerrero District, delivered a speech from the balcony expressing official, public recognition of the victors' heroic "courage," exemplary "citizenship," glorious "patriotism," and "pure love" of family:

> Noble warriors, sons of the historic state of Chihuahua, worthy ramparts of society, compatriots and friends, full of the most effusive gratitude I salute and congratulate you for the great triumph you obtained on the terrible field of honor, defeating in the sierra of Tres Castillos—a place that will perdure in memory—the barbarous enemy of civilization and humanity. You return crowned with laurels of unfading glory. (October 24, 1880; reproduced in Chávez 1939; my translation)

Through this "secular ritual" (which echoes Jordán's historical reconstruction of the macabre parade of scalp hunters), frontier warriors were officially accorded military honor. They were the "ramparts of society," men of extraordinary valor and virility who guarded the boundaries of the social from the deconstructing disorder of the wild.[41] Their masculinity, and their rectitude as subjects of the state and members of an imagined community, received public acknowledgment and acclaim. Clearly, this ritual and others like it were technologies of power deployed by the state to regulate the militarization of subjects and to reproduce the ideology of honor.

However, the production and reproduction of the meanings and values of gender honor were fomented not only by the state but also by the subaltern groups and classes themselves. The heroic construction of masculinity was exemplified in such forms of play as bullfights and rodeos. Through these games frontiersmen were able to display as well as compete for recognition of their masculinity, their horsemanship, and their ability to tame nature.

Like bullfights and rodeos, cockfights were (and continue to be) agons of gender honor. The cock engages in two activities: fighting and fucking. As a result, this bird is a privileged symbol of the macho; men who are extraordinarily masculine are often said to be "*muy gallo*," that is, very like cocks. In cockfights the roosters are icons of the men who own and support them with their bets. The victory of one cock over another increases the masculinity of the men identified with the winner and diminishes that of those who are equated with the loser. Gambling was a form of play that expressed this frontier vision:

> People constantly exposed themselves to risks: risks were considered inevitable, part of a flow of events over which one's actions had very little control. The underlying philosophy would seem to have been that in a frontier environment life and property could be lost at any moment in violent action: in that sense, existence took on the nature of a permanent gamble. The pervasiveness of games of chance among individuals was therefore an abbreviated statement of their views on life. This fatalistic approach was the other side of the constant pursuit of military honor, the only way one could sustain the . . . burden of permanent exposure to death (Baretta and Markoff 1978:615).

Games of chance articulated a paradox: mastery, as a quality of individuals and defiance of mortality, coexisted with acceptance of fate and of death as dimensions of existence that transcended the wills of individuals. Moreover, such forms of play affirmed the democracy of risk and the equality of men before fate and death.

Conclusions

On the Chihuahuan frontier the state did not have a true monopoly of force. However, it was able to regulate the use of force through three strategies. First, the state retained a great measure of control over the supply of arms and ammunition. Second, it arbitrated the use of force by fostering, legitimating, and rewarding only certain forms of violence, those that advanced its goals of territorial conquest and domination. Third, through secular rituals, moral and material incentives, the counting and registering of "able-bodied men," and other technologies of power, the state was able to militarize subaltern social identity and to inscribe the norms and values of warfare in the construction of social subjectivity.

Gender became a primary site for the militarization of subjects, the production of relations of power, and the achievement of status honor.

By deploying discourses and practices that advanced an ideology of honor in which valor and military skills were central to the construction of masculinity, the state turned peasants such as the Namiquipans into warriors. Subjection took the form of a military investment of bodies and identities through which masculine virtue and prestige became contingent on performance in warfare.

The social value accorded to gender honor, however, was not just the result of a discursive construction advanced by the state; it was also a consequence of the process of warfare itself. An uncanny parallel between certain Hispanic descriptions of Apache warriors and characterizations of frontier fighters suggests that warfare involved an exchange not only of weapons and strategies but also of meanings and values. Ironically, as a reciprocal specialty in violence developed among self and other, some of the same meanings and values came to be privileged by both colonists and colonized: valor, stoicism, and fighting skills became integral to the construction of Hispanic as well as Apache masculinity.[42]

In addition, the frontier settlers themselves, especially the members of subaltern groups, actively fostered, inflected, and reproduced the ideology of military honor. For Namiquipan men and other peasant warriors of Chihuahua, the social significance accorded to masculine valor and military prowess became a source of rights and privileges, as well as status honor. For Namiquipan women the significance accorded to sexual purity and virginal maternity was a source of value, respect, and protection, as well as confinement and subjection. For the members of rural frontier communities as a whole, the constant affirmation of military honor legitimated the right to state-conferred honors, including land, and became integral to the reproduction of the pueblo.

Distinction in warfare was one of the few sources of prestige open to "pacified" Indians. Tarahumara Indians who fought the Apache alongside the gente de razón acquired a military honor that conflicted with and at times overrode their ethnic status as *mansos*. As the killer of Victorio, the Tarahumara Indian Mauricio Corredor received two thousand pesos for the Apache leader's scalp and became a regional hero (Chávez 1939). Not surprisingly, Corredor's community, the sierra pueblo of Ariseáchi, received more land than other Tarahumara settlements when the Cantón Guerrero was surveyed in 1885.[43]

In short, subaltern groups actively reproduced the state's militarization of honor because it was a source of value and prestige that enabled them to improve their status position and class situation. As Baretta and

Markoff point out, on the frontier, "military honor could be achieved by all people, without distinction of birth or possessions. In other words, achievement of honor through exposure to risk was a democratic affair. . . . The cult of military values, a basic element in the life of the Spanish aristocracy, became for the lower classes a sort of ideology of the oppressed, their only route to the achievement of recognition" (1978:613). Ironically, military honor at once constituted and mitigated subalternity.

The militarization of frontier settlers was a paradoxical phenomenon. On the one hand, it was a product of strategies deployed by the state in order to create militarily effective subjects and to foment as well as to regulate warfare with indigenes. As such, it represents a form of domination and exploitation. On the other hand, this form of subjectivity-subjection simultaneously empowered subaltern groups, particularly after independence when the social organization of warfare became more decentralized.

Subaltern access to and skill in deploying the means of violence acted as a brake on exploitation and domination and allowed a wider latitude in the negotiation of the terms of subjection. Until the attenuation of warfare, military prowess was rewarded with access to the means of production and with a great measure of community autonomy. The social value accorded to military honor became a basis for frontier egalitarianism: subaltern groups that distinguished themselves in warfare commanded more military prestige than the majority of the members of dominant groups and classes. Ironically, in order to reproduce their privileged social position, Chihuahua's military peasants needed the very enemies they were trying to annihilate.

Ethnic and military prestige, however, were not the only sources of honor in frontier society. Occupation and class were also important to the construction of status honor.

CHAPTER FOUR

Honor and Class
Wealth and Occupation

In Spain, according to Pitt-Rivers, wealth in itself does not convey social esteem, for "honor derives from the domination of persons rather than things" (1965:60). Instead, honor is accumulated through "the act of beneficence," that is, through the generous disposal of what has been acquired rather than through "the fact of possession," as in Anglo societies (1965:60–61).

As a basis for the formation of patron-client ties, the capacity to redistribute wealth is a sign of power over others. But it is also a sign of mastery over the self. As Wolf notes, for the conquerors of the New World, wealth was an index of "spiritual autarchy," that is, of "personal liberty" and freedom from domination by other men (1959:161). Unlike children and women, who were recipients of the bounty produced by others and therefore dependent beings, hombres were givers and therefore masters of themselves and of others.

On the Chihuahuan frontier in the eighteenth and nineteenth centuries, beneficence was critical to the acquisition of honor.[1] Largesse was (and continues to be) central to the construction and legitimation of patriarchal and patrimonial authority; magnanimity is a stereotypic virtue of padres and hombres, whereas selfishness is a stereotypic vice of machos and padrastros.

The generous disposal of wealth was one way of transforming economic capital into symbolic capital. For the economic elite this included making financial contributions to the Apache campaigns, to the church, and to public works projects. Moreover, honor required that relations between patrons and clients be mediated by the values and norms of a reciprocity in which beneficence disguised and legitimated the asymmetries of exchanges between superiors and inferiors. Grounding precedence in virtue, largesse reproduced patriarchal and patrimonial relations of domination and exploitation.

Nevertheless, in the clash between "civilization" and "barbarism," the "fact of possession" became one of the signs that differentiated "rational beings" from "creatures of instinct." Possession of and property in land, as well as the right to freely alienate or acquire the means of production, were privileges accorded to the gente de razón, signs of civilization and of the mastery integral to the honor of men. The Apache, in the colonists' eyes, had no rights in land whatsoever. Because tame Indians were minors and wards of the Crown, the members of Indian communities were forbidden to buy and sell lands. They had usufruct rights rather than derechos de posesión, or property rights.[2]

Serrano peasant-warriors held the land granted to their pueblos as corporate groups. However, in contrast to the members of Indian communities, male family heads were given absolute rights of possession— derechos de posesión—to their lots. They could buy and sell lots, as well as transmit them to their heirs. In contrast to both the Indians and the peasant-warriors, hacendados and rancheros held land as individuals rather than as members of corporate groups. They tended to have legal title to their lands rather than derechos de posesión or usufruct rights.

Wealth, derechos de posesión, and property in land became signs of culture and mastery, indexes of the gente de razón's active role in the transformation of "nature" and in the refinement of the "natural" self. Culturally, accumulation was counterbalanced and restricted by the moral imperatives of beneficence and reciprocity, as well as by the morally ambiguous but heroic squandering of wealth in gambling. But although risked and redistributed rather than just hoarded and saved, wealth and "the fact of possession" were still indexes of civilized production.

Not only the types of rights to land and wealth but also work became a sign that differentiated the "civilized" from the "savage." From the colonists' point of view, Indians did not work. Although the mansos and the bárbaros were viewed as lazy (*flojos*) by the colonists, the Apache were regarded as the laziest of all: their natural "indolence" and "love of liberty" led them to live through "theft" (e.g., see Escudero 1834:243).

From the colonists' point of view, Apaches lived from the fruits of nature or from the spoils of theft, not from the products of their own toil. Machos who had honor-precedence but who lacked honor-virtue, Apache men were construed as purely natural. In the colonists' eyes, the "barbarians" had such a deficient sense of responsibility to wife and family that they let the women do the work. Indeed, one colonial text dwells on the "servile treatment" given to Apache wives by their husbands (Cordero in Matson and Schroeder 1957:342). Purchased by the men, who were "masters even of their lives," indigenous wives were like beasts of burden rather than civilized "guardian angels" of home and hearth: they did all the work (Cordero in Matson and Schroeder 1957:342).

> The [Apache] man knows no other obligation than that of the hunt or of war, of making his weapons, saddles and other trappings necessary for its exercise. The women care for the animals they own; make the utensils *needed in their work*; cure and tan the hides of the animals; carry water and firewood; seek and collect the seeds and fruits which the region produces; dry them and make bread and cakes; sow a little corn, beans, etc.; water them and reap at the proper time, and they are not exempt from accompanying their husbands on their expeditions, in which they are extremely useful for driving the stolen animals, acting as sentinels and serving in whatever capacity is commanded them. (Cordero in Matson and Schroeder 1957:339; my emphasis)

More than fifty years later General Emilio Lamberg advanced a similar (if somewhat more ironic) reading of the Apache division of labor: "The men never occupy themselves in any other work [*trabajo*] but hunting, fighting and stealing, for everything else is done by the women" (in Lozano 1949:275; my translation).

The colonists interpreted what they construed as a gender inversion in wholly negative terms. The work of Apache women was not valued as an active transformation of nature (for such females were "savages," after all) but instead was devalued as a sign of exploitation. For the colonists' this inversion became one more index of barbarism: of the savagery of the woman who worked like a beast and of the brutishness of the man who commanded her to do so.

In the confrontation of "civilization" with "barbarism," a "work ethic" emerged on the frontier. As an activity that transformed nature, work became a sign of ethnic honor that distinguished the gente de razón from the bárbaros. In contrast to the Center, where to work with one's hands was a sign of infamy, on the frontier even forms of manual labor, such as agricultural work and livestock herding, became signs of ethnic honor (Jones 1979:passim).

Work was also a sign of both the "natural" and cultural dimensions of masculine honor. Since undomesticated nature was viewed as sterile, harsh, and inclement, it took *huevos* to tame the wilderness and to make it produce. In a sense, the agricultural field was also a battlefield, a site of struggle with nature (as well as with the Apache, who often attacked peasants while they were working on their lands). Production itself was an education in maleness; indeed, the masculinity of frontiersmen is often represented as a product of the struggle with a hostile wilderness. Work tamed and feminized a land that was barren in itself but could be fecundated and rendered productive by masculine activity.

Not just a sign of macho precedence but also a sign of patriarchal honor-virtue, work made serrano warriors life givers and differentiated them from life-taking Apache braves. Men who did not work were construed as exemplars of a "bad mode of life" (*malo modo de vivir*): laziness made them prone to such vices as drunkenness (*embriaguez*), illegitimate sex (*amancebamiento*), and theft (*robo*).[3] The 1848 Register of Vagrants (Registro de Vagos) from Namiquipa makes clear that to be without a "recognized occupation" (*oficio conocido*) demonstrated a lack of verguenza and respeto. Neglecting their duties to family, community, and society, "vagrants" (*vagos*) were men of "perverse and vile sentiments" (*perversos y viles sentimientos*).[4] They were machos who were more like "barbarians" than like "civilized" hombres. Rather than being good *vecinos* (inhabitants of a settled place, often used as a synonym for *gente de razón* and rarely used to characterize Indians), they were vagos, men as propertyless, as placeless, and as lazy as the "savages" themselves.

As the key sites for peasant-warrior destructive and productive activity, the agricultural and battle fields were the principal domains of masculine value. By contrast, the fields of honor for serrano women were the female body and its metaphorical extension, the home. Lacking in huevos, women were considered "naturally" incapable of either domesticating the wilderness or of conquering its "barbaric" inhabitants. Moreover, as we have seen, on the frontier women were held to need special enclosure: the boundaries of the fields of feminine honor had to be maintained and guarded by men. However, although women's work was largely confined to the domestic domain, it was highly valued and construed as a key contribution to both the household and the community.

Pace Ortner (1974), the work of women was not seen as any less "cultural" than that of men. On the whole, work was a source of value for both men and women. The lazy woman was as dishonorable as the vago.

Registers of vagrants, such as the one discussed above, attest to the role played by the state in the construction of a frontier work ethic in which laziness became a form of infamy that had to be socially controlled. In Namiquipa today it remains the case that to "feel lazy" (*tener flojera*) is to be in a liminal state akin to illness.

For the state the frontier presented special problems of social and labor regulation. The indigenes' unwillingness to work for the gente de razón created a labor shortage. At the same time, the devastation wreaked by the Apache wars led to the growth of a vagrant population. Such vagrants sometimes became bandits and on occasion redefined their ethnic affiliation and became "Apaches." The registration, roundup, and allocation of vagrants to military service were state strategies aimed at regulating the subjectivities and the productive capacities of frontier men. Such technologies of power contributed to the emergence of a frontier work ethic in which productive activity became a sign of honor, one that articulated the meanings of gender and ethnicity as well as of class.

Not all forms of work, however, accrued the same social esteem. Hacendados garnered a great deal of social esteem. Entrepreneurs who wished to become part of the Chihuahuan elite invested in the acquisition of cattle haciendas; landed property was a privileged sign of personal prestige and social status. To be a peasant was less honorable than to be an hacendado, but tilling one's own land was far more honorable than selling one's labor to another man.

Significantly, in nineteenth-century documents wage labor is sometimes referred to as "personal services" (*servicios personales*).[5] To sell your labor power is to sell your self, to renounce the self-mastery integral to gender honor, and to experience a loss of masculinity. Today in Namiquipa, to work as a wage laborer is still considered dishonorable by agricultural producers who own their means of production. Although the peasants of corporate communities generally did not have title to their individual plots, in practice their rights to these parcels were no different from those of legal proprietors; peasants were their own masters and were able to freely dispose of their lands.

Finally, as we have seen, military prowess was a sign of honor. Soldiering was a prestigious occupation. Many of Chihuahua's nineteenth-century governors were career soldiers or men who had distinguished themselves in battle (Almada 1980).

The differential social prestige accorded to distinct occupations, as well as the access to social honor afforded by landed property and wealth, indicates that class situation was a determinant of status position on the Chihuahuan frontier. However, status position was not the a priori product of an immutable structure but the complex outcome of multiple and contradictory processes of political and discursive construction. Thus, agents and groups with divergent status and class positions construed the relationship between honor and class differently. Whereas economically dominant classes stressed the inequalities of honor based on wealth and property, subaltern groups such as the peasants of Namiquipa emphasized their privileged access to military honor and to an ethnic honor they shared with the elite. Moreover, members of subaltern classes insisted on their right to pride irrespective of their class position.

Documentary evidence and oral tradition indicate that even hacienda workers, especially the cowboys who had access to military-gender honor and who tended to be armed, demanded to be treated with a respect that recognized their rights to honor.[6] Cowboys and other hacienda workers who felt mistreated or insulted by hacienda administrators and *caporales* (cattle bosses) sought, and sometimes succeeded in obtaining, legal redress for their grievances.

Legal redress was often sought after workers and bosses had exchanged insults and even come to blows. These disputes, which often involved physical violence, were frequently cast in the idiom of gender honor. For example, one cowboy who was insulted by a cattle boss stated to the judge that "he obliged me to tell him to contain himself, for neither he nor anyone had the right to abuse and insult me so immorally."[7] Such cases suggest that the prestige and status of agents was the product of different and contradictory subject positions; class oppression was offset by access to other dimensions of status honor.

On the Chihuahuan frontier class situation—defined here in the Weberian sense of relationship to the means of production, distribution, and exchange—was one of the principles of social stratification (Weber 1978:302, 927–28). However, two factors limited the growth of class inequalities on the Chihuahuan frontier until the 1880s. First, economic development as a whole and the accumulation of wealth and property were hampered by the Apache wars. Second, the general economic depression that affected Mexico until the 1870s further curtailed economic growth on the frontier.[8] In addition, class was not the only basis for the creation of social hierarchy. As we have seen, status, the distribution of honor in society (Weber 1978:305, 927), was also a key principle of stratification. Moreover, one principle did not predominate over the other; instead, both were central to the construction of relations of super- and subordination.

On the one hand, status position conditioned class situation. For example, the serranos' relatively privileged access to the means of production was predicated on ethnic and military honor. On the other hand, class itself was a dimension of status. Wealth, property, and possession rights, as well as occupation, were sources of social prestige. But class was only one criterion of status honor, and it frequently came into conflict with ethnic and military-gender honor. On the whole, status inequalities based on class were mitigated by the effects of a widely accessible military and ethnic honor. But this relationship between class and status was to be altered once the Apache wars ended and economic development took off.

Order, Progress, and Resistance

2

State Formation, Hegemony, and the Construction of Subjectivities

Abrams long ago pointed out that by positing a mystifying separation of the political and the social, scholars have objectified and personified "the state" (1988:76). A product of the practices of politically organized subjection in capitalist societies, this misplaced concreteness resonates with and is reinforced by everyday experience and becomes "commonsensical" (Gramsci 1971:323–33). As an alternative, Abrams proposes that we study the "state-system: a palpable nexus of practice and institutional structure centred in government and more or less extensive, unified and dominant in any given society" (1988:82), as well as the "state-idea," a "message of domination—an ideological artefact attributing unity, morality and independence to the disunited, amoral and dependent workings of the practice of government" (1988:81). Understanding "the state" as a "mask" entails grasping its importance as a historically constructed and contested "exercise in legitimation, in moral regulation" (1988:77).

That modern relations of rule and forms of discipline—the other side of the coin of the rise of modern capitalism—construct and are constructed in everyday practices is demonstrated by Corrigan and Sayer's work on English state formation. Drawing on Abrams, Marx, Weber, Mao Zedong, Durkheim, and Foucault, Corrigan and Sayer argue that state formation is "cultural revolution," foregrounding in their analysis the ways in which everyday state routines, rituals, activities, and policies, which are themselves material cultural forms, constitute and regulate the social making of meaning and of subjects (1985:2–3). Anchored in relations of inequality, cultural revolution is not "merely an ideational matter, and cannot be considered independently of the materiality of state formation—what state agencies are, how they act, and on whom" (1985:191). Their work "draws attention to the *totalizing* dimension of state formation . . . to its constructions of 'national character' and 'national identity' . . . and the *individualizing* dimension of state formation, which is organized through impositional claims embodied in distinctive categories . . . that are structured along the axes of class, occupation, gender, age, ethnicity and locality" (Joseph and Nugent 1994:20; see Corrigan and Sayer 1985:4–5). These totalizing and individualizing processes generate "a common discursive framework" (Roseberry 1994:361), articulated by nonlinguistic as well as linguistic signifiers, which forms and is formed by the lived experience of state subjects (Joseph and Nugent 1994:20). "Making this *conscience* genuinely collective is always an accomplishment, a struggle against other ways of seeing, other moralities, which express the historical experiences of the dominated" (Corrigan and Sayer 1985:6). Thus, an anthropology of state formation needs to consider what the state is formed against: "Neither the shape of the state, nor oppositional cultures, can be properly understood outwith [*sic*] the context of the mutually formative (and continuing) struggle between them: in other words, historically" (Corrigan and Sayer 1985:7).

Although there are some obvious parallels between Corrigan and Sayer's theorizing of state formation on the one hand and Gramsci's on the other, there are also key differences. Gramsci's double definition of "the state" has both a "narrow" and an "expanded" sense. In the narrow sense the state, equated with government, functions by "direct domination," that is, command and coercion (Gramnsci 1971:12; see Cain 1983:99–101). In the expanded sense the "State = political society + civil society, in other words, hegemony protected by the armour of coercion" (Gramsci 1971:263). Both formulations privilege "civil society" as the site of production of "hegemony" and hence provide no way of theorizing either "the process of penetration of civil society by agencies of government"—in other words, the ways in which the quotidian functioning of the state system and the everyday production of the state idea are crucial to the hegemonic process—or "what is special about nongovernmental forms of control" (Cain 1983:101; Eagleton 1991:112–13). Moreover, for Corrigan and Sayer, the power of the state "rests not so much on the consent of its subjects but with the state's regulative and coercive forms and agencies, which define and create certain kinds of subjects and identities while denying" others through everyday routines and rituals of ruling (Roseberry 1994:357).

Writing a historical ethnography of how rule is accomplished in everyday practice entails moving beyond a notion of power as interdiction and uncovering the ways in which the exercise of power produces meanings, truths, bodies, selves—in short, forms of doing, knowing, and being. It also requires displacing the disjuncture Foucault "interposes between the power that belongs to sovereignty and the microphysics of power that operates in everyday life and practices" (Hall 1988:70). Although Foucault's focus on power's "capillary form of existence" (1980:39) is a useful counter to a traditional notion of power as radiating from the state alone (Hall 1988:70), the disjuncture he posits obscures the importance of the dialectic between state forms and everyday life. Only by recognizing that power is "multidimensional, a reciprocal interplay between centers of authority and [quotidian] practices" (Hall 1988:70) can we grasp the interchanges between a "macrohydraulics of power and a microphysics of power" (Hall 1988:70) and come to understand how the state system and the state idea are critical to the construction of hegemony.

Hegemony, as Laclau and Mouffe argue, is not "an external relation between preconstituted social agents, but the very process of . . . construction of those agents" (1982:100). Such a notion of hegemony moves beyond an a priori class reductionism and economism and allows us to integrate dimensions of subjectivity such as gender and ethnicity into analyses of domination and subjection.

In the following chapters I use the concepts introduced above to analyze how interlinked processes of state formation and capitalist development transformed Mexican society from the late 1850s to 1910. Although the effects of these processes on frontier society are discernible in the 1860s and 1870s, the incorporation of the Chihuahuan periphery into the capitalist world market and its increased integration into the nation-state were limited until the defeat of the Apache in 1886. These large-scale transformations had enormous consequences for relations between the state and frontier groups, as well as for relations between dominant and subordinate classes. Capitalist development and state centralization redefined the forms of subjectivity-subjection; class acquired a new saliency in the calculation of status. Ethnicity and prowess in warfare—the main sources of social honor for the subaltern groups and classes of the frontier—lost their centrality in the calculation of status.

After the end of the Apache wars, dominant groups and classes needed the serranos to provide labor for new economic enterprises rather than to fight the indigenes. For the state the "warrior spirit" of the serranos became an obstacle to "order" and "progress"; ironically, these one-time agents of "civilization" became redefined as the new barbarians. In order to turn the serranos into docile subjects and servile workers, the state denied them the privileges of patriarchy and the emblems of honor. Not only did the corporate land grants and the relative political autonomy of serrano communities come under attack, but these specialists in violence also became the object of state-deployed technologies of order and power designed to "reduce" what was now construed as their wild and threatening masculinity.

Paradoxically, the "good" frontier subject—the Namiquipan peasant warrior or the hacienda cowboy fighter—was a potential rebel. Not only were members of these groups specialists in violence, but their very identities were products of a code of honor that privileged violence as a legitimate means of avenging affronts and insults and of defending rights to social prestige and respect. In order to maintain their privileged position, militarized settlers needed enemies. When the class and status rights of the "centaurs" of the Apache wars were violated by the state and the elite at the end of the nineteenth century, these specialists in violence became the "centaurs" of insurrection.

Beginning in the late 1850s but particularly after 1886, serranos engaged in nonviolent and armed forms of resistance. From 1910 to 1920 the Chihuahuan sierra became a key focus of peasant revolutionary activity. The discourses, techniques, and forms of resistance deployed by these peasant insurgents were strongly influenced by the cultural construction and social organization of frontier warfare. Ironically, those forms of identity and discourses of honor deployed by an earlier state project and reproduced by the serranos were to become counter-hegemonic in a subsequent conjuncture and were to motivate and orient resistance.

The Nation-State, Capitalist Development, and the Transformation of the Frontier

The colonial Mexican state was predominantly patrimonial. A logic of hierarchy, predicated upon ethnic honor, made subjects different in "nature" and generated groups and classes whose interrelations were conceived by analogy to that of the corporal organs and whose common subordination to the patrimonial ruler paralleled that of the body parts to the head (McAllister 1963; Gutiérrez 1980). After independence the struggle between "conservatives-centralists" and "liberals-federalists" began to frame national political life: a legal-rational ideology, advanced by an emergent bourgeoisie, entered into conflict with the patrimonial vision of society held by the old colonial elite (de la Garza et al. 1986; Cardoso 1980). Until the middle of the nineteenth century, however, the Mexican state continued to be predominantly patrimonial. *Caudillos* (strongmen) from the Center and South formed armed patron-client sets and battled each other to become heads of a patrimonial state decapitated by freedom from the Spanish Crown (Wolf and Hansen 1967).

Nation-State Formation and National Economic Development (1855–1910)

In the mid-1850s the liberals succeeded in gaining control of the state apparatus. The ensuing decades would be characterized by efforts to impose a legal-rational form of organization on government, economy, and society and to reconstitute the forms of subjection-subjectivity. Replacing patrimonial with legal-rational forms of political legitimation such as electoral democracy involved an undermining of the link between personal violence and social authority: violence became viewed as a negation of the free exercise of will and reason that legitimated the liberal contract between government and people. Punishments such as mutilation, whipping, or other torment that deployed physical force to inscribe subjects' lack of free will on their bodies and to dramatize personal subjection to a sovereign were banned by the constitution; the Criminal Code of 1871 outlined a system of incarcerative correction and banned public executions.[1]

Ironically, this cultural revolution implemented by liberal state formation gave rise to almost a decade of armed conflict between conservative and liberal factions (1858–66), during which Mexico was invaded by the French, who were allied with the conservatives. By 1876, however, many of the liberals' policies had been put into effect. The Porfirian regime (1876–1910), continued to implement certain aspects of the liberal project of nation-state formation and capitalist development while it transformed others.

The Liberal Project: 1855–1876

The liberal project had two interlinked and mutually reinforcing aims: the formation of a modern nation-state and that of a capitalist national market (de la Garza et al. 1986). In order to carry out this project, the liberals had to break the power of the church, of the traditional corporations, of the old creole elite, and of the regional caudillos. Corporate organizations, such as the church, the indigenous pueblo, and the peasant community, that stood between the nation-state and the citizen had to be eliminated so that the supremacy of the nation-state in the regulation and administration of collective life could be established. From the liberals' point of view, particularist loyalties and overtly hierarchical social ontologies were to be supplanted by universalistic and purportedly egalitarian forms of subjectivity and community. Moreover, protectionist impediments to the free functioning of the market were to be eliminated in order to create the national capitalist economy, which was to be as much a precondition for the formation of a legal-rational state as its result (de la Garza et al. 1986).

Secularizing Reproduction:
The Rationalization of Domesticity and Patriarchy

In the mid-nineteenth century, the church possessed considerable control over economy and society and was one of the biggest landowners and finance capitalists in Mexico. Moreover, through a monopoly over the legitimation of sexual unions and their fruit, as well as the collection of demographic statistics, the church played a key role in the regulation of social reproduction, patriarchy, and domesticity. In addition, education was in the hands of the clergy (Márquez Padilla 1986:57–62).

From 1856 to 1859 the liberal government passed the "Reform Laws" as well as a new national constitution, both of which promulgated religious freedom, prevented the church from owning property, and secularized education and marriage. Church land passed into private hands, and the state usurped ecclesiastical control over social reproduction, education, and domestic patriarchy (Márquez Padilla 1986; Ludlow 1986; Meyer and Sherman 1979:404–12).[2]

The redefinition of legitimate authority in the public sphere entailed a reciprocal transformation of authority in the domestic sphere. Mid-nineteenth-century legal commentary stated that in modern times the domestic authority of the patriarch was more that of " 'a legislator or judge' " than that of a sovereign (cited in Arrom 1985:78). Although liberals did not question a husband's right to govern his wife, they did redefine the basis of his authority: the subjection of woman to man in marriage was to be predicated on the legal contract—the epitome of free will, reason, and modernity—which was at odds with physical violence, a signifier of barbarism. Significantly, in his speech to the Constitutional Convention in 1856, Ignacio Ramírez, a prominent liberal, stated that it was " 'shameful in a civilized country' that 'many unfortunate women are beaten by their husbands' " (cited in Arrom 1985:237).

Prior to the liberal revolution of the 1850s, both church and state had condoned a husband's right to apply "moderate physical violence" to "correct the faults" of his wife, and according to Arrom's study of gender in Mexico City during the first half of the nineteenth century, men's and women's attitudes were largely in line with official policy (1985:236). However, under the 1871 criminal code enacted by the liberals, wife beating was dealt with as an instance of the general categories of blows (*golpes*) and lesions (*lesiones*) and was penalized regardless of its severity. Moreover, for the first time in Mexico's history, a man's murder of his adulterous wife became a criminal offense punishable by four years in prison.[3]

The criminalization of domestic violence was only one facet of the liberal revolution's secularization of the management of reproduction and extension of the rationalizing reach of the modernizing Mexican state into the domestic domain. State regulation of reproduction and the domestic sphere was a matter of public morality and social stability. For Mexican liberals the nuclear family rather than the individual was both the basic unit of society and a microcosm of the state. If the husband, as citizen, was the family's representative vis-à-vis the state, he was also the state's representative in the family, governing his household in accordance with the principles enshrined in law that refined and rationalized the gender asymmetry ordained by nature.

Read to couples by judges performing the ceremony of civil matrimony, the Epistle of Melchor Ocampo,[4] in an 1859 liberal law regulating marriage and divorce, provides an apt example of the normalization of liberal constructions of gender and sexuality in the legal rituals of everyday life. Civil marriage continues to be construed as a sacred union, but society, rather than the church—a moral *conscience collective*—and its representative, the state, is now the agent that blesses heterosexual, monogamous, procreative sex. Defined as a civil contract based on free will, state-sanctioned marriage is deemed "the only moral medium of founding the family, of conserving the species, and of supplementing the imperfections of the individual who cannot be sufficient unto himself in order to arrive at the perfection of humankind." The dividing practices of the epistle create an essential split between masculine and feminine subjectivity, one that provides an alibi for domestic patriarchy and women's subordination. Within "the conjugal duality,"

> the man, whose sexual endowments are principally valor and strength, should give and will give to the woman protection, nourishment, and direction, treating her always as the most delicate, sensitive, and fine part of himself and with the magnanimity and generous benevolence that the strong owes to the weak, especially when this weak one gives herself to him and when she has been confided to him by society. The woman, whose principal endowments are abnegation, beauty, compassion, perspicacity, and tenderness, should give and will give to the husband obedience, pleasure, assistance, comfort, and counsel, treating him

always with the veneration that is owed to the person who supports us and defends us and with the delicacy of she who does
not wish to exasperate the brusque and irritable part of herself.

Men and women can transcend their essential incompleteness, a product of gender difference, and achieve integrity by recovering the other
as part of the self only through marriage. But the lifelong exchange that
the liberal contract establishes is unequal, even if the rhetorical paral-
lelism of the epistle represents marriage as balanced reciprocity: protection and obedience do not have the same social and cultural value. The
epistle exhorts husbands and wives not to insult each other, as "insults
between spouses dishonor the one who proffers them," and condemns
maltrato de obra (abuse in deed), a gloss for wife beating, as "it is villain-
ous and cowardly to abuse force"; significantly, one of the impediments
to marriage cited in this 1859 law is the use of violence because it negates
freedom of consent. Although men's strength is still key to the symbolic
construction of their social authority, its deployment against women is
now deemed dishonorable by the state, construed as a threat to the stability of marriage and family, which is at odds with liberal forms of
governmentality and hence of society itself.

Changes in the state's sanctioning of men's domestic violence were
not correlated with any major transformation in legal status entailing a
greater equality for women. The Constitution of 1857 made no direct
reference to citizenship for women, implicitly defining citizenship as a
privilege of adult men, and continued to deny women the right to vote.[5]
Women's submission to men was reinscribed both in the Reform Laws
and in the civil and criminal codes. According to the Civil Code of 1870,
the obligation of the husband was to feed and protect his wife and that
of the wife was "to obey her husband as much in domestic affairs as in
the education of the children and in the administration of property."[6] A
wife's capacity for legal self-representation was contingent on her husband's permission, except when she was the object of a criminal case
or when the case involved her husband.[7] Legally, he had the right to administer joint property as well as any property she had brought into the
marriage, although she recovered the latter in case of divorce.[8] Divorce,[9]
a separation of bed and board, did not destroy the marriage tie and only
suspended some of its obligations. Whereas female adultery was always
cause for divorce (all children born to a married woman were presumed
legitimate and inherited equally), male adultery could lead to a separa-

tion of bed and board only in certain circumstances, for example, if it led to mistreatment or abuse of the wife. However, though it secured their general submission, patriarchal law accorded married women certain "protections," ensuring their economic maintenance even in cases of divorce, requiring that husbands obtain their permission for the sale of property and penalizing wife abuse.

Patrimonial states in Europe, Connell writes,

> operated through a hegemonic form of masculinity which prized personal and family honor, worked through kinship and patronage obligations, and connected the exercise of authority with a capacity for violence. . . . The creation of a liberal-constitutional order, and especially the creation of an impersonal bureaucracy in place of an administrative apparatus run by patronage, involved an attack on this form of masculinity and its ramifications. . . . The hegemonic masculinity of the old regime was displaced during the nineteenth century by a hegemonic masculinity organized around themes of rationality, calculation, orderliness. (1990:12)

A similar if not identical shift in gender politics characterized the project (if not wholly the reality) of liberal state formation in nineteenth-century Mexico. Moreover, if the "protection" of women was linked to the state's project to build a nation founded on the principles of reason — so putting an end to the "chaos" of the decades following independence when force of arms and not electoral democracy had been the main principle of succession to the *silla* (presidential chair), a chaos that re-emerged during the Wars of the Reform (1858–61)—it was also linked to the defense of Mexico's autonomy, to the protection of the madre patria symbolized by the feminine. After their defeat in the Wars of the Reform, Mexican conservatives had conspired with foreign powers, and the subsequent French invasion of Mexico (1862–67) even resulted in the naming of an Austrian archduke as emperor of Mexico.

The Transformation of Peasant Communities

The processes of liberal state formation had as their goals the destruction of the corporate character of peasant pueblos and the replacement of a particularist imagining of community with the universalistic consciousness of nationalism (Ludlow 1986:130–33; Tutino 1986:258,

260–62). The peasant, who for the liberals was above all the Indian of the Center and the South, became identified with the colonial past and became viewed as an obstacle to national development. "Progress" (*progreso*) required that the peasant be transformed into a wage laborer or a capitalist agricultural entrepreneur. Land and labor had to be put on the market in order to advance capitalist development and state regulation of the economy. Social "order" (*orden*) necessitated the reconstitution of the *campesinos* (peasants) and of the meaningful forms through which they identified themselves and their place in the world. The peasant was no longer to be first and foremost a member of a local corporate community but instead a citizen of the Mexican nation.

The commodification and alienation of peasant lands became the means used by the state to destroy the rural corporate community and to effect the totalization and individualization of peasant identity. The Ley Lerdo of 1856 prescribed the privatization and sale of all corporate lands, including those of the peasantry. This law entailed the destruction of the autonomous economic base of rural pueblos and the reduction of local control over the production and reproduction of social life. Attempts to implement this law sparked numerous regional peasant uprisings in the 1860s and 1870s and pushed the "people of the countryside" to ally themselves with the church and the old colonial elite against the liberal state (Tutino 1986).

Other measures taken by the liberals to further nation-state formation included the reorganization of the state apparatuses, the rationalization of the bureaucracy, the institutionalization of the electoral principle of succession to office, the creation of a uniform fiscal system, the amplification of the central government's tax base, and the suppression of *alcabalas*, tariffs that had been an important source of revenue for provincial governments (Ludlow 1986:92–122). Capitalist development was fostered by eliminating barriers to commercial exchange, by initiating the construction of railroads, and by encouraging foreign investment (Ludlow 1986:92–122; Meyer and Sherman 1979:404). Moreover, the reorganization of the repressive apparatus of the state was begun.

Not only were electoral reforms central to the construction of "citizens," but they were also essential to diminishing the power of regional patrimonial strongmen. During the first half of the nineteenth century, no one principle of succession to office had achieved predominance; many caudillos came to sit on the presidential silla by staging military coups. Moreover, the establishment of a regular, legal principle of succession was key not only to state centralization but also to the creation of a "safe" climate for foreign investment.

Since the chaos of the decades following independence was partly the result of coups staged by military caudillos, the army had to be firmly brought under state control. To this end, the liberals retired many army officers and turned them into capitalists by allowing them to obtain the lands of the church at a nominal price. In addition, they reduced the strength of the national army from 80,000 to 20,000 men (Ludlow 1986:134; Márquez Padilla 1986:77–78). Moreover, the president, Benito Juárez, created a parallel repressive apparatus. The Rurales, a rural police force controlled by the central government (Vanderwood 1981:45–50), were to play a major role in repressing the peasantry and in curtailing the power of regional patrimonial leaders.

Although the federalist Constitution of 1857 had won the liberals the support of many regional elites anxious to preserve some autonomy from the central government, in the late 1860s the liberals turned on their former allies. The formation of a legal-rational state required that the power of these patrimonial leaders be broken and that regional governments be more effectively subordinated to central authority. The liberals tried to achieve this end by rationalizing the institutions of the state, by making legally sanctioned elections the means of achieving access to political office and legitimating authority, and by passing legislation that would establish the predominance of the national executive power. They failed. Their successor, Porfirio Díaz, was to succeed. However, state centralization under Díaz was to be effected through other strategies.

The Porfirian Project: 1876–1910

Legislation rationalizing the exercise of authority remained on the books during the Porfiriato.[10] Nevertheless, in practice political centralization assumed the form of patrimonial absolutism, which conflicted with the democratic-republican values and norms that had been disseminated by the liberal state and had become important to the legitimation of authority. The centralization of power under Díaz was effected through a strategy of "*pan y palo*" ("bread and club"), that is, through a combination of cooptation and repression of rival strongmen and regional elites. The result was a patrimonial oligarchy of gerontocrats who were members of the dominant classes and who were tied to the central head of state through a hierarchical network of patron-client lines.

Regional functionaries obtained office through the favor of Díaz; their power came to depend, above all, on patronage ties to the central government. As Knight points out, "a large proportion of Porfirian governors—maybe 70 percent—were presidential favorites, imported into alien states, where their prime allegiance was to their president and maker, rather than to their provincial subjects" (1986:17, vol. 1). Since provincial state functionaries were no longer as dependent on regional and local constituencies for access to office, the tendency toward personal arbitrariness that inheres in traditional authority came to the fore. The norms and values that legitimated the exercise of traditional and legal-rational authority were violated. Subaltern groups and classes were excluded from any intervention in the "political process." Although "citizens" on paper, in practice they became the personal subjects of sultanistic caciques.[11]

In addition, the implementation of liberal policies entailing the proletarianization of the peasantry and the destruction of rural corporate communities was accelerated. The politico-legal and repressive apparatuses of the state were deployed to effect the alienation of the lands of peasant communities.

Land and labor were put on the market at an unprecedented pace. The representation of space on the frontier once again became the object of social contestation as *compañías deslindadoras* (surveying companies) were contracted by the central government in the 1880s to locate untitled, and hence "vacant," lands, which passed into the dominion of the nation and were subsequently put on the market; between 1883 and 1892 about one-fifth of Mexico's land was turned over to these compañías deslindadoras (Hamilton 1982:45). "Vacant lands" (*baldíos*) were acquired by European and American investors and by members of Mexico's dominant classes—hacendados, merchants, bankers, and industrialists who had ties of patronage to Díaz and his political favorites. Land ownership became concentrated in the hands of members of the national and regional oligarchies and the dominant classes: 1 percent of rural families came to own 85 percent of Mexico's land (Márquez Padilla 1986:82).

As Katz has observed, the state's assault on rural corporate communities represents "the greatest catastrophe in the history of the Mexican peasantry since the massive Indian mortality of the sixteenth and seventeenth century" (1988:56). The corporate landholdings of peasant pueblos were privatized and alienated. By the end of the Porfiriato, millions of Mexican campesinos had been transformed into landless laborers.[12] Other peasants retained rights to plots insufficient in size for household reproduction and became at least partially dependent on the sale of their labor power. By 1910, 50 percent of rural Mexicans lived and/or worked on haciendas (Meyer and Sherman 1979:45).

The commodification of land and labor was only one of the pillars of national economic policy. The Díaz regime eliminated barriers to the national market, developed communications and transport systems, encouraged the growth of manufacturing, and favored and protected domestic and foreign capitalists by granting them tax exemptions.

Development resulted in the expansion of the industrial proletariat. However, since the Díaz regime was concerned above all with maximizing conditions for capital accumulation, the policy of "pan y palo," of cooptation and repression, was used to limit efforts at labor organization (Hamilton 1982:52). Domestic and foreign capitalists, not peasants or workers, were to be the beneficiaries of Mexico's first "economic miracle." [13]

For the Mexican state, foreign capital was the precondition of this miracle. By the end of the Porfiriato, conditions for dependent capitalist development were in place (Coatsworth 1978). Foreign capital played a decisive role in the most important sectors of the Mexican economy, including mining and commercial agriculture. By 1911 foreign investment amounted to more than 3,400 million pesos, 62 percent of which was European and 32 percent of which was American capital (Márquez Padilla 1986:80). Most of Mexico's exports were raw materials, mainly precious metals, agricultural products, and petroleum, while its imports included manufactured products, machinery, and other capital goods (Hamilton 1982:44). Mexico's increasing dependence on the United States was reflected in the balance of trade. By the end of the Porfiriato, imports from the United States represented 55 to 60 percent of the total, and exports to the United States ranged between 65 and 75 percent (Hamilton 1982:45).

The Porfiriato saw the first sustained economic growth in Mexico since the colonial period. Although economic recovery had begun during the Restored Republic (1867–76), colonial per-capita income levels were not surpassed until the late 1870s (Coatsworth 1978:81). However, Mexico's dependence on foreign capital made it vulnerable to fluctuations in the world market; the world economic crisis of 1907–10 was to have a disastrous impact on the Mexican economy (Katz 1981:20).

That the economic miracle should benefit capitalists, not peasants or workers, that subaltern groups and classes should be excluded from participation in the formal political process was only "natural," according to the positivist, social Darwinist ideology constructed by the Porfirian state. Whereas for the liberals the main protagonist of the drama of "progress" was the "citizen," for the Porfirians it was the capitalist.

Despite the democratic character of the extant liberal legislation and the national constitution, hierarchy became reaffirmed through a new biology of society, one still founded on differences in nature but now indexed by the signs of capital rather than those of color. Economic class overdetermined social status: the richest were by "nature" the fittest (Córdova 1973:18–19, 65). In order for society to "progress," the fittest had to impose themselves on the weakest; for their own good, subaltern groups and classes had to submit to their "betters" (Córdova 1973:39).

Porfirian social biology was grounded in a teleological vision of history as the natural and progressive evolution of social organisms. Official history construed privilege as a natural necessity: the alternative to hierarchy was chaos. Indeed, for the Porfirians, Mexico's past represented a primal chaos that had to be transcended. At the apogee of sociohistorical evolution, the Porfirian regime was to redeem the nation from the disorder and backwardness of the past by creating a "strong" patrimonial government that could impose "order," maintain hierarchy and guarantee the "progress" of the nation.

This ideology of history made the agents of "order" and "progress," who had proved their superiority by transforming nature into capital, the true and only representatives of national society. It was their task to keep Mexico on the fast track by ordering and controlling the lives, identities, and bodies of the weakest, namely, the peasants and workers, whose poverty had become an emblem of biological inferiority.

To this end, the Porfirian state reproduced and continued to develop the technologies of power implemented by the liberals. Any archive in Mexico attests to the increase in state production of statistics during the Porfiriato: bodies; properties; businesses; school-age children; agricultural, mining and industrial products; trees; cows; pigs; chickens; pounds of meat consumed; inches of rain and days of sunshine—all were counted, registered, and reported on a yearly, monthly, and even weekly basis by state functionaries in Mexican pueblos, as well as in urban centers. These statistics were questioned and examined for signs of "progress" or retrocession. Compiled and published by the state, these figures became indexes of Mexico's stage in the history of "progress." In addition, state control over the forms of reproduction continued to be consolidated by civil judges who licensed, enumerated, and inscribed marriages, births, and deaths. Moreover, the official ideology of "order" and "progress" was disseminated in hundreds of new schools.

While the state developed the hegemonic apparatuses, it continued to reorganize and to prune the repressive apparatuses. Díaz himself had come to power through a military coup and still feared that rival military caudillos might challenge his dominion. So he further reduced the size of the army: whereas in 1888 the national army had 33,200 men, by 1896 the number had dwindled to only 8,600 (Márquez Padilla 1986:83). The bulk of these forces were conscripts from subaltern groups; only the officers were career soldiers with professional training (Katz 1981:27–29). However, "order" and "progress" required that the state be able to deploy force against recalcitrant subjects. The railroads built by British and American capitalists allowed for an unprecedentedly effective deployment of the means of force. But more importantly, while Díaz pruned the army, he expanded the rural police force. By 1880 membership in the Rurales had increased by 90 percent and the budget for the force had grown by 400 percent (Vanderwood 1981:70).

As patrimonial troops, the Rurales were under the direct control of Díaz; most of them were volunteers, recruited from the peasant and artisan classes of central Mexico (Vanderwood 1981:126, 107–9). Initially used to subject regional caudillos to central authority, the Rurales were subsequently deployed to make Mexico "safe" for capitalism. This force was used to drive peasants from their lands and to repress proletarian and campesino protest, as well as to patrol export-import routes (Vanderwood 1981:119). Although the number of Rurales never surpassed 3,000, a state-manufactured image of their professionalism and military skill, as well as their *machista* ruthlessness and invincibility, made them hated and feared by subaltern groups and classes throughout Mexico (Vanderwood 1981:132–38). The force of ideology is perhaps most evident in the ideology of force.[14]

To summarize, from the late 1850s to 1910, the processes of state formation and capitalist development transformed Mexican society. Mexican state formation was contradictory. Patrimonial and legal-rational ideologies and modes of constructing and legitimating power subsisted in uneasy tension. Moreover, although the state tried to gain control over the economy, dependent capitalist development made Mexico vulnerable to world-market fluctuations. In addition, although the state reorganized and expanded technologies of social and moral regulation, it pruned the repressive forces. When revolution broke out in 1910, neither the federal army nor the Rurales were able to curtail popular insurrection.

The main beneficiaries of "order" and "progress" were foreign and domestic capitalists and members of the oligarchy and their clients. Women and subaltern groups and classes, as well as members of the petty bourgeoisie who lacked patronage ties to those with economic and political power, were excluded from the economic miracle and from participation in the "political process."

The peasantry was perhaps the class most adversely affected by these social transformations. Not only did peasants lose their lands, but capitalist development and state centralization destroyed the relative autonomy of many peasant communities and undermined peasant control over the production and reproduction of social life. Moreover, the new social biology denied peasants all social honor and reconstituted them as those subjects who were by "nature" the least fit; the peasantry's poverty and style of life became a sign of retrogression, of identity with the colonial past. To be "modernized," peasants had to be proletarianized. In addition, their lives, activities, and identities had to be ordered by the state—purportedly for their own good.

Peasants did not submit willingly to these transformations. Throughout the nineteenth century, campesinos turned to nonviolent forms of resistance and to armed rebellion. However, many peasants lacked the means as well as the military skills to fight effectively. In the peasant-warriors of the military colonies of Chihuahua, the dominant classes and the state were to find more formidable adversaries.

The Closing of the Frontier

> Frontier populations came to be considered as "barbarians" by the spokesmen of the same civilization that had created them out of its clash with Indian societies. (Baretta and Markoff 1978:597)

The "transformation of the frontier into the border" (Katz 1981:7), that is, the incorporation of the periphery into the capitalist world market and its increased integration into the nation-state, was a long-term sociohistorical process that spanned several decades.[15] Three phases can be distinguished: 1855–1885, when the impact of state centralization and capitalist development began to be discernible; 1886–1903, when state centralization and capitalist development were consolidated; and 1904–1910, when state centralization and capitalist development intensified.

The First Phase: 1855–1885

Until 1886 endemic warfare with the Apache limited the impact of projects of nation-state formation and capitalist development on the Chihuahuan frontier. Nevertheless, the transformations entailed by these projects are discernible prior to the end of the Apache wars, as are the social dislocations and conflicts that change engendered.

During these decades center-periphery relations became a focus of contention between Chihuahuan elites and a central government attempting to limit the power of regional caudillos and to reduce the autonomy of provincial administrations. The relationship between frontier elites and the central government was characterized both by conflict and by collaboration. On the one hand, Chihuahua's dominant groups and classes were receptive to the capitalist ideology advanced by the liberal and Porfirian regimes. The importance that official ideology accorded to class situation as the basis for status position found resonances in the significance wealth and property had already acquired as indexes of social honor on the frontier. On the other hand, frontier elites opposed efforts by the central government to increase its control over the regional economy and the provincial state apparatus.

Paradoxically, Chihuahuan elites who allied themselves with the liberals were able to manipulate policies designed to foster centralization to increase their regional political and economic power. The sale of church and national lands at extremely low prices allowed members of dominant classes to expand their control over the means of production and to build political alliances by distributing land concessions.

Chihuahuan elite factions integrated by interlinked "grand-families"[16] struggled against each other during the second half of the nineteenth century, competing for control over new economic resources and over the local state apparatus (Wasserman 1984:12–25; Almada 1955). These competing factions allied themselves with opposed national groups and fought for provincial hegemony during the Wars of the Reform, the French Intervention, and the armed movement of 1876 that brought Porfirio Díaz to power.

In Chihuahua the grand-families of the elite were quasi-corporate groups that formed the nodules of the extensive patron-client networks through which factions were constituted. These groups were differentiated by locality as well as by descent and interlinked by affinal and patronage ties. They were headed by the eldest patriarchs, whose power over other members rested on the traditional authority of the father over family and household. Until the 1860s no single grand-family had achieved predominance in Chihuahuan politics or gained control over the regional economy (Wasserman 1984; Almada 1955). By the end of the 1870s, however, the situation had changed: the Terrazas grand-family had emerged as the victor of intraelite competition (Wasserman 1984: 26–70).

Ironically, the foundations for the first mayor *cacicazgo* in Chihuahua, that of Luis Terrazas, were laid in the 1860s and 1870s (Almada 1955, 1964, 1980; Wasserman 1984). In Chihuahua the efforts of the national state to break the power of regional patrimonial leaders backfired. The Terrazas and their allies gained increasing economic and political power through the 1860s and '70s. It was not until the mid-1880s that Díaz's policy of "pan y palo" enabled him to appoint one of his own clients to the governorship of Chihuahua. And this by no means broke the power of the Terrazas clique. By the turn of the century, they controlled both the Chihuahuan economy and the local state apparatus.

Until the end of the Apache wars, the impact of the processes of state centralization and economic development on subaltern groups and classes was uneven and contradictory. On the one hand, peasant-warriors were still needed by the state and by regional elites to fight raiding indigenes. Moreover, rival elite and national factions relied on these specialists in violence for military support in the power struggles of the 1860s and '70s. On the other hand, the Chihuahuan government tried to deploy new technologies of power that increased state penetration into peasant communities and challenged local control over key aspects of the production and reproduction of social life. In addition, elite factions competing for lands put on the market began to violate the agrarian rights of peasant pueblos and to erode corporate control over the means of production.

As early as the late 1850s, the corporate land rights of Guerrero District peasant-warrior communities began to come under attack. For example, beginning in November of 1856, the indigenes and settlers of Santo Tomás began to complain that some of their lands, a flour mill, and a spring of water had been adjudicated to Jesús María Casavantes, a member of one of the Guerrero District's grand-families.[17] However, subaltern land rights were not seriously challenged until after the mid-1860s. In subsequent years the Mexican and Chihuahuan governments increased sales of baldíos to members of the dominant classes who had patronage links to regional and national oligarchs.

Even communities such as Namiquipa, which had legal title to their corporate holdings, began to see their rights to land challenged by the state and by members of the Chihuahuan elite. For example, between 1855 and 1863, Enrique Müller, an immigrant of German origin and American citizenship and the future business partner of the Chihuahuan governor Luis Terrazas, bought up the colonial titles to haciendas and ranchos in Namiquipa; two of these titles were invalid, since the owners had ceded their property to the Crown for the establishment of the military colony. In addition, in 1865, Müller received title from the liberal government for the baldíos located between these haciendas.[18] By 1871 he had acquired de jure rights to thousands of hectares of Namiquipan lands; from the 112,000 hectares accorded to Namiquipa by its colonial charter, the pueblo's legal corporate holdings had been reduced to 11,000 hectares, one-tenth of its former land area.[19] Similarly, in the 1860s and 1870s, Cruces, the other pueblo in the municipality of Namiquipa, saw its rights to land attacked. In 1865, Müller acquired de jure rights to more than 37,000 hectares in Cruces, approximately one-third of the pueblo's colonial grant, and later, in the 1870s, he bought up nineteen lots of ejido lands.[20]

The agrarian rights of serranos from the municipality of Namiquipa were menaced not only by Müller's purchases. Members of Guerrero District grand-families, such as Celso González and Jesús María Casavantes, began to buy other "vacant" lands in the municipality.[21] In addition, as land became privatized and commodified, the municipal authorities of Namiquipa were ordered to charge rent to peasants who in the past had acquired rights to corporate lands by virtue of community membership and through the fulfillment of military obligations.

For the serranos of the municipality of Temósachi, the situation was even worse. The pueblos of this municipality had rights to much smaller extensions of land than those of Namiquipa and, as a rule, lacked legal title to corporate holdings. In the 1860s members of the Casavantes, González, Herrera, Dozal y Hermosillo, and other grand-families of the Guerrero District, as well as district authorities, began buying up baldío lands in the pueblos of Temósachi.[22]

For example, Yepómera, a pueblo that had produced one of the most well-known Apache fighters, Santana Pérez, and whose settlers had played an important role in frontier warfare, began to lose its corporate holdings.[23] By 1869 the Yepomerans did not have sufficient land to meet the exigencies of household reproduction and were forced to request that the national government sell them lands at a reduced tariff; their petition was denied.[24]

As numerous peasant complaints evince, a subaltern frontier ideology—in which rights to land were contingent on the fulfillment of military obligations to the state—began to enter into conflict with a capitalist ideology in which land was a commodity to be held by individuals and acquired only through legal purchase. The commodification of land eroded not only the peasants' class situation but also their status position. The expropriation of corporate holdings represented the loss of the honors these communities had "justly" won for their role in frontier warfare. Moreover, the loss of lands had consequences for serrano identity. As we shall see, land rights were essential to the serrano vision of self-realization through dedication to work for the self and the family (*dedicarse a sus labores*) as opposed to wage labor (*trabajo de raya*). In addition, attacks on the pueblo's economic base menaced its existence. Peasant-warriors had a localistic sense of community not only because their principal military obligation had been the defense of their pueblos but also because locality was a key principle of social relatedness, one that defined rights and membership in these closed corporate communities. For the serranos the alienation of community lands was an attack on their patria chica.

Not all peasant-warrior communities, however, were equally affected by the commodification of land rights, and some, like Namiquipa, were able to retain de facto possession of their lands. Both the state and the elite were still dependent on the military services of these specialists in violence and therefore pursued a contradictory policy vis-à-vis their communities. In some cases district- and provincial-level authorities tried to protect the lands of peasant-warriors from alienation by the national government. For example, Luis Terrazas, governor of Chihuahua, urged the national administration to nullify the sale of Yepómera's land to Dozal y Hermosillo or to recompense the pueblo for this loss with other baldíos.[25] Likewise, the Guerrero District jefe politico and the Chihuahuan government protected the lands of the peasant-warriors of Bachíniva against a local hacendado.[26] Nevertheless, the erosion of the peasants rights to land had begun and was to have decisive consequences for community-state relations. Once peasants perceived that the state had broken the tacit compact it had with their communities, they began to question the legitimacy of authority. Frontier warriors began to deploy both violent and nonviolent forms of resistance against the state and the elite.

Not only agrarian dispossession but also other attempts by the state to gain control over key aspects of the production and reproduction of social life became seen by the serranos as attacks on local sovereignty and as unjust impositions of illegitimate forms of subjection-subjectivity. New taxes, compulsory education, and the civil inscription and legitimation of marriages became foci of contention between serrano communities and the state.

A law enacted in 1842 made education compulsory for girls and boys aged seven to fifteen (Arrom 1985:20), and in the 1860s and 1870s state-run public schools further undermined the role of the church and the family in the production of new social subjects. Although the Chihuahuan government subsidized part of the costs of education, parents had to contribute to the financing of local schools. District- and local-level archives are full of documents attesting to the serranos' resistance to state regulation of the socialization of children: educational taxes went unpaid, school attendance was poor, and teachers who were outsiders were ostracized and, at times, driven from the community.[27] The serranos valued literacy as a sign of "civilization." However, state-controlled compulsory education not only diverted children from the tasks that were assigned to them by the division of labor in the household but also represented the usurpation by the state of one of the family's key functions.

In serrano communities women were accorded a great deal of social respect for their role as mothers (*madres*) and for the part they played in the education (*educación*) of their offspring; it was from their mothers that children learned the values of verguenza and respeto. The socialization of children was one of the key activities through which femininity was constructed. Moreover, the exclusive right to discipline offspring physically was integral to masculine identity and self-mastery and underpinned the reproduction of patriarchal authority within the family. Thus, state usurpation of the household's role in socialization was viewed as a challenge to community and family sovereignty, one that interfered with the production and reproduction of identity, that is, with the self-realization of men as fathers and women as mothers.[28]

Likewise, the central government's attempt to appropriate the church's role in the regulation of the forms of reproduction was viewed by the serranos as an illegitimate intervention that contravened the character of marriage as a divine sacrament and stained the honor of women, men, and their offspring. For the serranos there were only three partners to every marriage—God, man, and woman. The government had no right to intercede in matters beyond the temporal jurisdiction of secular authority. From the Namiquipan point of view, civil marriage allowed men to dishonor the consanguineal female relatives of other men. For example, Francisco Vásquez of Namiquipa adamantly denounced civil marriages, declaring them to be *amancebamientos*, that is, illegitimate, sinful, and dishonorable forms of cohabitation.[29] For the serranos sexual unions lacking divine sanction were a form of concubinage that stigmatized women as whores (*mujeres prostituidas*) and offspring as "natural" children (*hijos naturales*).[30]

Such unions dishonored the men, whose identity was predicated on the protection of female purity and family honor. Since legal sanctions could not be brought to bear on men who refused to marry women by the church, civil marriages challenged patriarchal control over female sexuality and generativity. For decades serrano men had been fighting the Apache to defend the sexual purity of their women and hence their own honor. Now the purity of women was being threatened by the state.

The state's attack on the church and on its control of social reproduction affected not only the power and identity of peasant men but also that of women. In serrano communities the sanctioning of sexual unions by the church was critical to the mediation of the contradictory "nature" of femininity and was key to the construction of female honor. Church sacralization of marriage publicly purified women of the pollution engendered by the "natural facts" of sexuality and conception. The rites of Catholicism made every honorable woman a "María," a token of the ideal type of femininity of which the Virgin was the symbol. Paradoxically, church regulation of gender both subjugated and empowered women. Since women participated in the purity of the Virgin, they were considered to be more spiritual than men. Thus, although men controlled temporal power in serrano communities, women were primarily responsible for mediating between the community and God. Because of their spiritual "nature," women commanded a moral authority that they were able to deploy to gain a measure of informal power in serrano communities. The state's attack on the church threatened to undermine forms of feminine empowerment.[31]

In short, the desacralization of marriage implicit in state regulation of sexual unions contravened the frontier logic of gender and had consequences for the construction of social identity. Beginning in the late 1850s, the national and provincial governments' attempt to break the power of the church and to usurp its role in the regulation of social reproduction became one of the foci of conflict between serrano communities and the state. In Namiquipa the legitimacy of the authority of the Chihuahuan governor, Luis Terrazas, became compromised because of his personal acquisition of church lands and his sales of ecclesiastical properties to political allies and clients. As one inhabitant of Namiquipa recalled, "If the whole pueblo was Catholic, and if no one ignored what Luis Terrazas did with the clergy's properties, how could there not be discontent? Men and women spoke of nothing else but the abuses General Luis Terrazas had committed with the church's lands. How could they silence the clamor of a whole pueblo offended in its sentiments?"[32]

However, not all liberal policies were contested by the peasant warriors of the Guerrero District. From the serrano point of view, the institutionalization of the electoral principle as the basis for succession to political office enhanced local sovereignty. For the serranos elections were a form of popular empowerment. Since authorities remained dependent on local constituencies, they were subject to community sanctions that ensured that the exercise of authority would be oriented by the norms and values of honor. During these decades the exercise of authority was still regulated by traditional norms and values of patrimonial beneficence. During the famine of 1878, for example, the Chihuahuan governor ordered district authorities to procure corn, beans, and wheat and to sell them at cost to the peasants; this order was put into effect.[33]

Complaints about vote fraud were rare during these decades. Thus, it is likely that local elections were actually "clean" and that the participation of subaltern groups and classes in the formal political process was not just another paper policy. When suffrage ceased to be "effective" (one of the slogans of the revolution was "Effective Suffrage"), popular resistance was immediately galvanized in defense of electoral freedom.

To summarize, beginning in the late 1850s and increasingly through the next two decades, processes of nation-state formation and capitalist development began to have an impact on the frontier. Land, taxes, education, and social reproduction became the foci of contention between peasant-warrior communities and the state and between subaltern and dominant groups and classes. Yet some state policies, notably the legislation criminalizing domestic violence, continued to be applied when they intersected with local projects.

During these decades (1855–85), the relations between the state, the regional elite, and the serrano specialists in violence were fraught with contradiction. Although the serranos were still agents of "civilization" who were needed to make the frontier safe for "progress," they began to be seen by the elite as members of "backwards" classes who had to be controlled and ordered by their social "betters." From the serrano point of view, the transformations of the period simultaneously threatened and advanced community sovereignty and locally valued forms of social identity.

The effects of the policies of centralization and development on peasant communities were uneven. The expropriation of the corporate holdings of peasant-warriors was to prove difficult; initial efforts to put pueblo lands on the market were by no means always successful. Whereas some Guerrero District communities began to lose their lands, others managed to hold on to them. Moreover, at times the state supported peasants against elites and at other times it supported elites against peasants. A contradictory policy allowed the state to divide and rule discontented serranos.

The resistance of peasant-warriors to the transformation of the frontier during the 1860s and 1870s began to configure them in eyes of the elite and the state as agents of disorder and retrocession who, like the Apache they fought, possessed the fierce and barbaric instinct of rebellion. In 1876, for example, the peasant warriors of Santo Tomás, who had rebelled against the Chihuahuan government, wrote to the provincial legislature complaining that the pueblos downriver from Guerrero City were considered to be "a threat against power and legality: this more than unjust asseveration is highly dishonoring for us; its results have exasperated us, like he who is entirely sane and is nevertheless declared mad. . . . we have never fallen into errors because we felt in our souls the fierce instinct of rebellion; we are peaceful landowners, constantly dedicated to work in our fields."[34]

The serranos found this construction of their collective identity highly dishonoring because it implicitly likened them to the Apache and constructed them as men whose natural and unruly masculinity was in need of culturalization. Entirely "sane," they had been declared officially "mad," transformed into the legitimate object of technologies of "order" and power. However, it was not until after the Apache had been subjugated that the peasant-warriors of the Guerrero District were to be definitively constituted by the state and the elite as the barbaric other, in need of the "order" and mastery that could be imposed only by those whose wealth proclaimed their fitness to rule and to regulate the collective life of society.

The Second Phase: 1886–1903

The end of the Apache wars paved the way for the integration of the frontier into the nation and the world market. Beginning in the 1880s, railroads and systems of communications were constructed linking the frontier to the Center and to markets in North America (Almada 1955:passim). Not only did the construction of communications and transport systems facilitate the integration of the frontier into the nation, but it also made the development of an export economy possible. Northern commodities such as precious metals, beef, and hides could now be sold in both internal and external markets. Economic development proceeded at a vertiginous pace, largely, but not exclusively, fueled by foreign, especially American, capital. By 1902 more than 22 percent of all U.S. investment in Mexico was concentrated in the northern provinces of Sonora, Coahuila, and Chihuahua, mainly in mining, farming, and transportation (Katz 1981:7). By the turn of the century, large foreign and domestic capitalists controlled the frontier economy.

The consolidation of the state's monopoly of force was critical to the closing of the frontier. During the Apache wars the central government had always tolerated a degree of regional military autonomy in Chihuahua. In the 1880s, however, the Porfirian regime began to augment central control over the organization of warfare in the province and to increase the number of federal forces on the frontier (Almada 1955:324; Terrazas 1905:71–73 and passim).

In 1886 the government of Chihuahua officially declared the Apache wars to be at an end. As a result, in the 1880s and 1890s the government demilitarized the peasant-warriors, dismantled the organization of warfare that had subsisted on the frontier, and developed a repressive apparatus more fully under state control. A professional police force was created, and detachments of Rurales were stationed in Chihuahua to "keep order" in the countryside (Almada 1955: 339, 354).

Whereas the state had fomented the militarization of subaltern groups and classes during the decades of Apache raids, the armed peasantry of Chihuahua now became viewed as an obstacle to state centralization and capitalist development.[35] Accordingly, the state began to demilitarize these part-time specialists in violence. Arms and munitions that had been given to peasant-warriors by the Chihuahuan government were reappropriated. Full-time specialists in violence—federal soldiers, policemen, and Rurales who were maintained by the state—now fulfilled the repressive functions previously exercised by part-time military specialists from the subaltern groups and classes of the frontier. In addition, peasant-warriors' access to the means of force was now much more rigorously regulated by the state. In order to possess firearms, serranos had to request permits from local authorities, who were ordered to keep track of the number granted and to report the results to higher-level functionaries on a weekly basis.[36] As a result of these measures, serranos lost access to the personal prestige and status honor that their military obligations had conferred on them in the past. Ironically, the frontier peasants' military prowess now became a sign of disorder, of a "natural" masculinity that, like that of the Apache, had to be tamed for the good of society.

Those who could not successfully be "reduced" were viewed by local authorities as potential rebels. Serranos who were seen as a threat to "public order and tranquility" (and who would probably have been charismatic military leaders during the Apache wars) became officially defined as vagrants, evildoers, or vicious elements and hence dishonored. These potential rebels were drafted into the federal army, ostensibly through a lottery but in practice through designations made by local authorities. Through this strategy the state removed potential and actual rebels from frontier pueblos and "reduced" recalcitrant serranos by making them the object of the technologies of power, of the humiliations and abuses that passed for order and discipline in the federal army. Ironically, these measures recalled the colonial state's efforts to "reduce" Apache warriors by incorporating them into the frontier military forces.

In short, not only did demilitarization deprive the peasant-warriors of one of their key sources of personal and social honor, but in addition, remilitarization humiliated and dishonored those who were seen as threats to "order" and "progress." Not surprisingly, the *leva*, the forced conscription of serranos who had been redefined as the barbaric other, became a focus of nonviolent and violent forms of resistance in the peasant-warrior communities of the Guerrero District.[37]

For the state and the dominant classes, the barbarism of the serranos was not only that of the frontier specialist in violence who was a threat to "order" but also that of the peasant who was an obstacle to "progress." In the new logic of society, an opposition between "progress" and "backwardness" replaced that between "civilization" and "barbarism" in the construction of identity and status. Capital became the privileged sign of "progress."

The peasant became identified with nature and with the colonial past. In order for nature to be transformed and for the economy to be developed, the lands and labor of the peasants had to be put on the market. Considered not just commodities but also resources to be developed, lands had to pass into the hands of the fittest in order for Mexico to emerge from the dark ages. And the peasant had to be proletarianized: labor had to pass into the control of those who could best deploy it to develop the nation.

During the 1880s and 1890s land and labor were put on the market at an accelerating pace in Chihuahua. Surveying companies received concessions to locate baldíos which were then sold by the central government to members of Chihuahua's elite and to foreigners. The result was an unprecedented concentration of land in the hands of foreigners and members of the regional oligarchy. Whereas before 1880 there were very few great latifundios in the province, by the turn of the century sixteen had been formed (Almada 1955:334–35). Fourteen proprietors, all members of the Chihuahuan oligarchy or foreign capitalists, possessed lands whose total extension exceeded 103,145 square kilometers, or more than two-fifths of the province's total area (Almada 1955:335). The Terrazas grand-family controlled the greatest amount of land; Luis Terrazas himself owned 2,659,953 hectares, distributed in more than twenty haciendas, and had become the largest landed proprietor in all of Mexico (Almada 1955:335).

In the Guerrero District peasant rights to agricultural lands, woods, and pasture were violated and the holdings of most pueblos were limited to 1,755.5 hectares each.[38] The notable exception was the pueblo of Namiquipa. The resistance of the Namiquipans had allowed them to retain de facto if not de jure possession of the community's corporate holdings. Representatives of the peasants managed to convince the surveyors to respect the colonial titles of Namiquipa and Cruces.[39] However, unlike Namiquipa, Cruces had already lost de facto possession of almost 38,000 hectares to Enrique Müller.[40] Although the Jesús E. Valenzuela surveying company respected the title of Cruces, the hacendados did not; in 1884, Cruces lost an additional 1,884 hectares to the hacienda of San Miguel de Babícora, owned by Luis Terrazas.[41]

Members of the Chihuahuan elite and foreign capitalists were not the only ones who sought to acquire the lands of peasant pueblos. After the end of the Apache wars, a rural petty bourgeoisie composed of small ranchers and merchants began to emerge as a result of economic development. Many of these entrepreneurs were outsiders who had emigrated to the peasant pueblos of the Guerrero District from elsewhere in the province after the Apache had been subdued. Members of this class could not compete with the elite for the baldíos put on the market and therefore began to encroach upon the limited corporate holdings left to the serrano communities. They were able to gain the leverage to do this by becoming clients of the oligarchs who controlled the state apparatus and who appointed them to key posts in municipal administration.

Increasing social differentiation in rural pueblos opposed peasants to petty bourgeois and led to a struggle for control of lands and of the apparatus of municipal administration. In May of 1889, for example, Santana Pérez, the former Apache fighter and important rebel leader, complained to the Guerrero District head that the municipal authorities of Temósachi had stolen his land and allocated it to one of their clients.[42] Again, in July of 1891, some peasants from the same municipality complained to the Chihuahuan government that the municipal authorities were expropriating the community's lands.[43] Although the peasants tried to regain control over municipal administration, their efforts were a failure because the state government supported its petty-bourgeois clients. When Santana Pérez and Celso Anaya lost to "official" candidates in local elections, their defeat became the immediate grievance that precipitated an armed uprising in Temósachi in February of 1892 (Almada 1938:35; Almada 1964:99, vol. 1).

Control of the politico-legal apparatus of the state was essential to the monopolization of economic resources by the elite and to the implementation of protectionist measures that favored domestic and foreign capitalists. In contrast to the discourse of the liberals, Porfirian ideology affirmed that "order" depended on a benevolent patrimonial dictatorship, not a democracy. In the new social biology of the Porfiriato, subordinate groups and classes were considered too "uncultured" and "uneducated" to be accorded a role in the formal political process; it was absurd to respect the electoral rights of a mass of uncouth and illiterate peasants.[44] Mexico was not ready for democracy. Such freedoms could only be implemented after the nation had evolved to a higher stage and the "backwards" classes had been mastered and improved by the more "advanced" classes. In the meantime, Mexico's peasants needed to be ruled and disciplined with the firm hand of the patriarch.

For the good of society, subaltern groups and classes had to be excluded from the formal political process; their constitutional rights to elect authorities began to be undermined. In 1887 the new Chihuahuan constitution suppressed the popular election of the jefes políticos, or district authorities, and made succession to this post contingent on appointment by the governor (Almada 1964:23–25, vol. 1). In 1889 an amendment was passed replacing the municipal presidents of district capitals with the jefes políticos and increasing the latter's authority over the municipal councils of their jurisdictions (Almada 1964:23–25, vol. 1).

Consequently, as in the rest of Mexico, the form that the centralization of power assumed in Chihuahua during the 1880s and 1890s was that of patrimonial absolutism. At all levels power began to be wielded by caciques, sultanistic strongmen who depended on patronage ties to higher-level functionaries for access to office, rather than on the support of local constituencies. Not only the legal-rational values of democracy but also the traditional norms and values of honor, of respeto, verguenza, and beneficence, which had legitimated the exercise of authority on the frontier, began to be violated. For the cacique social honor was above all determined by wealth. In those sierra pueblos where the peasants had lost control of local administration to petty-bourgeois immigrants, caciques and their clients used the politico-legal apparatus of local administration to dispossess peasants of their lands, to implement new taxes and extract a larger share of peasant surpluses, part of which went into their own pockets, and in some pueblos, to force the peasants to pay labor tribute.[45]

Since the state had endowed these caciques with the exclusive franchise on the legitimate exercise of force, they used the local police and the Fuerzas de Seguridad Pública (Forces of Public Security) to repress dissident peasants. Those who refused to comply with the caciques' orders were labeled vagrants and evildoers and thrown in jail, where they were beaten and deprived of food and water until they agreed to do the caciques' bidding, or consigned to the federal army if they continued to resist.

For example, several peasants from the sierra pueblo of Tomochi refused to work for the local cacique, Juan Ignacio Chávez, who had been imposed by the Chihuahuan government as president of the Tomochi's *ayuntamiento* (administrative council). A relative of Joaquín Chávez, the sierra cacique and captain of the Forces of Public Security, Juan Ignacio Chávez was an outsider who lacked local popular support. These Tomochis were accused of being "pernicious vagrants"; some were consigned to jail in the district capital, while others were threatened with conscription into the federal army (Almada 1938:21; Chávez Calderón 1964: 10-13). What this and other cases demonstrate is that state functionaries and members of the dominant classes defined peasants who attempted to defend their rights as agents of disorder who had to be forcibly repressed and disciplined (Chávez Calderón 1964:10-13).

Not all sierra pueblos lost control over local government to petty-bourgeois caciques at this time. The peasants of the pueblo of Namiquipa, for example, managed to retain control over the institutional foci of local power. However, those serranos who became subjects of local caciques were highly dishonored by the sultanistic exercise of power. As we shall see, the hundreds of complaints about *caciquismo* are couched in the idiom of honor. Caciquismo violated the norms and values that had legitimated the traditional and legal-rational exercise of authority. For the serranos the cacique lacked verguenza and respeto, and instead of exemplifying beneficence, his actions indexed his avaricious and thievish disposition; the caciques were machos but they were not hombres. Moreover, caciquismo had implications for the construction of subjectivities. Men who were unable to avenge the abuses of caciques were emasculated and hence dishonored.

Some caciques, such as Luis Chávez of Cruces, went so far as to dishonor the virgins of serrano communities, and hence their consanguineal kinsmen, by imposing their own version of the droit du seigneur (Calzadíaz Barrera 1969:passim). Ironically, the technologies of power deployed to "tame" the peasant-warriors of the sierra relied on the same signifiers as those used to "pacify" the Apache: for the dominant classes and the state, the extraordinary masculinity that empowered these serranos was to be "reduced" by emasculating and dishonoring its bearers.

The Third Phase: 1904–1910

The year 1904 marks another turning point in Chihuahuan history, the beginnings of Enrique Creel's term as governor of Chihuahua and the return to political power of the Terrazas grand-family.[46] State centralization and capitalist development were intensified from 1904 to 1910.

For the peasants of the Guerrero District, three of the measures passed by Creel's administration were to further erode their class situation and status position, as well as to advance the implementation of the new forms of subjectivity-subjection that the state and the elite had been trying to impose on them for decades. These three measures intensified and generalized rural class conflict and further delegitimized the authority of the provincial and national governments in the peasants' eyes.

First, Creel's revision of the Chihuahuan constitution in 1904 eliminated the last vestiges of peasant control over municipal administration, doing away with local elections and legalizing the direct appointment of *jefes municipales* by the governor (Almada 1964:21–26, vol. 1). Although elections continued to be held in Namiquipa and other serrano towns because of popular pressure, they were merely a secular ritual designed to legitimate the exercise of authority by providing a public simulation of popular participation in the selection of political incumbents.[47] In many sierra pueblos this "reform" gave the victory to petty-bourgeois immigrants who had been battling the local peasants for control of the apparatus of municipal administration. The last obstacles to the consolidation of local cacicazgos were removed.

Second, in the same year Creel passed a municipal tax law that substantially increased the state's share of peasant surpluses, shifting the fiscal burden even further from domestic and foreign capitalists to subaltern groups and classes (Almada 1964:81–83, vol. 1). During the Apache wars peasant-warriors had rarely paid taxes. Exemption from these contributions was one of the honors the state had accorded the serranos. Thus, increased taxation was yet another sign of state denial of social prestige and status to this group. In addition, since a portion of these revenues went into the pockets of hated local caciques, the payment of taxes was viewed as theft; to be forced to collaborate in one's own dispossession became one more sign of dishonor. Moreover, a crisis in agriculture that coincided with a world-wide economic depression in 1906–7 further undermined the economic situation of the peasantry and made state demands on peasant surpluses harder to bear.

Third, the Municipal Land Law of February 1905 decreed the privatization of the remaining corporate holdings of peasant communities. By exploiting this law, petty-bourgeois immigrants were able to expand their holdings at the expense of serrano peasants. Ostensibly designed to deliver the benefits of "progress" to the "backwards" classes, that is, to transform peasants into capitalist farmers, as well as to "modernize" the last vestiges of colonial modes of corporate land tenure, this law put the remaining lands of rural communities onto the market and furthered the internal social differentiation and polarization already evident in sierra pueblos (cf. Lloyd 1988). Dispossessed peasants had to turn to wage labor, at least on a part-time basis, or to sharecropping and tenancy arrangements.

Namiquipa: 1904–1910

The impact of the measures adopted by the Creel administration on Guerrero District peasant-warrior communities can best be illustrated by focusing on one specific case, that of the pueblo of Namiquipa. In 1904, Namiquipa had about 1,500 inhabitants; the pueblo was the administrative center of a municipality with a population of more than 3,000.

The bulk of Namiquipa's inhabitants were middle peasants engaged in subsistence production on small plots of land that ranged from one to ten hectares in size. Most of the middle peasants were *originarios*, that is, descendants of the original colonists, although some of them were immigrants who had arrived as late as the 1880s and had been accepted by the community. Some of them had legal titles to their plots, but many of them only had derechos de posesión.

Corn, beans, and wheat were the main crops. Most households also kept domestic animals such as pigs, chickens, horses, mules, oxen, and cows. Domestic and agricultural tasks were largely carried out by household members according to a division of labor based on gender and age. Adult men and their older unmarried sons worked in the fields and looked after the horses, mules, and cattle, while adult women and their single daughters cooked, washed, sewed, raised the children, and looked after the chickens and pigs. At key points in the agricultural cycle, friends and kin might also engage in labor-sharing arrangements. Although in local ideology the household and the nuclear family coincided, in practice some households also had other members.

A small proportion of Namiquipa's inhabitants consisted of a rural

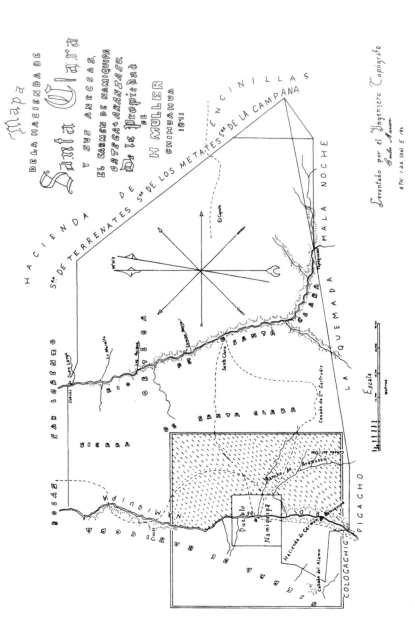

Map 2. Hacienda de Santa Clara Y Anexas. More than 40,000 of the 377,000 hectares claimed by Muller were part of Namiquipa's colonial grant. The large double-lined square around Namiquipa shows the full extent of the pueblo's colonial land grant and was not part of the original map drawn by C. Marion. It has been added here, as has the cross-hatching, indicating Namiquipan land invaded by the Hacienda de Santa Clara y Anexas. Map reprinted with permission from Daniel Nugent, *Spent Cartridges of Revolution: An Anthropological History of Namiquipa, Chihuahua*, p. 49 (University of Chicago Press, 1995).

petty bourgeoisie who bred cattle for the market and invested in small-scale commerce. Most of the members of this group were *foráneos* (outsiders) who were related to each other by kinship and *compadrazgo* (spiritual kinship) ties and who had immigrated to Namiquipa after the end of the Apache wars. By and large, they did not enter into compadrazgo or affinal relations with the middle peasants, although some of them did establish alliances with the richer peasants of the community. Referred to as *los ricos*, "the rich," by local peasants, these immigrants comprised not only a distinct class but also a discrete status group. They aspired to the style of life of the elite and tried to imitate it as best they could. Moreover, their vision of society was that advanced by the state and by dominant groups and classes; unlike the peasants, the foráneos were advocates of "order" and "progress."[48]

The agrarian situation in Namiquipa at the turn of the century was somewhat unusual. As previously mentioned, since the mid-1860s the community had been involved in a protracted agrarian conflict with Enrique Müller and his descendants, owners of Santa Clara y Anexas, one of the largest haciendas in Mexico, which claimed a total land surface of 377,000 hectares, more than 40,000 hectares of which belonged to Namiquipa's colonial grant (see map 2).[49] Although the Namiquipans were able to prevent the Müllers from taking de facto control of the contested lands, the conflict had important repercussions. It effectively froze the global commodification and the privatization of corporate holdings.

After 1891 the national and provincial governments repeatedly ordered the community to divide and privatize its corporate holdings, locally referred to as *los terrenos de común repartimiento* (the lands of common distribution). However, because of the conflict with the Müllers, the privatization of common lands was never carried out. As a result, although the community had legal title to its corporate holdings, most peasants had derechos de posesión to specific plots but no formal titles.[50]

Although during the colonial period settlers were supposed to be issued property titles to their plots by the presidial captains,[51] in practice they received derechos de posesión. After independence they continued to be issued derechos de posesión by the *ayuntamiento*, or municipal council. In Namiquipa, until 1904 household rights to particular agricultural and house lots were vested in heads of families who petitioned the municipal council for permission to plant and build on these plots. This derecho de posesión was obtained through the fulfillment of four conditions.

First, until the end of the Apache wars, the most important criterion for obtaining land in the community was the fulfillment of military obligations. Even as late as 1903, Namiquipans were soliciting derechos de posesión from the municipal council based on their role in the Apache wars.[52] Second, locality was critical to the securing of land rights; these generally went to *hijos del pueblo* (sons of the pueblo). However, immigrants who arrived before the end of hostilities with the Apache and fulfilled their military obligations tended to be granted the same rights as the originarios, or descendants of the original colonists. Third, rights to land depended on the fulfillment of obligations to the pueblo through participation in community projects organized by the ayuntamiento. Fourth, derechos de posesión were also contingent on working the land. If a member of the community abandoned his plot for more than a few years, it could be reallocated to another peasant by the municipal council.[53]

In practice these derechos de posesión differed from property rights only in that they were not legitimated by individual, legal titles but by permission granted by the municipal council, which administered the pueblo's corporate property. Land held in posesión could be bought and sold and transmitted to heirs. Moreover, the municipal council could not revoke the rights granted to households once they had been allocated unless jefes de familia violated the conditions governing rights to land. Although in practice posesión was not very different from property, the logic informing these diverse ways of acquiring rights to land was quite distinct.

Whereas property was acquired through market transactions, posesión was obtained by virtue of membership in a closed corporate community that had been allocated corporate property rights by virtue of fulfilling military obligations to the state. Moreover, being a "good community member" (*buen vecino*) was key to posesión. In order to conserve their rights, family heads had to work their lands and fulfill their obligations to the community.[54]

By 1889 some immigrants had begun to secure rights in the común repartimiento lands. Significantly, they did not acquire these rights by purchase but rather by what was construed as "cooperating in the defense of the lands." This no longer consisted of fighting Apaches but instead involved contributing money to pay the pueblo's legal representative, who was trying to secure recognition of Namiquipa's land grant by the state. By 1900, however, the market in land began to have a local impact. Some of the *comuneros*, that is, those heads of families who had *derechos* (rights) to común repartimiento lands by virtue of their descent from the "original colonists," began to sell these rights to foráneos. This did not mean that land had become a commodity for the Namiquipan peasants. Those who alienated their rights did so as a swindle; originarios continued to retain derechos whether they had sold them or not.[55]

By 1900 an internal conflict had developed between petty-bourgeois foráneos and middle peasant originarios over control of the community's extensive holdings. Although the ayuntamiento of Namiquipa, still controlled by originarios, backed the peasantry, the Chihuahuan government supported the petty bourgeoisie. A number of future revolutionary families, all originarios, were forced to stop planting certain plots of land because petty-bourgeois cattle breeders, all foráneos, claimed that these fields "prejudiced" their access to pasture. This agrarian conflict became directly linked to the internal struggle for control of the municipal administration as a dispute developed over the local elections of 1903. Reyes Ortiz, one of the leaders of the peasants, was elected municipal president, but petty-bourgeois complaints to the Chihuahuan government culminated in his ouster in 1904.[56]

Victoriano Torres,[57] a prominent member of the petty-bourgeois faction, was chosen by the Chihuahuan governor to replace Ortiz, the locally elected peasant leader. Torres was notoriously unpopular and had no local following outside the members of his faction. The peasants considered him a *sinverguenza*, an improperly socialized man whose actions indexed his lack of the cultural dimension of masculinity. Moreover, Torres was a foráneo and therefore not a true member of the community. Don Victoriano proceeded to construct a local cacicazgo through ties of clientage to higher-level government officials and ties of patronage to local petty-bourgeois immigrants. Revenues from increased municipal taxes and other sources allowed him to generously reward his followers and to expand the local forces of repression. More important, Torres was in a privileged position to control the redistribution of municipal lands put on the market by the 1905 law, since all such land sales had to be approved by the jefe municipal.[58]

Having gained control of local administration and the support of higher-level government officials, Torres and the faction he represented immediately began to undermine the peasantry's rights to land. The first step was to charge the comuneros rent for the small plots they cultivated, to which they had derechos de posesión. By 1906 approximately half of the peasant families were paying rent for their plots.[59] For the peasants the issue was not a financial one but instead an ideological one. The exaction of rent denied the legitimacy of their rights to land. By paying rent, they were forced to participate in and acknowledge the symbolic expropriation of their own holdings.[60] Moreover, the exaction of rent implied that land rights could be obtained only through legal purchase. This vision of land as a commodity conflicted with the peasant ideology of land as a birthright and an honor. The second step also involved the manipulation of meaning and focused on creating a definition of the municipal ejido that would increase its size by a factor of more than six, from the standard 1,755.5 hectares to 10,972.7 hectares, thus freeing more común repartimiento land for the market.[61] The third step was the alienation of these 10,972.7 hectares under the umbrella of the 1905 Municipal Land Law.

Although this law placed limits on the size of lots sold, the legal niceties were either ignored or easily circumvented. Of all the municipalities in the Guerrero District, Namiquipa was the most affected by the municipal land sales, precisely because until 1905 it had been the most successful in resisting the alienation of its holdings. Of a total of 456 lots sold in the Guerrero District between 1905 and 1909, 303 were in the municipality of Namiquipa, and of these, 181 were in the pueblo of Namiquipa itself.[62] A few of these sales to foráneos, such as the 300 hectares bought by Pedro Loya in 1905, the 200 hectares bought by Victoriano Torres, and the 495 hectares bought by José Casavantes in 1906, directly contravened the legal limit.[63] However, the standard practice was to disguise the consolidation of tracts of land that exceeded the legal limit by having relatives purchase adjacent 25-hectare lots. Through this strategy petty-bourgeois families such as the Comaduráns, who acquired 325 contiguous hectares, were able to amass land without contravening the law.[64]

The municipal land sales begun in 1905 encroached on the lands of Namiquipan peasants in three ways. First, originario peasants who had derechos de posesión to plots within the municipal ejido had their lands sold from under them. Second, the jefes municipales favored petty-bourgeois buyers over peasants, who were largely excluded from purchasing land. Third, the land sales invaded more than 9,000 hectares of the terrenos de común repartimiento. Moreover, common usufruct rights to water and timber were violated as these were transformed into commodities and sold or rented by the jefes municipales to foráneo entrepreneurs.[65] In addition, since the local cacique forced peasants to pay rent for land possessed outside the ejido, the originarios effectively lost the rights to the entire corporate grant.

For the petty-bourgeois immigrants, the expropriation of the peasantry's lands was necessitated by "order" and "progress." Ironically, foráneos legitimated their usurpation of the holdings of originarios through an exegesis of the very same colonial charter that the peasants used to justify their rights to land. However, the petty-bourgeois reinvention of the past was structured by a very different logic from that deployed by the peasants.

This logic of "order" and "progress" was articulated by Luis J. Comadurán in his response to a complaint voiced by Manuel Antillón, a comunero who accused Comadurán of expropriating his cattle ranch.[66] According to Comadurán's interpretation of the community's founding charter, the peasants had no land rights: "It is clear from the philosophical nature of this concession that the vacant lands . . . should be considered public property . . . reserved to establish municipalities" as the population grows and new towns are founded, "in accordance with the development of industry and capital." Comadurán added that to "concede the property of all these lands to a few natives would be as antipatriotic as impolitic" and would contravene the interests of "progress and development." In short, for Comadurán and his allies, the peasants were "ignoramuses" who engaged in a backwards form of production that had to be displaced by capitalist agriculture so society could "progress."

The petty bourgeoisie shared the capitalist ideology of the dominant classes who controlled the state apparatus. Not surprisingly, after 1904 the state supported and used them against the peasantry. As we shall see, the logic the peasants used to legitimate their claims to land was not that of gold but of blood: it was a frontier idiom in which land rights were not commodities but honors acquired by fighting the "barbarians." Class conflict was also a conflict of interpretations.

As should be apparent, the form of rural class conflict in Namiquipa between 1904 and 1910 is analogous to that described for Temósachi in the 1890s. The emergence of a rural petty bourgeoisie was the result of broader processes of centralization and development, as well as of local conditions. This class did not emerge in all the sierra pueblos at the same time, but by 1910 the struggle between the petty bourgeoisie and the peasantry was generalized throughout the serrano pueblos of western Chihuahua.

The measures passed by the Creel administration eliminated the last vestiges of peasant control over municipal administration and alienated the limited corporate holdings left to the pueblos. Even the peasants of Namiquipa, whose efforts to resist the impact of development and centralization had been relatively successful, finally lost control over the local state apparatus and saw the lands they had fought for years to retain sold to outsiders. Community sovereignty was violated. Depeasantization humiliated and emasculated serrano men, while caciquismo dishonored all members of the community who did not belong to the coterie of clients and favorites.

Lloyd's discussion of the impact of the 1905 Municipal Land Law on the Galeana District demonstrates that what happened in the sierra towns of Guerrero was not unique (1988). In Galeana the same social conflict occurred between a petty bourgeoisie of rancher-merchant immigrants and a native peasantry that had played a key role in frontier warfare. As in Guerrero, the petty bourgeoisie gained control of the municipal administration and used their political power to dispossess the peasants of their remaining lands. Thus, not only in the Guerrero District but elsewhere in the state, the reversals suffered by the peasants who had fought to conquer the frontier were to be a key impetus to insurrection and revolution.

Conclusions

[The Tomochis were a] fanatical tribe of mountain men, haughty in their tremendous and savage ignorance, wild and fierce sons of the sierra, eaglets perched on their formidable nests, obstinate in the barbarous caprice of their supreme pride . . . their delirious and puerile dream of absurd, savage liberty. (Frías 1983:110; my translation)

And the strangest thing was that they did not constitute a barbarian tribe. They were not indigenes but creoles. (Frías 1983:26; my translation)[67]

Broad processes of nation-state formation and capitalist development began to transform frontier society as early as the late 1850s, although their impact was limited by ongoing warfare between colonists and indigenes. Once the Apache wars ended, the stage was set for the closing of the frontier. In the following decades, state centralization and economic development were consolidated and intensified. Subordinate groups and classes, above all the peasant-warriors of the Guerrero District, became the objects of processes of "modernization" and of new technologies of power, which were deployed by the state and by the dominant classes in order to control these new barbarians and transform the militarized agents of "civilization" into the docile subjects of "progress."

Images of alterity have their histories. English stereotypes of the Irish informed images of Indians and blacks in British New World colonies (Muldoon 1975; Baretta and Markoff 1978: 597n). In Mexico the Iberian image of the Moor underpinned the colonial construction of the Indian. Thus, it is ironic but not surprising that as the frontier was integrated into the nation-state and into the world market, past constructions of alterity were revalued and deployed by the state and by the dominant classes to construct as the new "others" those who resisted "order" and "progress" as tenaciously as the Apache had earlier resisted conquest and "civilization."

As is evident in the characterization of the Tomochis (above) advanced by Heriberto Frías, one of the federal officers who fought the serrano rebels in 1892, the reconstitution of the social identity of the one-time Apache fighters reproduced many of the elements of the frontier construction of the "barbarian." Since frontier warfare had involved an exchange of meanings and values, as well as fighting styles, strategies, and technologies, the state and the elite's reinvention of the serranos could be grounded in what were construed as the natural signs of an unmediated reality. The serranos' style of fighting, their superlative marksmanship, their extraordinary horsemanship, their tracking skills and knowledge of the landscape, their physical fortitude and stoicism, and their courage echoed that of their one-time enemies and now proclaimed their own "barbarism." Their resistance to new forms of subjection became identified with that of their past enemies, the Apache, who had also fought for an "absurd dream" of "savage liberty."

For the state and the elite, the serranos, like the Apache, became the epitome of an unruly and threatening "natural" masculinity that had to be socialized and tamed through the technologies of "order" and "progress." The serranos' attempts to affirm and defend their honor and rights became essentialized as a manifestation of their barbaric and rebellious nature. Their rebelliousness, in turn, further legitimated their "reduction." Like the Apache, the serranos became viewed as natural rebels; they also carried in their hearts and souls the wild lust for liberty and the "fierce instinct of rebellion."

If "civilization" was the mother of barbarism, "progress" was the mother of rebellion. The more the serranos resisted the effects of "order" and "progress," the more they became construed as agents of disorder and retrogression. Those who fought back became constructed as vagrants, thieves, and bandits. The state and the elite depoliticized the serranos' struggle, as they had once done that of the Apache. Official discourse denied that these peasant-warriors were fighting for a legitimate or even identifiable political cause; instead, their object, like that of the Apache, was merely to "pillage" and "steal." However, the official reinvention of the serranos did not simply reproduce frontier categories of alterity. It also revalued them. According to the new biology of society, the "self" was no longer the ethnic but the economic superior.

Throughout the decades from 1855 to 1910, land, politics, the character of authority, the principle of succession to office, education, forced military conscription, the civil inscription of marriages, pueblo sovereignty, and taxation were the foci of contention between dominant and subordinate groups and classes as well as between peasant communities and the state. However, what was at issue here was not simply class situation but also status position and social identity.

State formation and capitalist development entail a "cultural revolution." Domination is not simply based on the power to issue commands and to enforce their obedience but also on the power to construct and to order the identities of the subjected and to inscribe docility into their natures.

Serrano resistance was not just a struggle over land or electoral rights or taxes but also a dispute over the meanings and values that orient the production and reproduction of social life and social identity. The new forms of subjection-subjectivity implemented by "order" and "progress" were apprehended as signifying the alienation, emasculation, and dishonor of the self, as well as entailing the erosion of status position and class situation. Nineteenth- and early-twentieth-century serrano rebels were affirming and defending locally valued forms of identity, which had their roots in the frontier past, as well as fighting to conserve the sovereignty of a local community for which countless men and women had sacrificed their lives.

CHAPTER SIX

The Forms and Organization of Serrano Resistance, 1858-1920

Scott has remarked that much of the recent work on the peasantry has been concerned with resistance, above all with those "organized, large-scale, protest movements that appear if only momentarily, to pose a threat to the state" (1985:xv). He argues that the almost exclusive focus on revolution and rebellion has rendered invisible "everyday" forms of peasant protest (1985:xvi). Scott's observations are apposite, for "the revolution" has become the privileged "case" of peasant resistance in the historiography of Mexico. Not only has the historical literature largely ignored individual, quotidian forms of protest, but it has also neglected more collective, organized, and overtly confrontational instances of peasant rebellion that antedate the events of 1910-20.

Scholars have been rightly puzzled by the apparent lack of peasant resistance prior to 1910. But recent research has demonstrated that state centralization and capitalist development engendered peasant insurrection well before the revolution (Tutino 1986). Ironically, what has been construed as an objective fact—the lack of popular resistance prior to 1910—is itself a product of historiographical practices.

Serrano peasant resistance prior to 1910 has been ignored or minimized for several reasons. The ideological saliency accorded to the revolution as the founding event of the modern Mexican state has led to an almost exclusive focus on the events of 1910-20. Developments prior to 1910 are teleologically labeled precursor movements and, with the exception of Magonismo,[1] are given a cursory treatment at best. Moreover, until recently, the official interpretation of the revolution characterized the Chihuahuan peasants and their leader, Francisco Villa, as "bandits" lacking in any serious sociopolitical purpose: Villismo has been widely construed as an "aimless, mercenary rowdyism" (Knight 1980:19). As a result, relatively little research has been done on the popular northern revolutionary movement, let alone on the decades of peasant resistance that preceded it. In addition, investigators' dependence on official archives for information on the forms of popular protest has contributed to the erasure of peasant resistance prior to 1910. First of all, individual, everyday forms of protest are not usually reported in official archives; since such covert acts of resistance tend to take place "off-stage," they are rarely recorded by state functionaries (Scott 1985:28). Also, even when peasant struggles pose an overt threat to the state, official ideology strives to manage this threat by minimizing it, by inscribing popular rebellion as crime, as "aimless, mercenary rowdyism," rather than as a challenge to hegemony.

For example, the government records that contain most of the documentation on the serrano rebellion of 1887–96 depoliticize this movement and minimize its unity and impact. Major encounters between rebels and the forces of repression are treated as discrete "uprisings" with no broader social or temporal connections. Minor skirmishes are presented as the operations of "gangs of bandits." This is not to deny the usefulness of archival sources (indeed, my own work is founded on them). It is only to point out that official representations of events need to be deconstructed rather than objectified as factual.

Clearly, Scott's observations are both insightful and important. However, by privileging everyday forms of resistance over others, he risks reproducing some of the antinomies that have bedeviled the literature on peasant protest for so long. Different forms of resistance may be analytically distinct, but in practice they are not mutually exclusive. Everyday and armed forms of struggle can occur simultaneously as well as sequentially (though not in any necessary progression), depending on historical circumstances, the shifting balance of forces, and the politics of social and cultural struggle. Rather than focusing on one form of resistance ("the most effective") to the exclusion of others, I think it more worthwhile to examine the different forms taken by protest over time, in relation to a wider balance of social forces and broad politico-economic and sociocultural transformations.

Nonviolent Resistance (1858–1886)

Between 1858 and 1886, but especially after the mid-1860s, the peasant warriors of the Guerrero District, particularly those of the municipalities of Temósachi and Namiquipa, both as individuals and as members of corporate local groups, deployed various strategies of non-violent resistance in order to impede the implementation of policies that abrogated rights to land and community sovereignty and threatened the reproduction of locally valued forms of social identity.[2] Foot dragging, dissimulation, feigned ignorance, and outright refusal were deployed to avoid compliance with new policies. Taxes and educational subsidies were not paid, and many children were not sent to school. Moreover, peasants refused to cooperate with government plans to map, measure, and limit corporate landholdings.

Government orders to map and measure peasant holdings were an essential step in the commodification of land. In order to become an object of capitalist exchange, land had to be represented in terms of ab-stract, uniform, and quantifiable spatial units. But official technologies of quantification, which presumed that land was a commodity, came into conflict with local agrarian ideology.

In the pueblos of the sierra, agricultural fields had been "measured" in terms of the amount of seed that could be planted on them, a quan-tity that varied with the quality of the land. Fields had been delimited by situating them in relation to neighboring holdings or local landmarks. For the serranos land was an object of productive activity, a sign of honor, and an index of social rights rather than a fetishized commodity that could be quantified abstractly and sold to anyone who had the means of exchange. Thus, not only did peasants withhold their compli-ance from state attempts to rationalize and quantify corporate holdings, but they also refused to recognize the status of land as a commodity that could be freely exchanged. Moreover, peasants opposed sales of lands they considered to be part of their corporate patrimony.

The peasants of Namiquipa prevented outsiders from occupying the baldíos they had purchased within the limits of the pueblo's corporate holdings. In 1871 the justice of the peace for Namiquipa wrote to the jefe político that the vecinos had informed him that they would not allow Celso González to occupy the lands he had "bought."[3] Likewise, although Enrique Müller had obtained de jure rights to thousands of hectares of Namiquipa's corporate lands, the Namiquipans never al-lowed him to take de facto possession of these holdings.

The peasant-warriors also made use of legitimate, institutionalized channels of protest. Numerous collective and individual complaints were sent to government functionaries. Sometimes the peasants even hired bourgeois and petty-bourgeois representatives who knew how to effectively exploit the channels of grievance and redressal. In the late 1860s, for example, after their land grant was reduced to one-tenth of its size, the peasants of Namiquipa organized themselves to hire a legal representative to defend their agrarian rights.

The withholding of military services to the state was a another key form of nonviolent resistance. Since warfare against raiding indigenes was critical to the survival of their communities, the serranos continued to fight the Apache. After the mid-1860s, however, the Chihuahuan government's efforts to recruit the peasant-warriors of the Guerrero District to fight both French invaders and conservative insurgents[4] were resisted.

Since local authorities could not raise the required number of men, the Chihuahuan government began to send military recruiters to sierra communities in search of "volunteers." For the serranos, forced military service was a degrading form of exploitation, which they resisted. Eligio Cisneros, a forced recruit from Namiquipa, recalled: "It was with all the cynicism possible that they called them 'volunteers.' That government never respected anybody's will. Poor men were taken as if they were wild animals, donkeys without a master" (in Calzadíaz Barrera 1969:83; my translation). Some men were unable to elude the state's representatives, and others were "persuaded" to fight by offers of financial reward. However, most serrano peasants did their best to avoid becoming "donkeys" by fleeing to the mountains, where they could hide for several days and evade the representatives of the state.

In pueblos where the apparatus of local administration was still controlled by the peasants, municipal authorities tolerated, attempted to justify, and in some cases overtly supported the serranos' noncompliance with government orders. Sometimes they even provided leadership and helped to organize peasant protest. For example, the elected representatives of the pueblo of Namiquipa did their best to ignore superior dispositions that ordered the measurement of corporate holdings and decreed their alienation to the Müllers. Moreover, they allowed the vecinos to continue to use the lands Müller had purchased from the national government. In addition, they defended the agrarian rights of the community to superiors, restating the terms of the frontier charter and arguing that Müller's land purchases were illegal.

The support of such local authorities was critical to the success of nonviolent forms of resistance in Namiquipa; however, as agents of the state, municipal presidents could be forced by superiors to comply with government orders and to subvert peasant attempts at resistance. In doing so, of course, they risked losing the support of their local constituency. For example, in August 1871, Jesús Burciaga, the president of Namiquipa, was finally forced to allow an engineer hired by Müller to measure the community's lands. As a result, Burciaga was soon removed from office through a local peasant uprising.[5]

However partial and uneven, the backing of local authorities was crucial to the efficacy of nonviolent forms of resistance. Thus, in the pueblo of Namiquipa, where local authorities did their best to support the peasants, nonviolent forms of resistance were quite successful. By contrast, in the municipality of Temósachi, where this was not the case, nonviolent forms of resistance were less effective and more peasants turned to armed struggle.

Armed Struggle (1858-1886)

Between 1858 and 1886 the peasant-warriors of the Guerrero District rebelled against the Chihuahuan and national governments on several occasions.[6] By and large, armed struggle was not initiated by the serranos themselves. Instead, they took advantage of national insurrections, as well as of foreign invasions, to ally themselves with those seeking to overturn the regime in power.

In 1858 some peasants from the municipality of Temósachi joined conservative rebels in order to "fight for the lands that have been taken from them."[7] The conservatives also managed to glean some support in Namiquipa and Bachíniva. However, prior to the mid-1860s, only a few members of serrano communities joined insurgent movements. A more extensive mobilization did not occur until 1865, when serranos from the Guerrero and Galeana Districts allied themselves with the conservatives and the clergy and supported the French invasion of Mexico.

Peasant-warriors, particularly from the municipalities of Temósachi and Namiquipa, formed a Coalition of Pueblos that fought against Mexican liberal troops until March of 1866, when the Chihuahuan conservatives who supported the French were finally defeated (Almada 1955:277–85). Serrano support of the French invasion indicates that adherence to the patria chica took precedence over nationalist loyalties at this time and implies that popular grievances were pronounced enough to override patriotic sentiments. Indeed, the degree of serrano discontent was such that most of the rebels refused to sign the Certificate of Adhesion, a statement of subordination to the Chihuahuan government and of personal loyalty to Governor Luis Terrazas, which would have given them amnesty.[8] This implies that the Chihuahuan government, specifically the administration of Luis Terrazas, was as much a focus of opposition as the national regime.

In 1876, Porfirio Díaz led a national insurrection against the regime of Lerdo de Tejada. Once again serranos allied themselves with an insurgent movement in opposition to the national and Chihuahuan governments. Most of the serrano armed support for the Porfiristas came from the municipality of Temósachi. Although only a few serranos from other municipalities actually joined the armed movement, they supported it and refused to fight against it.[9]

Armed support for the Porfiristas in Temósachi was organized by the well-known Apache fighter Santana Pérez. In 1879, Pérez once again "raised men" (*levantar gente*) in Temósachi in order to join rebels led by Mayor Francisco Bastarrechea, who were trying to depose the Chihuahuan governor, Angel Trías, Jr.[10] Finally, in 1886 the Temósachis allied themselves with rebels from Cusihuiriáchi and Guerrero in a movement initially sparked by an electoral dispute in the Cantón Abasolo.[11]

Agrarian rights, control over municipal administration and effective suffrage, taxes, education, and the civil inscription of marriages were all overt foci of contention between serrano communities and the state between 1858 and 1886. In addition, serrano dissatisfaction with the government's conduct of the Apache wars was probably a factor in their support of the conservatives and the French in the 1850s and 1860s. However, these foci of contention were only the nodal points of a more diffuse and comprehensive struggle against the new forms of subjectivity-subjection that the processes of state formation and capitalist development entailed.

Since the Chihuahuan government still needed the serranos to fight the Apache, rebels were treated with clemency and were offered concessions as an inducement to lay down their arms. In 1877, for example, the Temósachis asked the Chihuahuan legislature to allow them to secede from the Guerrero District because members of the Guerrero elite were using their control over the apparatus of local administration to expropriate peasant holdings; the petition was granted. Since one of the grievances that sparked the 1879 rebellion of the Temósachis was the behavior of the district boss, Luis Comadurán, he was immediately removed from office.

On the whole, the government pursued a policy of cooptation, making concessions to some discontented serranos and not to others. This strategy succeeded in dividing the peasants and in containing the spread of armed insurrection. Ultimately, however, these concessions entailed only token changes. The transformation of the frontier into the border was already underway, and the impact of the processes of state formation and economic development on peasant pueblos was only softened by the policy of cooptation.

Nonviolent forms of resistance were relatively successful at this time. The Namiquipans, for example, were able to retain control of their local administration and conserve de facto possession of their lands because of the Chihuahuan government's dependence on the serranos' military services and its lack of a true monopoly of force. But the success of nonviolent resistance also hinged on the role played by municipal authorities. Where peasants could count on the support of local leaders, nonviolent resistance was more likely to achieve results.

In municipalities such as Temósachi, where the peasants had lost control over local administration, nonviolent resistance was less effective. For this reason Temósachi rather than Namiquipa became the focus of serrano armed struggle in these decades.

On the whole, serrano rebellion was informed by the experience and knowledge gained in frontier warfare. The fighting style, strategies, and forms of organization deployed by rebels were the same ones they continued to use in warfare against the Apache. Charismatic Apache fighters, such as Santana Pérez of Yepómera and Jesús María Vásquez of Namiquipa, played key roles in organizing the rebellion, providing not just leadership but also arms; they were able to furnish their men with guns and ammunition they had obtained from the Chihuahuan government to fight the indigenes.

Nonviolent Resistance (1887–1910)

Between 1887 and 1910 serranos continued to deploy the forms of nonviolent resistance they had utilized earlier to impede the effects of new technologies of power, to resist unjust demands on economic surpluses, to retain de facto possession of agrarian holdings, and to conserve some control over municipal administration.[12] Foot dragging, temporary flight, dissimulation, assumed ignorance, "trespassing," destruction of wire fences (symbols of agrarian dispossession), and noncompliance were deployed to defy official orders. Children were kept out of school. The payment of taxes was constantly put off. Serranos forced into wage labor refused to comply with degrading orders. Small merchants who charged outrageous prices or were members of the petty-bourgeois faction became victims of peasant-engendered theft and arson. In pueblos such as Namiquipa, where settlement had never been nucleated, peasants tried to construct new houses and plant new fields as far away from the administrative center as possible in order to elude surveillance by agents of the state. Peasants also continued to seek legal redressal of grievances and official recognition of agrarian, political, and social rights.

Cattle rustling, which became widespread in the Guerrero District after 1886, represented a new form of serrano resistance. For the serranos, taking cattle from wealthy hacendados was not "theft," just as continued use of community pastures and woodlands that had been sold by the state to outsiders was not "trespassing." Until the end of the Apache wars, wild cattle had roamed free in the sierra and had been hunted by any man who had a rifle and some bullets. After 1886, however, hacendados such as Luis Terrazas had their cowboys round up these *orejones* and brand them with the signs of private property. Cattle rustling was simply a way of laying claim to what the serranos considered to be rightfully theirs, of resisting the unjust alienation, commodification, and privatization of collective resources. From the serrano point of view, the hacendados were the thieves, for they were the ones who were appropriating for themselves what had once belonged to all and to no one.

Serrano rebels who had to leave their pueblos to avoid repression at the hands of local caciques and who were unwilling to put up with the humiliations of wage labor were able to subsist in the mountains from the proceeds of cattle rustling. Many future revolutionaries, including Andrés Vargas, Telésforo Terrazas, and Manuel Baca of the municipality of Namiquipa, and, of course, Francisco Villa himself, took to "cattle rustling"; by 1902 these Namiquipans had developed contacts with Villa and would join him from time to time to steal from the rich.

Protests against caciquismo became more widespread after 1886, as the effects of state centralization began to be generalized and as a sultanistic form of domination began to be imposed on peasants who had formerly exercised the right to elect their own authorities and who had enjoyed a great deal of control over local administration. Resistance to caciquismo was both individual and collective.

As individuals, serranos affirmed their right to social honor and avenged the affronts and injustices to which they were subjected by state functionaries in hundreds of everyday acts of defiance, which are unrecorded in official archives. Reminiscing about conditions in the 1890s, the serrano Eligio Cisneros stressed the significance of these acts of resistance:

> In Chihuahua the common man was beginning to gain consciousness, as is proved by his attitude to the protected cacique. . . . I will cite a case in point. On the road from Guerrero City to the pueblo of Tomochi . . . Alisandro Rascón and Martín D. Rivera [future revolutionaries from Namiquipa] encountered the . . . cacique, Joaquín Chávez,[13] a twisted assassin. . . . Chávez tried to interrogate them, as was his custom. But not taking him seriously, Alisandro Rascón said to him: "When will you stop meddling in what does not concern you?" And in case [Chávez] was going to draw his gun, Alisandro added: "You are nothing but an . . . *espanta pendejos* . . ." The renowned assassin . . . continued on his way, murmuring, "We will meet again." . . . Observers sensitive to changes in the atmosphere noted and understood that in such individual acts of rebellion was to be found the flame, which would later be lit, of collective retaliation and vengeance. The desire to be free of the tyrant became a stimulus to action. The cacique Joaquín Chávez kept his silence, but news of the state of shame and humiliation in which the two young men— Alisandro and Martín D. Rivera—had placed him was spread by word of mouth, indicating that the hour of the common, humble, and dispossessed man was in sight. (In Calzadíaz Barrera 1969: 186–87; my translation)

An *espanta pájaros* is a scarecrow. In everyday contexts a *pendejo* is a good-for-nothing. Although *pendejo* is commonly used to disparage a man's honor, *espanta pendejos* is an unusual and imaginative insult. To call Chávez an *espanta pendejos* is to say that he is only capable of scaring tame men who lack the huevos to defend their honor and therefore that he himself is a coward. Since huevos are viewed as the "natural" basis of power, to diminish Chávez's machismo is equivalent to stripping him of his power.

This symbolic act had practical consequences; in a society where masculine reputation is central to almost every aspect of everyday life, to be bested in a conflict of honor is to be emasculated and disempowered.

The cacique, whose power rested on a terror grounded in the symbolism of machista preponderance, was humiliated and shamed. Henceforth known in the pueblos of the sierra as an espanta pendejos, he became a ridiculous figure, one to be mocked rather than feared.

As peasants' political rights were increasingly abrogated, protest against caciquismo began to take on a more organized, collective, and overtly confrontational form. Serranos organized themselves to prevent electoral fraud and in some cases destroyed electoral records or refused to vote, in the hope that the rigged elections would be annulled. In 1908 more than fifty Namiquipans went to Chihuahua City to ask the governor to remove the cacique, Victoriano Torres, from his post as municipal boss. The independent newspaper *El Correo de Chihuahua* characterized this manifestation of popular discontent as an act of "civil valor" without precedent.[14]

After 1905 resistance to agrarian dispossession also assumed a more organized and collective form. In May of 1906, for example, originario peasants from Namiquipa formed the Sociedad Civil Particular (SCP), an organization whose goal was to administer the común repartimiento lands in accordance with the provisions of the community's colonial charter and to defend corporate holdings from encroachments by both hacendados and local petty-bourgeois entrepreneurs.[15] Membership in the SCP was overtly restricted to "descendants of the original colonists"; in practice this meant any peasant who was either born in Namiquipa or had immigrated there prior to 1886, and who had defended the community from the raiding Apache and thus established his rights to land. Members of the petty bourgeoisie who had contributed to the costs of the legal defense of the pueblo's lands or who had bought rights to the común repartimiento were explicitly excluded from the SCP and thus were denied any legitimate claim to Namiquipa's corporate holdings.

The SCP and organizations like it were important for several reasons. First, the SCP directly challenged the right of Namiquipa's petty bourgeois–dominated ayuntamiento to administer and to dispose of the community's lands and acted as a brake on the process of peasant expropriation. Second, it provided an alternative organization that united peasants in opposition to the local cacique and his petty-bourgeois clients. Third, it gave peasants valuable experience in collective organization, resistance, and mobilization; many of the SCP's members were to join the ranks of the revolutionaries in 1910. Fourth, collective organization made resistance more effective. For example, in May 1908 the president of the SCP, which at the time comprised 118 members, rode with an armed force of 50 originarios to the neighboring Hacienda de Babícora, property of the American Hearst family, which had invaded more than 9,000 hectares of común repartimiento lands. The SCP members tore down the hacienda's new fence and repositioned the boundary markers, forcing the Hearsts to move their fence and preventing them from taking possession of the peasants' lands.[16]

Armed Struggle (1887-1920)

From 1887 to 1896 a rebel movement developed in the Guerrero District. Peasants from the municipalities of Guerrero, Temósachi, and Namiquipa took up arms with the explicit goal of overthrowing the Díaz regime. Although some historians have disaggregated this rebellion into more than twelve localized uprisings, continuities of leadership, personnel, grievances, and ideology suggest instead that it was a loosely organized but nevertheless unitary guerrilla movement.

Even the Chihuahuan historian Francisco Almada, who tends to treat each confrontation between rebels and federal forces as a separate revolt, has recognized these continuities, noting that the rebels of 1893 were "the same group" who had conspired against the government in 1889 and had fought the federal army in the intervening years (1938:24). Significantly, another Chihuahuan historian has observed that the rebels themselves viewed their struggle as a unitary movement; according to Rubén Osorio, those who rose up after the defeat of the serranos of Tomochi in 1892 indexed their identification with these rebels, most of whom had been killed by federal forces, by calling themselves Tomochis (pers. com.). Indeed, this self-identification was proclaimed in a manifesto issued by Santana Pérez and other insurgent leaders in 1893.[18]

The rebellion was largely a peasant movement, although a few discontented members of the rural middle classes also participated. Simón Amaya, former jefe político of the Guerrero District, was a middle-class rebel who became one of the leaders of serrano insurrection. As a military broker during the Apache wars, Amaya had gained experience in the coordination of warfare. Moreover, he had contacts with members of the middle and dominant classes. If, as has been alleged, the serrano rebels did indeed receive some financial support and armament from Luis Terrazas, the one-time governor of Chihuahua who had been temporarily removed from power by Porfirio Díaz, it is likely that men such as Amaya acted as intermediaries.[19] However, as in earlier armed struggles, the leadership came from among the peasants, from charismatic Apache fighters such as Santana Pérez from Yepómera and Benigno Arvizo from Cruces.

As in earlier struggles, locality was a key principle of organization. The movement really consisted of allied contingents of men from several sierra pueblos who fought under their own local leaders but joined together to oppose the regime, much as they had earlier cooperated to fight the Apache. The rebels waged a guerrilla struggle, mobilizing to attack or defend key pueblos and scattering to the sierras surrounding their communities of origin when defeated. The forms of organization and leadership, the strategies, and the techniques of frontier warfare were perpetuated in the serrano rebellion. There were no rigid military hierarchies or forms of discipline. Rather, the rebels formed a charismatic and egalitarian community of comrades in arms.

Although resistance continued to center on the same grievances that had generated serrano protest prior to 1886, popular outrage with caciquismo became a more important factor in mobilization as the state increasingly marginalized subaltern groups and classes from participation in the formal political process. Conflicts between peasants and members of a rural petty bourgeoisie over control of the apparatus of municipal administration, generally sparked by elections, were a key "trigger" of armed serrano insurrection. Significantly, after taking a town, the rebels would appoint new local authorities and destroy the archives that legitimated the caciques' abuses.

The burning of archival records was much more than a symbolic protest against the new technologies of power deployed by the state. These documents not only codified but also legitimated and made possible the expropriation of corporate lands; the categorizing of dissidents as bandits, cattle rustlers, and criminals; the charging of unjustly high taxes—nowhere is the "materiality" of language clearer than in official records. To demolish them was to sabotage an instrument of power and to erase the traces of the changes that order and progress had brought to serrano communities.

Agrarian dispossession continued to be a critical impetus to mobilization. Although historians have underestimated the importance of agrarian grievances at this time, Porfirio Díaz himself linked the abortive 1889 serrano conspiracy against his regime to popular discontent with the state's alienation of corporate pueblo lands:

However much, we should not grant a great deal of importance to the daily rumors circulating about adjudications of land . . . it is certain that in some parts [of the republic] they have served as a stimulus to the malcontents, and in others they may serve to foment attempts against the public peace, as happened in a conspiracy that was just uncovered in Chihuahua, the members of which are now at the disposal of the local authorities.[20]

Díaz himself points out that these grievances were not confined to the Chihuahuan serranos. As processes of state centralization and economic development began to impinge on the lives of the Mexican peasantry as a whole, alliances between rebels from places as distant as Oaxaca and Chihuahua began to be forged. Significantly, Díaz adds:

Among the plans and documents taken from [the Chihuahuan conspirators] are some that make reference to an imminent uprising in Juchitán over this question of land, and they exploit this possibility to animate and convince otherwise vacillating followers. At the least, these rumors give hope to those who would upset the order, and although in the last analysis the rebels will be repressed, we were incapable of preventing this attempt, which could have been so damaging at this time.[21]

The armed movement of 1887–96 differed from earlier forms of serrano insurgency in several respects. First, instead of taking up arms to join rebellions initiated by others, as they had done prior to 1886, the serranos developed their own movement. Second, they began to forge alliances with rebels in other parts of Chihuahua, such as the peasant-warriors of the Galeana District, as well as in other areas of the Republic as distant as Juchitán, Oaxaca. Third, like the Apache, they took advantage of the proximity of the border, crossing into the United States to evade pursuit, to form new alliances, to obtain arms and munitions, and to organize attacks on Mexican pueblos and customs agencies. The strategy of exploiting the border for insurgent ends, developed during these years, was to be critical to the success of the 1910 revolutionaries.

After the defeat of the Apache in 1886, the state and the dominant classes were no longer dependent on the serranos' military services. These one-time agents of "civilization" became redefined as barbarians who had to be forcibly "reduced to order." Hence, an official policy of violent repression supplanted the pre-1886 strategy of cooptation.

The Chihuahuan government tried to recruit serrano auxiliaries to fight against rebels from their own area. By using serranos to fight serranos, not only would the government "divide and rule," but it would be able to vindicate and legitimate its construction of serrano rebellion as "banditry." However, men from serrano towns who were not themselves involved in the rebellion actively sympathized with the insurgents and refused to fight against them. As Eligio Cisneros recalled:

> In Namiquipa, when Don José Casavantes [the municipal president] received the order to recruit men to form a corps of auxiliaries, many were the Namiquipans who manifested their unwillingness and many others left the pueblo. He found it so difficult to recruit volunteers that he was unable to participate in the combat of Santo Tomás and he was barely able to assemble thirty-five men, all forced, for the combat of Cañón del Manzano. (in Calzadíaz Barrera 1969:180; my translation)

Cisneros's recollections are borne out by numerous archival documents. Indeed, attempts to recruit the Namiquipans to fight against the rebels in 1893 precipitated a shoot-out that almost sparked an uprising in the town. Other sierra pueblos also refused to "cooperate" in the repression of the rebels.

Unable to use serrano auxiliaries, the state had to rely on federal forces. Between 1891 and 1892 three separate federal army expeditions, integrated by hundreds of soldiers, were sent to subject about one hundred Tomochi and serrano rebels. Although the rebels were vastly outnumbered and short of ammunition, their fighting skills were so superior to the federals' that they were able to rout two of these contingents. However, by the end of 1892 the Tomochis had been defeated: the army razed the pueblo and came close to exterminating almost the entire population, including women and children. In 1893 and 1894 federal forces were again sent to repress the rebels. Again outnumbered and short of guns and ammunition, the rebels could not secure a military triumph; by 1896 they had been defeated militarily.

Although the scope and unity of the serrano guerrilla movement have been underestimated in the historical literature, several factors operated to constrain the process of armed rebellion and ultimately to preclude its success. Prior to 1904 the effects of state centralization and capitalist development on the serrano peasantry as a whole were still uneven; some communities, such as Yepómera, in the municipality of Temósachi, and

Cruces, in the municipality of Namiquipa, had fallen victim to agrarian dispossession and caciquismo, while others, such as the pueblo of Namiquipa itself, had managed to retain de facto possession of corporate lands and to conserve a measure of control over the apparatus of municipal administration. Moreover, nonviolent forms of resistance could still be successfully deployed in some pueblos. For these reasons, not all serranos were willing to take up arms at this time, which weakened the movement.

Ethnic differences between serranos and Indians hindered an alliance between these groups and limited the rebels' base of support. By and large, very few of the Sierra Madre's Tarahumara Indians were involved in the serrano movement. Although the Tarahumara rebelled during these decades, they did so independently, as a distinct ethnic group opposed to all the gente de razón.

Serrano pueblos were interconnected by ties of kinship and friendship and linked by a tradition of solidarity and cooperation rooted in the common struggle against the Apache. Nevertheless, a highly localistic consciousness, a concern first and foremost with intra-community affairs, hampered the development of a more viable sense of unity.

Serrano pueblos were internally divided by three of the overt foci of resistance, namely, the expropriation of lands, the contravention of the electoral process, and the increase in municipal taxes. Wealthier peasants and petty-bourgeois immigrants, who joined together to seize control of local political institutions, benefited from land expropriations and from increased municipal revenues and obviously did not support the rebels. Because outside sources of support were limited, the rebels were plagued by a shortage of arms, ammunition, and horses.

On the whole, the serrano movement was unable to obtain sufficient resources, and its leaders were unable to generate a base of support wide enough to ensure a military victory, even just within Chihuahuan territory. In addition, new means of communication allowed the government to deploy the forces of repression with unprecedented speed and efficiency. Although the serranos scored some important victories, by 1896 the movement had been defeated and the rebels disbanded.

After 1904 the effects of state centralization and economic development became generalized throughout the sierra peasant communities. Even the peasants of the pueblo of Namiquipa, who had successfully resisted agrarian dispossession and political marginalization until this time, lost their rights to land and became the victims of the abuses of caciquismo. After 1904 popular discontent spread throughout the sierra; the pool of potential serrano rebels was much larger than it had been in the 1890s.

During these years Magonistas operating on the U.S. side of the border tried to organize a rebel movement in Mexico and succeeded in obtaining support from serrano communities in the Galeana and Guerrero Districts. In October of 1905, for example, Concepción Cervantes, uncle of the revolutionary leader Candelario Cervantes, wrote to Ricardo Flores Magón, saying that the Namiquipans were ready to fight against "the authorities governed by the Dictatorship" of Díaz.[22] However, steps taken by the American government, which still supported the Díaz regime, precluded the success of the Magonistas' efforts. In the face of the American government's arrest and imprisonment of key leaders, the betrayal of rebel plans to the Díaz regime, and the limits placed on access to supplies of arms and ammunition, the Magonistas were unable to organize an armed movement of any significance. The suppression of the Magonista movement illustrates the impact U.S. policies could have on the process of rural revolt in Mexico (on this topic, see papers in Nugent 1988).

By 1910, American support for the Díaz regime had declined; the shifts in U.S. policy provided a more favorable climate for revolution in Mexico. Moreover, by 1910 discontented members of the middle class, supporters of Francisco I. Madero, had spearheaded the organization of a national network of Liberal Clubs, which were able to provide rebels with arms and ammunition as well as to coordinate diverse locally and regionally based insurgent movements.

On November 20, 1910, serranos from Namiquipa, Bachíniva, Temósachi, San Isidro, and other Guerrero District pueblos rose up in response to Madero's call to arms. Serrano revolutionary mobilization was so extensive that the Guerrero District is often characterized as "the cradle of the Mexican Revolution."

Significantly, one of the first acts of these peasant revolutionaries was to depose the hated caciques and appoint new municipal authorities who would be the padres rather than the padrastros of the pueblos.[23] These local authorities became the "fathers" of the revolutionaries' families and were responsible for providing economic support to women and children and guarding the honor of mothers and daughters, wives and sisters. They also acted as political and military brokers, mediating between the peasant insurgents and the Maderista leadership. Indeed, their role in the revolution recalls that played by their frontier predecessors in the Apache wars.

As in earlier struggles, the serranos continued to fight under the supervision of charismatic local leaders and to deploy the techniques of warfare and the forms of organization developed during the Apache wars. Madero himself did not take active command of the Liberating Army until March of 1911, just two months before the rebels took Juárez City and brought down the Díaz regime. Although he tried to impose rational military disciplines on the serranos, he was not able to do so. Popular leaders had de facto control of revolutionary warfare, and popular authorities had substantial autonomy in the sphere of local administration.

Madero's policies were more conservative than his promises. For example, his administration did not act upon repeated requests from peasants for land reform. Since the state was weak, armed peasants were often able to take matters into their own hands and achieve a local resolution of their grievances. Such was the case in Namiquipa, where members of the SCP initiated a local agrarian reform (Alonso 1986). Significantly, the vision of agrarian reform put into practice by the SCP in Namiquipa echoed the conditions set out in the pueblo's colonial charter of 1778. Derechos de posesión were to go to those who had defended the lands of the community; the derechos were transmissible to heirs, but they could not be sold.[24] Serrano peasants understood what the commodification of land entailed.

The Maderista regime's inattention to popular grievances was one of the factors that helped to mobilize limited support among Chihuahua's peasants for the Orozquista counterrevolution of 1912, which was backed by the Terrazas-Creel grand-family, as well as by other prerevolutionary Chihuahuan oligarchs. Pueblos such as Namiquipa, however, stayed loyal to Madero and fought the Orozquistas.

After Madero's assassination in 1913, Namiquipans and other serranos from the Guerrero District joined the forces of Francisco Villa. The Namiquipans soon became Villa's favorites, members of his elite corps of warriors, the Dorados, or "Golden Ones."

Born in Durango, Villa had been a sharecropper on a hacienda. According to popular tradition, while attempting to defend the sexual purity and honor of his sister, Villa shot and wounded the hacendado who had tried to exercise the droit du seigneur. Forced into "banditry," Villa roamed the sierra of Durango and Chihuahua for a number of years. By 1902 he had struck up close friendships with a number of serrano rebels from Namiquipa and often visited the pueblo, where he was known as El Guero, that is, "The Fair-Skinned One" (Calzadíaz Barrera 1979).

Villa was the embodiment of all the antinomies of serrano masculinity. Known as the Centaur of the North, he was a charismatic macho who knew how to use force, as well as a traditional patriarch who conducted himself in accordance with the norms, meanings, and values of the frontier code of honor. The parallels between Villa's style of leadership and fighting and that of serrano frontier warriors are also remarkable (Campbell 1985). But more interesting is the similarity between Villa's dream of postrevolutionary society, as told to John Reed in 1914, and the form of organization and ideology of the military colonies of the Chihuahuan frontier (Katz 1981:142–43):

> We will put the Army to work. In all parts of the Republic we will establish military colonies composed of the veterans of the Revolution. The State will give them agricultural lands and establish big industrial enterprises to give them work. Three days a week they will work and work hard, because honest work is more important than fighting, and only honest work makes good citizens. And the other three days they will receive military instruction and go out and teach all the people how to fight. . . . My ambition is to live my life in one of those military colonies among my compañeros whom I love, who have suffered so long and so deeply with me. (Reed 1969:144–45)

This dream of a peasant republic based on popular self-defense represented a vindication of frontier forms of social reproduction, ideology, and identity, which had been undermined by the processes of state formation and economic development. Condensed in this vision were the aspirations of the serranos, whose own dreams were as inflected by the frontier past as Villa's. The serrano men of this postrevolutionary utopia would once again have honor-precedence and honor-virtue: they would be life givers and life takers, peasants and warriors.

Serrano peasants continued to support Villa through the end of 1915. By then he had lost control of Chihuahua to the bourgeois opposition led by Venustiano Carranza, and he formally disbanded what was left of his army.

Convinced that Carranza planned to sell the northern provinces to the United States, Villa attacked Columbus, New Mexico, on March 9, 1916 (Katz 1977). Although a large proportion of the force that attacked the town consisted of veterans from Namiquipa, the majority of them had been forcibly recruited. Many of Villa's Namiquipan followers simply did not share his nationalist anti-imperialism (Alonso 1988c). In the conjuncture of 1916, most Namiquipans were primarily concerned with the achievement of localistic goals, with reconstructing the patria chica. Although willing to support Villa against the Carrancistas, they could not see any significance in Villa's plans to attack the United States. (Alonso 1988c).

On March 16, 1916, the U.S. government sent 6,000 troops into Mexico on a "punitive expedition" with the ostensible purpose of capturing Francisco Villa and destroying his forces. The American military made Namiquipa a prime objective, and by the end of March the area had been occupied by thousands of U.S. troops (Alonso 1988c). Two months later, in response to a "suggestion" of General Pershing's, Namiquipans formed a local militia that was to actively collaborate with the U.S. military in pursuing its objective. Similar armed nuclei were formed in other Guerrero District towns (Alonso 1988c). After the American withdrawal in 1917, these local militias continued to operate under the umbrella of the Carrancista government.

The reasons for this radical change in the Namiquipan attitude toward Villa are too complex to go into here (they are treated in detail in Alonso 1988c). Ironically, in local ideology these *defensas sociales*, or "home guards," became construed as heroic forces of order bent on defending the patria chica from the incursions of "vandalic hordes." In this case, however, the "barbaric" other was no longer the Apache but Villa himself: indeed, one member of the Namiquipan defensa social expressly likened Villa to an Apache. "Guero" in 1902, "Apache" in 1916: perhaps these ethnic categories are the most apt indexes of the shifting relations between the Namiquipans and the leader who, paradoxically, had best articulated their visions, aspirations, and interests.

Conclusions

[It] is also necessary to consider the effects of the social organization of frontiers upon the forms given to rebellion by frontiersmen. (Baretta and Markoff 1978:607)

Clearly, state centralization and capitalist development engendered a long-term process of resistance in the Chihuahuan sierra. Beginning in 1858, violent as well as nonviolent forms of resistance were deployed by peasants. The revolution was one of several conjunctures in a process that antedated 1910 by several decades. Although land, taxes, and control of municipal administration were the overt foci of contention, what was at issue was a more general discontent with the imposition of new forms of subjection-subjectivity, which eroded community sovereignty and impeded the reproduction of honorable forms of social identity, as well as of a whole way of life.

The reversals suffered by the serrano peasants not only eroded their class situation and status position but also humiliated and dishonored them. Resistance was an affirmation of honorable forms of social identity whose roots lay in a frontier history that was perpetuated in social memory, as well as in the values, meanings, and norms that oriented the practices of everyday life. In this sense the frontier past was critical to the serranos' subsequent mobilization against the state and against the dominant classes, whose interests, properties, and lives they had once defended and protected from the indigenes. In addition, the forms, the organization, and the tactics of serrano resistance were shaped by the tradition of frontier warfare. A frontier code of honor provided the vision of the just society and the idiom of both individual and collective resistance to the injustices of the present.

CHAPTER SEVEN

Progress as Disorder and Dishonor
Discourses of Serrano Resistance, 1858–1920

Social beginnings are important because the possibilities of the future are inflected by the past. But this relationship between present and past is not one of mechanistic causation. The prefiguring of the present by the past is always mediated by the meanings inscribed in culture and memory, as well as by the sociohistorical circumstances of groups and classes. If social action is mediated by a history, it is because the past has significance.

The serrano peasants' history as members of frontier military colonies was to inform their resistance to the transformations engendered by the processes of state formation and capitalist development. A frontier ideology of honor and a vision of the past provided the bases for the perception of injustice and for the imagination of a utopian future. The forms of organization, the style of fighting, and the types of leadership that had characterized frontier warfare were redeployed in armed insurrection.

But social groups reconstruct their histories as the history they live changes; the past is not a given. Ricoeur's observation is very much to the point: "It is always through interpretations which reshape it in a retroactive way that the founding act of a group keeps being re-enacted. . . . no social existence is possible without this indirect relation to its own foundation" (1978:46). The Namiquipans' vision of utopia was a return to the frontier past. Their denunciations of present injustices were couched in historical terms and constantly referred to the community's founding charter. But the past they wished to reclaim was not a "given" but instead an object of discursive and political construction, a past whose signs were oriented by the struggles of the present.

Capitalism as the Midas Touch:
Honor and Wealth, Blood and Gold

What is significant is that capitalism cut through the integu-
ment of custom, severing the people from the accustomed social
matrix in order to transform them into economic actors, independent of prior social commitments to kin and neighbors. (Wolf
1969:379)

While in Namiquipa, I often went to visit my good friend Doña
Aurora,[1] who was born at the turn of the century and had lived through
the revolution. Like others of her generation, Doña Aurora had a highly
developed historical memory and a great interest in and concern with
the past. When we talked about people and events long gone, we often
spoke in the present tense.

One day I asked Doña Aurora to tell me about the Müllers, the
owners of the Hacienda de Santa Clara who, from the 1860s on, had
repeatedly tried to appropriate thousands of hectares of Namiquipa's
corporate land grant. "Were they good or bad people?" I asked. Doña
Aurora put away her sewing, lit a cigarette, and answered my question:

> Well, I heard that the daughter, María Müller, was intimate with
> her own brother. Imagine! She became pregnant and they locked
> her up in a *carcel de agua* [jail of water] for a week. When they
> took her out of there, she was so swollen she never walked again.
> She was enormous. Everywhere she went, she had to be carried
> about by servants, whom she constantly abused. That's what rich
> people are like. But don't think that she didn't find someone to
> marry her. The administrator of the hacienda. A Mexican. He
> knew where the money was.

"What happened to the brother and the baby?" I asked. She told me
that after being disinherited by his father, the brother went to "the
other side," taking the baby with him. On another visit she continued
the story:

> One day many years later, the Müllers had a big *pachanga* at their
> ranch in Cruces. There was a lot of meat. They butchered many
> cows. And there was music. María Müller was sitting there, sur-
> rounded by her servants, when a young man came up to her.
> They stared at each other for a long time. "You're my mother,"
> he told her. At that moment, he fell in love with her.

"He was the child she'd had by her brother, right?" "Yes," replied Doña Aurora, "the son came back and fell in love with the mother. And what's more, he went to live at Santa Clara with her."

All sorts of unusual things happened at Santa Clara. Some of Müller's sheep were born with human faces. But one of the most bizarre events, from Doña Aurora's point of view, was the birth of a fetus from the feces of an Indian peon that had been heated and quickened into life by the sun. The hacendado sent the cowboys out to find and bring the fetus to the house, where it was kept and where it grew into a baby.

What is the meaning of these stories? What do they say about the ways in which the peasants constructed the identities of the rich and powerful?[2]

Doña Aurora often commented that *los ricos* (the rich) formed illicit sexual unions and "made a mess of kinship." Her Santa Clara stories are about the disordering of reproduction. Fetuses are born from excrement; babies are conceived through incest. The reproduction of human life is a synecdoche for the reproduction of social life. In the world of los ricos, reproduction has become disordered: life comes into being in unnatural, polluting, and immoral ways. Nothing is what it should be: the boundaries that separate and distinguish between the social and the natural, the pure and the impure, the human and the animal, no longer exist. Norms of honor are violated, and prescribed obligations to kin are unmet or transgressed.

For the Namiquipans, the socially and divinely sanctioned form of sexual union entails the commingling of divergent "bloods." Significantly, the only stories of incest I heard in Namiquipa involved either ricos, caciques, or *hijos naturales* (natural children), who are believed to carry in their "blood" their unmarried mother's infra-sociality. Incest, the refusal to commingle blood, is a transgression of divine law and social morality, associated with the realm of the devil and with infra-social being.

In Doña Aurora's story about María Müller, incest becomes a privileged symbol of an illicit hoarding of substance, which underlies the ricos' inability to reproduce human and social life in orderly, morally sanctioned ways. A metaphorical equivalence is established between the incestuous hoarding of bodily substance and the capitalist accumulation of wealth. Although wealth had been a sign of honor in frontier society, the social prestige of the dominant classes was dependent on patrimonial forms of redistribution. But after 1886 traditions of beneficence were displaced in the scramble for the spoils of "progress." For the Namiquipans, the failure to redistribute wealth, like the failure to commingle blood, became a sign of the dishonor of the rich and of the evil of capitalist accumulation.

But incest is a multivocal symbol. In Doña Aurora's story María Müller's permanent and unnatural bloating is an enduring sign of the rich's violation of other norms and meanings that regulated social personhood and relations among kin. The Müllers' incestuous unions transgressed the values of sexual chastity central to the honor of women and were a breach of the duty to protect the sexual purity of sisters and mothers key to the honor of men. A sign of evil and infra-social being, of an illicit hoarding of substance and wealth, of a contravention of the norms and meanings that underwrote gender identities, and of a violation of prescribed duties to kin, incest indexed multiple dimensions of the ricos' lack of honor.

The symbolic link between the hoarding of wealth and the hoarding of substance, between accumulation and profane forms of reproduction, is articulated in another of Doña Aurora's stories, prompted by my queries about los ricos. Doña Aurora told me that Victoriano Torres, the local cacique, was so obsessed with gold that he even stole the "treasure" of the local church.[3] After his wife died, he married his co-mother (one of his children's godmothers). "You've heard the story about the man who sold his soul to the devil, haven't you?" asked Doña Aurora. "No? I'll tell it to you." And she continued:

> A man who sold his soul to the devil noticed that his time was up. This man had a wife as wily as a fox. He didn't want to go to hell, so he asked his wife what he should do. His wife said, "When the devil comes for you, tell him you slept with your sister." That night, when the devil came, the man told him, "I slept with my sister!" But the devil was not impressed. "That's all right," he said; "we have many worse ones down there." The man pleaded for more time and in the morning asked his wife, "What should I do? He says he'll still take me!" His wife counseled him to say he had slept with his mother. The next night the devil returned and the man protested, "But I slept with my mother." "Is that all?" the devil responded. "Come on. It's time to pay your debts." By morning the man was really desperate. But his wife advised him not to worry; "Tell him you slept with your co-mother. He won't take you." That night when the devil came for his part of the bargain, the man insisted, "But I slept with my

co-mother!" And the devil screamed with fury, "Dirty old man! Not even in hell do we want the likes of you!"[4]

What this story makes clear is that incestuous reproduction is a sacrilege, associated with the realm of the devil. Those who commit incest dishonor themselves and their families. A man who deflowers a woman he knows to be his sister is one who inverts and subverts the code of honor; instead of protecting the sexual purity of his sister, he violates it. Incest between mothers and sons is even more "immoral" and "dishonorable" than that between brothers and sisters. Mother-son incest is not only a sinful commingling of the same blood but an inversion of the ideal type of the mother, the Virgin.

Interestingly, sexual relations with co-parents are regarded as more sacrilegious than copulation with blood kin. As Gudeman has demonstrated, in Catholic doctrine the sharing of "spiritual substance" makes co-parenthood a "higher," more sacred tie than those of marriage or parenthood, which entail carnal bonds that carry the stigma of original sin (1971). Because sex with a co-parent transforms a spiritual tie into a physical bond, it is sacrilegious, degrading, and dishonoring.[5] Like incest, it conjoins that which should be kept distinct and hence is a form of what Mary Douglas calls "dirt," a transgression of the boundaries of cultural order (1966).

At the same time, incest and sexual relations with co-parents represent a refusal to share substance with others to whom one is not already tied, a refusal that is analogous to a failure to redistribute capital. As Jean Comaroff notes, these stories index the elitism of the rich, as well as the "intransitivity" of capitalist forms of accumulation (pers. com.).

The peasants' attribution of incestuous relations to the elite indexed multiple dimensions of the latter's lack of honor. Hoarders of substance and hoarders of wealth, the rich were so evil that not even the devil to whom they had sold their souls would take them. In the eyes of "the tillers of the fields" (*labradores*), members of the dominant classes were improperly socialized beings who had not disciplined and tamed their "natural" selves. Incest was also a sign of the power of the rich. But for the serranos, this power, like that of the devil's, was evil and antisocial (cf. Taussig 1980).

The "surreal" quality of the stories I have discussed expresses the serranos' experience of social dislocation, of living in a disordered world where the implicit understandings that configure reality can no longer be taken for granted. Whereas official ideology construed "the rich" as the creators of order, popular counter-discourses represented them as the generators of disorder, of unnatural and immoral forms of human and social reproduction.

For the serranos, honor became the "capital" of the dispossessed. The rich had economic capital, but only the poor had the most precious capital of all—honor. This distinction between rich and poor, wealth and honor, is clearly articulated in the words of Plácido Chávez Calderón, son of one of the leaders of the serrano rebels of Tomochi: "My father and my uncles always belonged to the humble class and never disposed of [economic] capital: their only capital—one that was greater and more precious—was their work, their self-esteem, and their honor, an honor without flaw or stigma;[6] they conserved these gifts until the last days of their lives" (1964:6; my translation).

Lacking in virtue, the dominant classes did not merit the precedence that society accorded them. Since they did not possess personal honor, no social respect and esteem was due to them; nor did their authority have legitimacy. As was discussed earlier, the values and norms of verguenza and respeto prescribed obedience only to honorable and beneficent superiors.

On the frontier the transformation of economic into symbolic capital had been mediated by a patrimonial beneficence and by a logic of reciprocity that overtly recognized the social embeddedness of "economic" relations. Until the end of the Apache wars, money barely circulated in serrano towns.[7] The logic of the gift gave symbolic form to the exchange of goods and services; exchange was mediated by the norms and values of verguenza, respeto, and consideración. Thus, "economic" transactions created and cemented personal relationships between the parties concerned. This personalization of exchange relations was the very inverse of the logic of capitalism, which depersonalizes social relations while it endows things with social life.

As class became a more important criterion of status and as the impersonal logic of the marketplace began to regulate relations between dominant and subordinate groups, the elite began to contravene the norms and values of the frontier code of honor. At the same time, members of subaltern groups and classes affirmed the values of the frontier code against those of capitalism; honor became the ideology of the oppressed and exploited. They inverted the logic of the Porfirian social biology; for the serranos capital became a sign of dishonor. Thus, the revolt of the serranos against los ricos and the regime that served their interests came to be legitimated by a popular vision of the elite's dishonorableness. If human and social life were to be reproduced in orderly and moral ways, the elite had to be defied; their rule was not that of "progress" and "order" but instead that of moral corruption and disorder.[8]

This vision of progress as disorder and of its agents as dishonorable was articulated in a manifesto circulated in the Guerrero District in November of 1893, signed by important rebel leaders, including Santana Pérez.[9] The overt purpose of this text was to convince the soldiers of the federal army to join the rebels in the fight against the Díaz dictatorship. The manifesto is structured by an opposition between social relations mediated by a logic of kinship, identified with reciprocity, egalitarianism, "shared substance," and honor, versus social relations mediated by a calculus of money, identified with asymmetry, domination, difference, and corruption.

The manifesto establishes a bond of kinship between soldiers and rebels; they are "sons of the same mother," the patria. As members of a community of kin, soldiers and rebels have the same personal obligations, that is, the duty to defend and protect the honor of their families and, by analogy, that of the patria. In return they receive the same rewards, the love and nurture of their kin. Why, then, the text asks, are soldiers and rebels fighting each other?

The answer the text provides is that "the tyrants of the people are extremely astute and have deceived us." The rupture between brothers and the dismemberment of the patria are blamed on Porfirio Díaz, who is characterized as "Cain, the illegitimate son of greed" and "the fatal enemy of justice." Díaz is "that bad Mexican who has mortgaged Mexico in the foreign market." He is a "tyrant" who "enslaves" and "degrades" the people, seeking only "his own aggrandizement." The Díaz regime has inverted the moral order of kinship and reciprocity and replaced it with an unjust disorder in which money mediates relationships, creates asymmetry and domination, and "corrupts" the people.

Like Doña Aurora's stories and Plácido Chávez's recollections, this manifesto deploys a symbolic idiom to articulate a critique of capitalism, construed as the mediation of social relations by money rather than by the reciprocity of kinship, which it inverts; an implicit contrast between gold and blood is established in these texts. More tellingly, money is again associated with immorality and with the profane realm of the devil. As Cain, "the illegitimate son of greed," Díaz is also "that damned son."

The transformations and dislocations engendered by capitalism were experienced by the serranos as the moral and sacred disorder of a world turned upside down. Money, not honor, had become the measure of value—of the worth of people as well as of things. The obligations of blood integral to the definition of personhood, the duties to kin, neighbors, and dependents, were no longer being fulfilled. Personal obligations to kin, friends, and clients are irrelevant to capitalist economic rationality. Money, not blood, mediates social relations. This has consequences for social identity. The person embedded in a web of social ties is replaced by the isolated individual living in a world of commodities. The serranos' rebellion against "progress" was a resistance to the imposition of new forms of subjection-subjectivity. The peasants of the sierra had a concept of identity antithetical to that advanced by capitalism, one that stressed the social dimensions of personhood and grounded the value of human beings in honor.

After 1886 the serranos began to be dispossessed of even their most "precious" capital, their honor. Doña Aurora told me that rich entrepreneurs, many of whom had immigrated to Namiquipa after 1886, seduced and impregnated the virgin daughters of the local peasants. Kinship was really in a disastrous state, she declared angrily. Others told me that prior to the revolution, landowners and estate administrators cuckolded hacienda peons and defiled their brides by exercising the droit du seigneur on the wedding night.[10] Located at the gateway between the social and the infra-social, the female body was construed by the serranos as a point of great vulnerability for the honor of both men and women, one that had to be constantly guarded or reputations would be destroyed and society would be plunged into a state of disorder. The rich had disordered human and social reproduction not only by hoarding their own bodily substance but also by illicitly appropriating that of others.

Recall that in one of Doña Aurora's Santa Clara stories, the baby that the cowboys were ordered to take to the hacendado's house was born from the excrement of an Indian estate worker. Doubly subjected, the Indian peon is the epitome of a tamed and feminized being whose body and activity are the object of others' control and appropriation. This story creates a set of metaphorical equivalencies that link disordered reproduction, the appropriation of workers' bodily substances, and capitalist accumulation.

That the rich reproduced themselves and their wealth by illicitly expropriating the bodily substances of the poor is made quite explicit in a speech given by one serrano revolutionary at the beginning of 1911. Speaking to the peons and cowboys at the one of the haciendas of Luis Terrazas, Chihuahua's biggest landowner and political boss, this revolutionary exclaimed: "We consider it unjust for one sole man to possess all the land. Your patron is the owner of much hoarded/stored[11] wealth, unjustly obtained from the toil and the sweat of so many poor workers" (cited in Duarte Morales 1968; my translation).

While the subjectivity of peasant women was reinscribed through sexual defilement and rape, that of men was reconstituted through agrarian dispossession and proletarianization. For the serranos, depeasantization was as dishonorable as rape. How was agrarian dispossession perceived as both dishonorable and dishonoring? What was the logic that construed the appropriation of surplus value as a loss of the value attached to the social self?

Blood, Gold, and the Rhetoric of Agrarian Grievance

The rhetoric of grievance and redressal deployed by members of the one-time peasant military colonies of the Guerrero and Galeana Districts, whose rights to land were being contravened, is organized by a symbolic contrast between blood and gold.[12] Like the narratives and texts discussed so far, these agrarian petitions (*ocursos*) are rich in bodily symbolism.

The ocursos of the serrano peasants were grounded in a history that, if not wholly "an invented tradition," was produced in the context of struggles that oriented the construction and representation of the past. This history idealizes the time of community origins and locates utopia in a heroic frontier past that is construed as an epic world: "a world of 'beginnings' and 'peak times' . . . a world of fathers and of founders of families, a world of 'firsts' and of 'bests' " (Bakhtin 1981:30; see Koreck 1986a for use of Bakhtin's concept of the epic to discuss the historical traditions of Cuchillo Parado, Chihuahua).

By grounding their aspirations in the world of "immemorial time," the serranos endowed them with authority and legitimacy. As Bakhtin has commented:

> The absolute past is a specifically evaluating (hierarchical) category. In the epic world view, "beginning," "first," "founder,"

"ancestor," "that which occurred earlier," and so forth are not merely temporal categories but valorized temporal categories, and valorized to an extreme degree. This is as true for relationships among people as for relations among all the other items and phenomena of the epic world. In the past, everything is good: all the really good things (i.e., the first things) occur only in the past. The epic absolute past is the single source and beginning of everything good for all later times as well. (1981:15)

Epic discourse, Bakhtin adds, is an authorized and authoritative discourse, for its signs articulate "the word of the fathers" (1981:342).

Authority and legitimacy were critical to these texts because their purpose was to secure the state's recognition of the peasants' rights to land by restating the terms of the traditional frontier compact: agrarian rights in return for fighting the Apache. The serranos claimed to have fulfilled their obligations. For example, the Namiquipans affirmed that their colonial land grant "was protected and validated until the present through [the fulfillment of] the same conditions which were [originally] consigned to them [i.e., their ancestors]; honor was defended, as were the legitimate rights with which they were graced." [13] Consequently, the state should honor its obligations to the serranos and revalidate their rights to land.

Although these texts, addressed to the functionaries of the Chihuahuan and national governments and signed by the communities' patriarchs and their sons, span the decades from the 1860s to the 1900s, the rhetoric is always the same, indicating that a frontier construction of agrarian rights, in which land was not just a means of production but also a sign of honor and of social personhood, continued to be reproduced and affirmed by the serranos in the face of a new official discourse in which land was a sign of capital, a commodity whose value was determined by the market. [14]

Peasant petitions for the redressal of agrarian grievances begin with a historical account of the state's establishment of frontier military colonies. All the agrarian complaints from Namiquipa recall the establishment of the town by Teodoro de Croix in 1778 and recapitulate the terms of the pueblo's founding charter: the settlers were obliged to fight the Apache, to work the land and make it bear the fruits of their toil, and to contribute their labor to community projects. The frontier compact between the state and the peasant-warriors is restated: land and privileges were to be exchanged for military obligations.

The texts from Galeana construct an analogous history:

> The town of Galeana, to which we belong as members/inhabitants,[15] is situated in the foothills of the Sierra Madre, in the most dangerous and deserted part of the territory that comprised the ancient Spanish dominions. . . . In order to settle this region, so as to benefit the civilized race, it became necessary for the Crown of Castille to create vital social interests, through a truly wise and politic measure . . . in order to attract a civilized population who should put an end to the vandalic warfare of the savages, so that the richness contained in the breast of its minerals could be brought forth, and so that from a wild soil the rich fruits of agriculture and cattle breeding could be produced.[16]

Although this text advances a frontier construction of "civilized" production as the transformation of wild nature, land here is represented not as a commodity but instead as a sign of honor and "civility."

These ocursos continue by providing a history of the Apache wars in which the role of the pueblos' "civilized" settlers in the conquest of the "barbaric Indians" is idealized and heroized. For example, the peasants of Namiquipa affirm that their pueblo was "the sole bulwark of civilization in these isolated regions"; in contrast to neighboring pueblos and haciendas, Namiquipa was never abandoned, and its original settlers and their descendants, not the hacendados or the new immigrants, were the ones who "sustain[ed] that destructive struggle" against the "savages."[17]

In these texts a subaltern, frontier ideology of agrarian rights is reaffirmed: possession of land is a sign of ethnic, class, and gender honor, acquired in the struggle of "civilization" against "barbarism," an index of men's abilities to domesticate a wild nature. Writing in 1894, the municipal council of Namiquipa affirms that "since the year 1778 and until very recently, the descendants [of the original colonists] and those who actually possess the aforementioned [común repartimiento] land have defended it . . . against the frequent and tenacious attacks of the barbaric Indians, irrigating with their own blood, as with that of their ancestors, the land that until now they have peacefully possessed."[18]

As the figure *irrigating the land with blood* indicates, there is a reciprocal metaphorization between warfare and agriculture. Possession of land on which blood has been shed is simultaneously a sign of men's capacities to destroy and to regenerate life. Possession of land is also a sign of community membership and family continuity. The blood on the land is a mediating symbol that links the living to each other and to the dead and conjoins place and identity. The land belongs to those who have been born in the pueblo, to those whose blood links them to the past generations who struggled to defend the patrimony of the community and of their families. Honor—and the land that is its emblem—is won through the sacrifice of blood, not the payment of gold. Writing in 1865, the Galeanans assert that their land "was to be bought not by gold but by torrents of blood." [19]

The signs of blood—of the struggle of the "civilized" against the "savage" and of the sacrifices that the compact of conquest entailed—were inscribed in the land itself: "There still exist, in the contours of this population, signs which indicate the places where our grandfathers, fathers, and brothers succumbed to the knife of the savage, fulfilling the obligations which had been imposed on them.[20]

For the serranos, the community had the right to sovereignty over the territory its "sons" had lost their lives defending. The sacrifice of blood was what had reclaimed the land from the wilderness and redeemed the "civilized" from the "savage." The land belonged to those who had fought for it, not simply because this was the condition of the compact between state and settlers, but also because by spilling their blood on the land, by inscribing their deaths in the contours of a territory, the peasant warriors and their descendants had transformed it, had inextricably linked it to their bodies and made it their own.

Not just the signs of blood but also those of the toil of generations were etched in the land and were the legitimate indexes of its ownership, as well as the true measure of its value. As the Namiquipans wrote in 1908: "We see with deep sorrow that those lands which we justly esteem to be ours, received from our fathers and fecundated with over a century's constant work, are passing into the hands of strangers through a simple petition and the payment of a few pesos." [21] How can gold buy what the sweat and blood of both the living and the dead have earned, claimed, and transformed?

Represented as the recipient of personal bodily substances, the land was both an object of social activity and its symbol. Embodied in the land—blood, as shed in fighting and as inherited from ancestors—and sweat, as shed in work—were signs of the self, of the continuity of family and community, and of the human activity that had domesticated a wild nature. Notice that the serranos drew an analogy between production and reproduction. With their bodily substances, men irrigated and fecundated both the land and women. As immutably as the conjugal tie conjoined men and women by commingling their blood, the shedding of bodily substances in production and warfare linked life and death, destruction and regeneration, place and being, land and person-hood, activity and its object. The inscription of the self and of the self's productive activity in the object of work was the privileged sign of pos-session, not the payment of gold or the procurement of a title.

In these petitions the serranos ask the state for "justice," that is, for the honoring of the frontier compact and the reestablishment of the symbolic ties to the land broken by agrarian dispossession and com-modification. Justice is located in an epic frontier past that is contrasted to the injustices, humiliations, and disorder of the present. The serranos invert the logic of official history; "progress" has not meant social ad-vance but retrocession. Indeed, the peasants of Janos overtly state that they were better off in the colonial period:

> Today in 1910, which marks the one hundredth anniversary of our national independence, in this pueblo we receive a coarser treatment than when there were viceroys on our soil; just the fact that the aforesaid title [to our lands] was issued in those times, by the Caballero de Crois [*sic*] who ceded the aforementioned ejidos to our ancestors, so that they would come [and populate the region], without mentioning [the payment of] rents, or the exaction of small or large taxes, indicates the truth of this with-out any doubt.[22]

Not only the peasants of Janos but also those of Namiquipa re-presented the founding charter of their communities, Teodoro de Croix's decree of 1778, as constitutive of a utopian society, of a benign, patri-archal social order. Writing in 1908, the Namiquipans located an ideal of social reproduction in the colonial past. Croix's decree of 1778, the word of the founding father, was presented as constitutive of a utopian society, of a benign, paternalistic, social order: "In the said decree, with paternal care, are fixed all the measures necessary to the formation and conservation of these pueblos."[23] They wanted to continue to hold the land according to the terms specified in their colonial charter, that is, as a corporate group represented by a locally controlled organization that regulated collective usufruct rights to common pasture and wood-lands and distributed individual derechos de posesión to household and family heads in equal shares.

"Justice," then, was the recovery of the epic past. But it must be remembered that this vision of history was constructed in relation to and inflected by the struggles of the moment. Moreover, although this popular memory delegitimated the official history of "progress," it reproduced much of an earlier version of history organized by the state, which heroized the struggle of "civilization" against "barbarism." Although the effects of power entailed by "progress" were exposed and criticized, those imposed by an earlier state project of "civilization" were rendered invisible.

Not surprisingly, the frontier logic invoked by the serranos to legitimate their claims was no longer effective; all the petitions for the redressal of agrarian grievances were rejected. One Chihuahuan government report goes so far as to say that the peasants' claim to such a huge extension of land is "monstrous."[24] Others affirm that corporate groups cannot own property.[25] By the last decades of the nineteenth century, the transformations and dislocations of "order" and "progress" had created an "ideological disjuncture" (Nugent 1987) between the frontier peasants on the one hand and the dominant classes and the state on the other.

Whereas for the state and the elite, land had become a commodity, for the serranos, it continued to be a sign of ethnic, class, and gender honor obtained through the work and warfare that had domesticated the wilderness, a right sanctified by the sacrifice of blood and sweat. The ideology and interests of the state and the elite were not consistent with a reaffirmation of the rights of a frontier peasantry that had become identified with disorder and retrocession. The relative autonomy of peasant corporate communities had to be undermined, and the social life of agrarian pueblos had to be regulated by the new technologies of power, which would proletarianize and transform the peasant into the docile subject of "progress."

Agrarian dispossession was one of the main grievances that spurred serrrano resistance. The frontier notion that land belonged to those who fought for it was particularly conducive to armed revolution. On the one hand, the state had broken the tacit reciprocity of the colonial pact, and the state's authority had lost its claim to legitimacy. Military obligations had been fulfilled, but once the frontier was pacified, the serranos were denied the fruits of their blood and the honors they had earned by fighting. On the other hand, armed resistance was a form of reaffirming the frontier logic of land rights. But it was not just as a material means of production that land was important to the peasants.

For the serranos, land was as necessary to the symbolic reproduction of the community, of the household and family, and of the self as it was to the material reproduction of human and social life. The bodily substances inscribed in the land were multivocal symbols of gender and ethnic honor and of community membership and continuity. Agrarian expropriation entailed a redefinition of subjectivities and a perceived alienation of honor, of the social value accorded to the self. It was construed as an illicit form of appropriation by the rich of the poor's bodily substances and of their very selves. This will become more evident if we examine the contrasting attitudes to working on one's own land for oneself, one's family, and one's community versus selling one's labor power and hence one's self to a master.

Productive Activity and Wage Labor

One day in Namiquipa we were admiring the chile harvest of a friend who was born around 1906. "I have always dedicated myself to my fields/tasks," he said with pride; "I have never had to work *de raya*." The expression *dedicarse a sus labores* (to dedicate oneself to one's fields/ tasks), is commonly used to characterize and to refer to productive activity on one's own lands. Here the noun *labores* means both fields and work on one's fields: the same term is used to designate the activity of work and its object. The verb *dedicar(se)* is reflexive: the self is both the subject and the object of the action. Moreover, the possessive pronoun is used to stress personal control over the land and over the activity of work.

By working on their lands, the peasants of serrrano towns like Namiquipa not only ensured the material reproduction of household and community but also realized themselves as honorable men. "Going to the labor" is an activity that is key to the production of masculine identity, since the socialization of the "natural" self is accomplished through the domestication of nature.

A man who is hardworking (*muy trabajador*) is an hombre de respeto who possesses verguenza, who fulfills the obligation to "maintain his family" (*mantener su familia*) entailed by a fully socialized masculinity. Such a man is a good jefe de familia, an honorable patriarch. By contrast, a man who is lazy (*flojo*) is a *sinverguenza*, a man without honor who neglects his duties to his family. Such men are commonly held to lead a life of vice (*vida viciosa*), drinking, stealing, and committing petty crimes. Unlike hardworking men, flojos are not considered to be "good members of the community" (*buenos vecinos*) nor good husbands and fathers.

Possession of land has always been key to this self-realization through productive activity. The self-mastery that is integral to masculine honor and identity is realized through work on one's own fields. Our friend who had always dedicated himself to his *labores*, and who claimed never to have worked *de raya*, went on to say, "*A mi nadie me manda*," that is, "Nobody bosses me about."

In contrast to salaried employees, who are thought to depend on others for their sustenance, men who work their own lands are perceived as maintaining themselves and their families. To call a man a *mantenido* (one who is maintained by others) is to defame him. Indeed, in the late nineteenth and early twentieth centuries, mantenido was used by peasants to insult policemen and other salaried municipal employees.[26] In contrast to the independent producer who is fully male, the mantenido is both like a child and like a woman because he relies on others for his sustenance.

Clearly, a man's status and identity as a jefe de familia, as an honorable patriarch, is contingent upon his role in production. Power and autonomy are viewed as aspects of personal identity that can only be realized if a man is his own master, that is, if he controls both his work and its object, the land. The self-mastery that control over one's productive activity and its the object implies is integral to men's embodiment of both the "natural" and the cultural dimensions of masculinity. The fields, which are willed to descendants, are the enduring symbol of a man's honoring of duties to kin and community and of his realization of the patriarchal ideal. In the construction of subjectivity, class situation and gender identity are reciprocally defined.

The possession of land was critical not only to the embodiment of serrano ideals of gender but also to the reproduction of ethnic identity. On the frontier, possession of land and the practice of agriculture were signs that differentiated the "civilized" from the "savage." Derechos de posesión were a sign of ethnic honor, an index of the reason that allowed nature to be domesticated and socialized and of the self-mastery that distinguished "civilized" men from "tame" Indians. Like the peon in Doña Aurora's story, subjected Indians were dependent beings who were the object of others' control. For the serranos, to be deprived of agrarian rights was tantamount to being transformed into "Indians."

In contrast to *dedicarse a sus labores*, which implies self-mastery and control over the process and object of work, *trabajar de raya*, a phrase that continues to be used to designate wage labor, connotes dependence and self-alienation. On haciendas that retained their work force through debt peonage, the *raya* was the record kept of the debts owed by workers to the enterprise's store. Other signs of the idiom of wage labor also connote dependence, powerlessness, and emasculation. For example, during the Porfiriato, the verb *enganchar* (to hook) was used to refer to the hiring of workers. The figure recalls the sexual act, which is a trope for domination and subjection: those who were "hooked" were rendered as powerless as women. What the idiom of wage labor implies is that the worker's subordination to the master is predicated precisely on his humiliation as a man.

As the frontier was transformed into the border, capitalist development opened up new jobs in mining, in railroad construction, and on haciendas. Labor in the northern provinces was scarce because the frontier had always been less densely settled and because U.S. enterprises on the other side of the border attracted many Mexican workers (Katz 1981:10). In order to obtain workers, Chihuahuan capitalists had to offer better salaries and conditions; workers in Chihuahua were better paid and treated than those elsewhere in Mexico (Katz 1981:10; Wasserman 1984:118–20). Yet noncapitalist forms of labor retention, such as debt peonage, continued to be deployed. The symbolism of personal servitude coexisted uneasily with a capitalist rationality according to which the worker's labor was freely exchanged for wages.

Once hacienda workers no longer played a role in frontier defense, they began to be treated with less respect. Certainly hacendados' and cattle bosses' exercise of the droit du seigneur on haciendas dishonored their workers (Duarte Morales 1968). Even though the material conditions of work may have remained relatively good, workers' rights to honor and self-esteem seem to have been increasingly abrogated.[27] This would account for the antagonism between hacienda workers and their masters in Chihuahua on the eve of the 1910 Revolution (Katz 1981:12–13).

Different forms of productive activity involve the worker in distinct types of social relations and imply diverse forms of subjection-subjectivity (cf. Comaroff and Comaroff 1987). Despite the high pay and better conditions enjoyed by Chihuahuan workers—as opposed to those elsewhere in Mexico—for dispossessed peasants from the Guerrero District, proletarianization was a humiliating and dishonoring alternative. Wage labor represented the alienation of the self and the expropriation of personal bodily substances. The symbolism of personal servitude made evident the extent to which trabajo de raya abrogated the self-mastery critical to the production of masculine honor. The serranos were not willing to engage in symbolic practices that undermined their masculinity and threatened their personal autonomy. For example, one of the sons of Cruz Chávez, the famous rebel leader of Tomochi, refused to allow himself to be humiliated and symbolically emasculated by an administrator of one of Luis Terrazas's haciendas. Since Chávez would not kiss the hand of this administrator, he was told to find work elsewhere.[28] Not surprisingly, Chávez was later to join the revolutionaries of the municipality of Namiquipa.

The conflict between the values of masculine honor and the servility of wage labor was quite clearly illustrated by a dispute between Gregorio Calzadíaz and one of his hired hands, Abraham Ontiveros, which occurred in 1907.[29] Calzadíaz was the well-to-do tenant of one of the Müller's ranches in the municipality of Namiquipa. While working in the fields, he ordered Ontiveros to perform first one task and then another. According to one witness, Ontiveros told Calzadíaz "that he was not a boy to be going from here to there." Calzadíaz replied "that he paid him his money so that he would do what he ordered him to." Ontiveros answered that, "after all, he [Calzadíaz] was not a man" and tried to slap Calzadíaz on the face, but the latter hit him over the head with a goad stick first.

This dispute followed the lineaments of an affair of honor: a challenge to masculinity is issued and evokes a corresponding riposte. Calzadíaz's disrespectful mode of giving orders offended Ontiveros's sense of masculine honor because it made visible the asymmetry in power between master and worker. Moreover, Calzadíaz's remark implied that by buying Ontiveros's labor power, he had also purchased his self, and that Ontiveros owed him not just his work but also his personal subordination. Ontiveros rejected this claim on his self, affirming his honor by denying that Calzadíaz had bought the right to dominate and humiliate him: he insisted that he was not a boy but a man. He topped this by impugning Calzadíaz's masculinity and by slapping his face, the privileged index of a challenge to honor. Like Chávez, Ontiveros refused to accept the symbolic emasculation and dishonor that the alienation of one's labor power entailed.

Clearly, the frontier ideology of gender honor conflicted with the servile image of the docile worker. To be in the power of another compromised a man's personal autonomy and self-mastery. Wage labor implied a form of subjectivity-subjection that did not permit serrano men to embody their ideals of masculine identity. The dependency wage labor entailed made a man like a child, like a woman, and like a "tame" Indian. The emasculation of the worker was analogous to the tameness of the subjected Indian, a tameness that implied both docility and symbolic castration. Thus, despite relatively good wages and working conditions, the serrano peasants resisted proletarianization.

Resistance was not confined to personal disputes of honor between employer and employee but also included more organized, collective forms of protest. In 1909, for example, the future Villista captain Reydecel Aguirre organized a strike among fifteen fellow Namiquipans who had been hired as temporary workers by Agustín Domínguez, husband of María Müller and administrator of the Hacienda de Santa Clara. Domínguez complained to the jefe municipal of Namiquipa that, "after failing to respect his superiors and to fulfill his tasks, [Aguirre] organized a strike with the others [from Namiquipa] in order to completely abandon work, [an objective] that he had no difficulty achieving." [30] It is no coincidence that another of Namiquipa's revolutionary leaders, the Villista general Candelario Cervantes, had also worked at Santa Clara, probably as a sharecropper. For the Namiquipans, to work for the hacendados who were trying to expropriate their lands was a double humiliation, one more easily resisted than tolerated.

As Strauss observes, "Identities imply not merely personal histories but also social histories" (cited in Abrams 1982:230). For the peasants of Chihuahua's one-time military colonies, productive activity was not a commodity to be bought and sold but instead a sign of gender, class, and ethnic honor. The honorable man could not be the docile laborer. A whole history mitigated against the servile alienation of the self that wage-labor entailed. Subaltern forms of social identity, which were the historical product of the frontier struggle between "civilization" and "barbarism," conflicted with the new forms of subjection-subjectivity fostered by the processes of state formation and capitalist development. Honor could only be maintained through work on one's own fields. Land was a means of both material and symbolic reproduction; a sign of ethnic, class, and gender honor; an index of community and family continuity.

The alienation of corporate lands disrupted the peasant economy. Moreover, it threatened the reproduction of the peasant community, of the patria chica. Once tenaciously defended against Apache raids, the pueblo was now to be defended against the attacks of the agents of "order" and "progress." In addition, depeasantization and the loss of lands had consequences for the production and reproduction of locally valued forms of social identity. Resistance to proletarianization was not just a question of economic insecurity, as is commonly argued, but also a question of power and subjectivity. Class situation, status position, and social identity were all implicated in the peasants' attempts to maintain their frontier way of life and to retain control over their labor and the object of their productive activity: the land.

Caciquismo: The Idiom of Honor and the Delegitimation of Authority

Like all men of spirit, [the frontier soldiers] are extremely punctilious [about their honor]. This tends to degenerate into a defect for society: captains and officers are obliged to address their soldiers as companions in all conversations, and [soldiers] respond with defiance to any insulting threat from their superiors. . . . It can be inferred that these soldiers . . . require a different form of leadership from that which is usual in the army. When they are led with sweetness and respect, their docility and religious obedience are such that they do not complain or argue, even when led to the ultimate sacrifice. All in all, the presidial soldiers know through their reason that they should obey, but they want to be led with [the same] reason; in this I am their ally. I expect more from a man who knows how to conserve the privileges of being one, than from one who has been outraged and insulted a thousand times, and who is forever debased and degraded.[31]

"*Por las buenas, bueno, y por las malas, peor*," or "Through fair means good, and through foul, worse," is an adage used in Namiquipa that condenses the norms and values of the serrano code of honor and encapsulates the serrano conception of authority and obedience. What is articulated here is a logic of reciprocity that prescribes respeto and consideración for those who recognize one's rights as well as one's honor, and retaliation in worse coin for those who do not. Namiquipans quote this maxim to exemplify the norms and values that should orient all social relations, including those between political authorities and their subordinates. Deference and obedience are owed to legitimate authorities who rule *por las buenas*, that is, who respect the rights and the honor of their subordinates and exercise power with the pueblo's active consent. Caciques, "political bosses" who rule *por las malas,* that is, who violate the rights and the honor of the pueblo, and whose power is based on force and corruption are not owed obedience. Instead, the logic of honor prescribes that they be defied and resisted.

This vision of authority has a long history. Its genesis lies in the social relations, in the code of honor, and in the forms of social identity that were produced and reproduced during the centuries of frontier warfare. The militarization of members of subaltern groups and classes was simultaneously a form of subjection and a form of empowerment. Armed peasants with a highly developed consciousness of personal and social honor could not be ruled through coercion. Rather, domination had to rest on an honorable exercise of authority oriented by the logic of reciprocal respect, which entailed that superordinates recognize the rights and the honor of subordinates. As Gálvez, the colonial viceroy, pointed out, por las buenas, frontiersmen were docile and obedient, but por las malas, they were defiant and recalcitrant.

The conception of legal-rational authority advanced by a liberal discourse that grounded the exercise of power in the consent of citizens and in the representation of the popular will, and institutionalized an electoral principle of access to political office, was easily integrated with the traditional and charismatic vision of authority held by frontier peasant-warriors. The principle of effective suffrage resonated with frontier egalitarianism and was viewed by the serranos as a measure that enhanced local sovereignty and ensured that authority would be honorably exercised. Electoral rights provided *garantías individuales,* that is, individual guarantees, which ensured that subordinates' rights to honor would be respected by authorities.

The serranos' ideal of the political leader was the patriarch who integrated both the "natural" and the cultural dimensions of masculinity, that is, who had huevos but who also had verguenza, who exercised power in a way that demonstrated respeto and consideración for his subordinates. Moreover, after the 1860s, the ideal local leader became a son of the pueblo, a member of the local corporate group, elected to office by his equals. The elected leader represented the pueblo's will and ruled only with its consent, sacrificing his personal interests for those of the whole.

After 1886 the electoral rights of subordinate groups and classes were increasingly abrogated. The exercise of power assumed a sultanistic form in which the tendency to personal arbitrariness inherent in traditional authority became foregrounded. Local authorities became agents of the state and of the dominant classes. Caciques who exercised power through ties of clientage to higher-level officials and represented the interests of members of the dominant classes, as well as of a rural petty bourgeoisie, used the apparatus of political and legal administration to dispossess peasants of their lands, to extract a larger share of their economic surpluses, and to enrich themselves at their expense. Moreover, as the serranos became increasingly identified as the new barbarians, they became the object of forms of discipline and punishment deployed by local caciques to transform these paragons of defiant masculinity into docile, emasculated subjects.

After the end of the Apache wars, official discourse began to reconstrue these one-time agents of "civilization" as paragons of disorder and backwardness. For example, to the cacique of Namiquipa, Victoriano Torres, the peasants were members of a "lower class" that was a "social leprosy," a disease in the social body that had to be cured.[32] He considered the Namiquipans to be "drunks" who lacked honor and reason, rebels who had participated in the "insurrection" of 1893. Their resistance to the "wise and moral" measures of authority was an index of their "ingratitude and imbecility," as well as of their lawlessness, rebelliousness, and lack of reason:

> The ideal of the insensate people . . . and of the majority of the pueblo, as far as authority is concerned, is a personality in which the following qualities are conjoined: (1) that he dispense an absolute impunity to all forms of unruliness and misconduct; (2) that he allow the empire of the law to end; (3) that he tolerate the nonpayment of taxes of any type; (4) that he allow them to insult everyone in the world; (5) that he permit the most complete anarchy.

For Torres, this social disease had to be cured by force. The fomenters of anarchy could only be "reduced to order" by the strong hand of an authority who would discipline por las malas those who lacked the reason and the subordination to be ruled por las buenas. Writing about the Namiquipans, Torres commented to his superior, "Civil law is too soft for their good government, and the necessity to govern them militarily almost imposes itself." Such a military government would allow "men of order" to deploy extra-legal punishments that would tame the rebellious and intractable nature of the new barbarians.

Torres was impeded from fully implementing his vision of "order" by the resistance of the Namiquipans and by his inability to deploy other agents of force apart from the local policemen. By contrast, the caciques of Bachíniva had at their disposal the forces of the state police and thus were better able to impose on the serranos forms of punishment designed to reduce the "bandits" to order.

Perhaps some of the worst abuses of sultanism were committed in the municipality of Bachíniva, which comprised the territory just downriver from Namiquipa. Like the Namiquipans, the Bachinivans had once fought the Apache. Although they barely participated in the armed uprisings of the nineteenth century, some Bachinivans did join the Magonistas in 1905, and many of them were to join the revolutionaries in 1910 (Olea Arias 1961).

By the turn of the nineteenth century, a cacique named Luis J. Comadurán had consolidated his rule in Bachíniva and had placed his relatives and compadres in the key posts of municipal administration. Moreover, having acquired the titles to some of the peasants' lands, he proceeded to sell them for his own profit. As in many other serrano towns, those who opposed the cacique were forced to pay higher taxes, were unjustly accused of crimes they had not committed, and were subjected to punishments of the "law" or forcibly conscripted into the federal army.[33]

After 1905 things became even worse for the Bachinivans. Because local peasant leaders, including Heliodoro Olea Arias, the pueblo's elected official, had been involved with the Magonista's revolutionary project, the Bachinivans became even more identified with "banditry" and "disorder" in the discourses of the state and the dominant classes.[34] A new cacique, Pablo Barray, was imposed by the Creel regime after Olea Arias was forcibly removed from office.

Barray was much more of a sultan than even Luis J. Comadurán. Unlike Comadurán, Barray commanded not only the services of local policemen but also those of Captain Librado Galaviz, a member of the Fuerza de Gendarmes del Estado, or state police force, charged with maintaining order and apprehending "bandits." An outsider to the community and a specialist in the tactics of terror and torture, Galaviz did not hesitate but instead seemed to positively enjoy making the Bachinivans the object of practices designed to emasculate and humiliate, to replace the bodily rhetoric of honor with that of degradation and sub-jection.[35]

Since gender is the privileged site of masculine power and feminine virtue in Latin America, torture has taken (and continues to take) this dimension of social identity as its principal object. Torture is a type of negative rite of passage. Symbolic and material practices are deployed to destroy and to reconstruct the social identities of victims. The Latin American tactics of torture are designed to emasculate men and to de-file the sexual purity and chastity of women. Torture reconstitutes its victims as docile subjects by dishonoring them, by destroying their self-esteem and their pre-existing identities, while simultaneously affirming the masculine preponderance and hence the power of the torturer and those he represents.

Although Galaviz lacked the electronic technology of modern tor-turers, there is not much difference between what he did and what the contemporary agents of order and progress are doing. Like their mod-ern counterparts, Galaviz and Barray realized that terror is effective only when it is arbitrary, when anyone, at any time, for no apparent rea-son—other than the whim of those who wield power—can become the next victim. It is precisely this arbitrariness that indexes the sui generis character of the caciques' power, a power that recognizes no meaning-ful foundation other than the symbolism of its own prepotency. As one Namiquipan recalled, "The cacique was the law."

"To pursue bandits" and to "reduce them to order" was how Gala-viz defined his task. Men were the privileged objects of his efforts to "reduce" the Bachinivans to "order." With the compliance and support of the municipal functionaries, Galaviz would arrest men for no rea-son, search their houses for traces of wrongdoing, and consign them to the local prison, where they were kept incommunicado and rarely given food or water.

After isolating his victims in a space he totally controlled, a space de-fined as the locus of punishment, Galaviz would begin to systematically humiliate and dishonor them. Prisoners were slapped and whipped, ad-dressed as bandits, and insulted with words so obscene that most of the victims refused to reproduce them in writing, preferring to relate them verbally to the jefe politico. One witness characterized these insults as "the most offensive ones that could be directed to an honorable man."

In addition, Galaviz would threaten his prisoners with death so as to coerce them into confessing to false charges. The forcible extraction of "confessions" was intended not only to cloak Galaviz's practices with an appearance of legality but also to function as a sign of the victims' successful taming—of their willingness to agree to anything that those in power affirmed—and hence of their "reduction to order." In all but one case the men refused to confess to these false charges.

After a period in jail, the men would be taken out and forced to labor in "public works" that is, to work for the cacique and his clients for no payment. As we have seen, to work for another man was a sign of personal subjection—of the alienation of the self, of the loss of self-mastery, of emasculation. Then they were sent back to jail. Eventually, the victims were allowed to purchase their liberty through the payment of heavy fines. Those who lacked the resources to redeem their liberty were forced into "service" as debt peons of the cacique, Barray, who magnanimously offered to pay the fines he himself had unjustly imposed.

Men were not the only objects of these technologies of order and power. The virtue of women was sometimes defiled by the caciques (Calzadíaz Barrera 1969). For example, Galaviz offered the mother of a man who had been consigned to service in the federal army the freedom of her son in exchange for the virtue of her daughter; the mother refused to let her daughter be dishonored. Another of Galaviz's forced conscripts complained that because he had been impressed into the police force, he had to leave his wife and daughters alone, "exposed to being outraged by some evildoers." Thus, women became a vehicle both for the dishonor of serrano men and for the affirmation of the caciques' virility and power.

On the whole, the technologies of order deployed by caciques utilized the symbolism of degradation and dishonor to subject serrano men by "reducing" their masculinity, the "natural" basis of power. At the same time, they asserted the prepotency of the cacique and his cohorts. Through the humiliation of men and women, the caciques affirmed their superior machismo, that is, their "natural" power.

Octavio Paz has noted: "One word sums up the aggressiveness, insensitivity, invulnerability and other attributes of the macho: power. It is force without the discipline of any notion of order: arbitrary power, the will without reins and without a set course" (1985:81). The caciques' was a power without legitimacy, grounded solely in the personification of force and in the symbolism of dishonor and humiliation. As Paz adds: "The essential attribute of the macho—power—almost always reveals itself as a capacity for wounding, humiliating, annihilating. . . . He is not the founder of a people, he is not a patriarch who exercises patria potestas . . . He is power isolated in its own potency, without relationship or compromise with the outside world" (1985:82).

Not only adult men but also young boys were the victims of technologies of order that deployed the symbolism of degradation. The state-sponsored school became the locus of forms of discipline designed to tame serrano boys by "emasculating" them and by forcing them to accept dishonor and humiliation. As the Namiquipan revolutionary Teodosio Duarte Morales recalls:

> In those days they said that literacy was only "learned with blood"; the teachers would abuse their authority, beating the boys with ferules, rods, and clubs and [subjecting them to] other physical punishments. They humiliated them and they killed their morale. . . . I remember that one day, Carmen [Delgado] hit another boy and that the schoolteacher, who was like an inquisitor, then made him kneel in the middle of the street, so as to exhibit him before the whole pueblo, with his pants rolled down to his knees; he put a stone in each of his hands, which weighed about two kilos, and made him keep his arms extended; each time he bent them, he would order another boy to hit him on the elbows with a ruler, so that he was forced to hold them out. (Duarte Morales n.d.:101-2; my translation)

Duarte goes on to detail other forms of pedagogic discipline that make it evident that the schoolteacher was as much of an "inquisitor"— an agent of the state's technologies of power—as the cacique and that he tried to "reduce" serrano boys in much the same way that the municipal boss tried to tame serrano men: through humiliation, emasculation, and dishonor. These practices subverted the values and meanings inculcated by the everyday forms of pedagogy through which serrano boys learned to be men; for this reason, many parents tried to keep their children out of school. Duarte suggests that resistance to official pedagogic disciplines was important to the formation of a whole generation of future revolutionaries. Significantly, he asserts that defiance of "the inquisitor" made the future revolutionary Carmen Delgado "a warrior" even as a boy (Duarte Morales n.d.:101).

For the serranos, the cacique, the schoolteacher, and other state-supported "inquisitors" were the epitome of a "natural," unsocialized masculinity, of a power that transgressed the moral norms of honor and thus had no legitimacy and had to be resisted. And resist they did, first through legal means and later, when these proved ineffective, through armed struggle.

Not surprisingly, the idiom of honor framed serrano complaints against caciquismo. The cacique was represented as a threat to the honor of his subjects. His actions were construed as "vengeances" whose object was to humiliate the honorable men who would not lend their consent to his illegitimate rule. For example, the Namiquipans asserted that Torres's administration had as its "sole object the satisfaction of vengeances and our humiliation." They complained that Torres exacted labor for "public works" projects simply to "affront . . . the many honorable men who have fallen into his hands." They concluded by saying that owing to the procedures of these "social executioners," "each day we feel tied to the chains of a humiliating and shameful servility that we can no longer bear." [36] Similarly, the Bachinivans affirmed that they were the "victims" of the caciques' "bad actions" because of "the rancor that they profess towards us since we have never consented and will never consent to their perverse machinations." [37] Moreover, all of Galaviz's and Barray's victims complained that their honor had been "insulted" and "outraged" and asked that these "abuses of authority" be punished by the law.[38]

What the serranos found most degrading was the implicit analogy that official discourse had established between themselves and those other "barbarians," the Apache. They complained that although they were hard-working, honorable men who respected the law and the legitimately constituted authorities, they had been characterized as agents of disorder. As one of Galaviz's victims commented: "These outrages are only executed by inquisitors and are only deserved by bandits, and we who value ourselves as honorable men, who are submissive to the law, consider ourselves greatly offended." [39]

The caciques were portrayed as improperly socialized men who had violated the norms and values that legitimated authority and were therefore unfit to rule. Insulting and humiliating the people, ruling por las malas, the caciques had demonstrated their lack of verguenza, respeto, and consideración, the moral qualities possessed by men of honor. Thus, the Namiquipans characterized Torres as a "perfidious, impudent, disrespectful," and "unpopular man, lacking all sentiment of equity and love of justice as well as of the pueblo." [40]

By failing to fulfill his social obligations and by putting his own interests before those of the group, the cacique articulated a profane re-lationship between the individual and the social whole. As Pitt-Rivers observes, honor sanctifies power and legitimates authority by endow-ing it with virtue (1965:72–73). In the serrano amalgam of traditional and legal-rational ideals of authority, power was sacralized by the sym-bolic equivalencies that subsisted between the leader's dedication to the public good, the father's devotion to the well-being of his family, and God's guardianship over the destinies of men.[41] The patriarch was both a member of the social body and its symbol. By working for *el bienes-tar del pueblo*, for the well-being of the group, he sacrificed himself for the whole and reproduced a virtuous and sacred relationship between himself and the totality. By contrast, the cacique inverted this moral and sacred ideal and put his own interests before those of the group. Thus, the Namiquipans castigated Torres as "an enemy of the public good" whose administration left "no hope of bettering the condition of our natal pueblo."[42]

Like the ricos, the caciques put gold before blood. Instead of work-ing for the members of their "family," as a patriarch should, these "stepfathers" stole from the people in order to enrich themselves. This perception of the cacique was clearly articulated in a political poem written in 1905 by Heliodoro Olea Arias, a revolutionary leader from Bachíniva: "The cacique loses no sleep over the public good, / And only steals shamelessly" (Olea Arias 1961:9; my translation). This poem draws a contrast between the honorableness of hard-working peasants, who labored in the fields, and the dishonorableness of caciques, who enriched themselves by stealing from the people. By inverting the sacred and moral norms and values that regulate the exercise of authority and the reproduction of social life, the cacique undermined his own legiti-macy. Moreover, instead of producing order, his administration created the chaos of a world upside down.

For the serranos, the dishonorable exercise of authority plunged society into a state of sacred as well as moral disorder. The caciques' "tyranny," "abuses," and "arbitrariness" were tantamount to sacrilege. As the Bachinivans wrote to the Chihuahuan governor in 1898: "Even the most ignorant person understands that when an individual takes advantage of the sacred mission of authority with which he has been en-trusted, and uses it to execute personal wrongs, violating our institutions and the sacred temple of justice in the most atrocious manner . . . he ceases to be an authority and becomes a being unworthy of his office."[43]

Moreover, the caciques violated not only the sacred norms of authority but also those that ordered the reproduction of human and social life as a whole. For example, Torres's obsession with gold led him and his henchmen to defile the sanctity of the Namiquipans' church altar. His sexual union with his co-mother was yet another act of sacrilege, one that violated the divine sanctions of kinship and marriage. As one friend recalled: "Since Torres decided to marry his co-mother, he went to see the priest to ask for a special dispensation. The priest told him to go down to the river and to get into a canoe filled with sand. If the canoe floated, he would be granted his request." Defying the priest and the divine will he represented, Torres got married anyway; "he did whatever he wanted, whenever he wanted, with whomever he wanted, whether it was wrong or right.[44]

What this story stresses is that the cacique was the epitome of the unsocialized and egotistical individual who puts himself before all things—before the well-being of the community and before the will of God. This vision of the caciques—not only as dishonorable but also as evil and sacrilegious—was also articulated in Plácido Chávez Calderón's recollections:

> In the time of the regime of Porfirio Díaz, all of the cities, all of the towns, and all of the villages had their caciques and their Judases, and just as Judas Escariot, for thirty gold coins, sold his Lord so that he would be crucified, so in Tomochi the Judases . . . with lies, with intrigues, with calumnies, and with hatred and cowardice, consigned the pueblo to misery and poverty, to hardships, to suffering, and finally to the sacrifice and extermination of the majority of its inhabitants. (Chávez Calderón 1964:9; my translation)

Through metaphor, the caciques are equated to Judas, the Catholic personification of evil, and the pueblo to the sacrificed Christ. Like Judas, the cacique violates his obligations for the sake of wealth; his lust for money, his avarice, is at the root of his wickedness.

A parallel symbolic analogy is drawn in the 1905 poem of Olea Arias (1961:5–10). Through metaphor and metonymy, the people are equated with Christ, the sacrificial lamb. The local caciques and, more significantly, the Porfirian authorities as a whole, including Creel and Díaz himself, are equated with the sacrificers of Christ and by analogy are portrayed as the sacrificers of the people.

In short, in serrano discourse the sacred and moral disorder fomented by capitalism and that engendered by caciquismo are all of a piece: the political and the economic are interpenetrated and indistinguishable. Both caciques and capitalists put gold before blood and plunged society into a state of profane chaos.

This vision of social and sacred chaos made certain serranos, such as the Tomochis, receptive to the egalitarian, politicized, and anticlerical Catholicism of the Sonorense charismatic healer Teresa Urrea. Serrano adherence to Urrea's teachings seems to have been confined to the Tomochis.[45] However, even for the Tomochis, sacred chaos had its roots in the social disorder engendered by the policies of the Porfirian regime. Thus, the Tomochis' charismatic folk Catholicism was part of a broader, politicized, and this-worldly vision of social dislocation; theirs was not the millenarian ideology stereotypically assigned to peasants by some historians of Mexico.

Plácido Chávez Calderón, son of one of the Tomochi rebel leaders, affirms that the characterization of the Tomochis as "religious fanatics" was disseminated by the Porfirian government in order to depoliticize and trivialize the rebels' cause: "Fanaticism was unjustly attributed to Tomochi and viewed as one of the principal motives of the rebellion" (1964:12; my translation; see also 7, 13–16). From Chávez's point of view, for the Tomochis religious freedom was part of a broader struggle against caciquismo and the new forms of subjection-subjectivity advanced by the state; their so-called fanaticism was simply a demonstration that "they were free to believe [in what they wished] and to adore a ravine if they felt like it" (1964:12). In other words, for the serranos of Tomochi, the freedom to practice an anticlerical, charismatic, folk Catholicism was part and parcel of the defense of community sovereignty, of the affirmation of the right to self-mastery and social honor, and of resistance to caciquismo.

To summarize, caciquismo was a degenerate form of traditional domination in which the element of personal arbitrariness became foregrounded. The cacique put himself above the tradition that endowed his authority with legitimacy and had to increasingly rely upon coercion to maintain his power. Moreover, by manipulating the electoral process so as to "re-elect" himself, he violated the legal-rational norms upon which his legitimacy also rested. Lacking in virtue, the cacique, like the capitalist, did not merit the precedence society accorded him, nor did he deserve the obedience that was to be granted only to legitimate authorities.

For the serranos, caciquismo inverted the relationship that ideally subsisted between the leader and the community. The cacique sacrificed the well-being of the totality for the sake of his egotistical interests, thus, in a sense, becoming a whole unto himself. The asymmetrical flow of goods and services—from the people to the cacique—violated the logic of reciprocity and thus was tantamount to theft and exploitation. Since the group became a mere means to the cacique's personal ends, the people were reduced to a "shameful servility"; society became the servant of the individual.

Official discourse justified sultanism and the technologies of discipline it deployed as necessary to the "reduction" and taming of the serranos, one-time agents of "civilization" who had become redefined as the bearers of disorder. But the serrano conception of authority and obedience was predicated on a different logic, on a frontier code of honor that entailed a reciprocal respect between rulers and ruled, and on a populist rendering of the liberal vision of democracy, which made the leader the representative of the pueblo's will. Obedience was owed only to legitimate authorities, to *hombres de respeto*, who, as heads of the social group, were a fitting symbol of its honor. Leaders who violated the norms and values that underpinned the legitimate exercise of authority had to be resisted. This vision of relations between superordinates and subordinates had its roots in a frontier past and was inscribed in a social memory transmitted from one generation to another, as well as in the practices of everyday life. As Cenobio Rivera, a Namiquipan revolutionary, recalled, "the roots. . . of liberty were precisely the roots of the elders. . . . From their way of life . . . we learned the principle that regulates the conduct of citizens, that . . . a man has to be honest, just, and a fighter, rebellious before evil, before the despot, [and before] the tyrant" (in Calzadíaz Barrera 1979:304; my translation). A conception of manhood that was also a figure of resistance was inscribed in the word of the fathers.

For the serranos, caciquismo entailed a collective and personal emasculation and humiliation that could not be tolerated. "Order" and "progress" had plunged society into a moral and sacred chaos; its agents had to be resisted so that a just society could be restored and so that honor could be avenged.

Conclusions

[The rebellious] attitude [of the Tomochis] could signify nothing else; [it was] the very noble and dignified gesture of throwing
down the gauntlet to challenge the adversary, [a gesture of] fabu-
lous, ancient paladins. (Frías[46] 1983:13; my translation)

With respect to the military and to the human, the moral potency
of these unbreakable men [that is, the Villista serranos] is admi-
rable from all points of view. . . . The centaurs of the North—I
refer, as should be obvious, to the men born in the sierra—blazed
a trail of valor, a valor that was death, disintrestedness, and freedom. (Campobello[47] 1940:117; my translation)

From the serrano point of view, the pueblo was imagined as an
egalitarian community of kin and vecinos whose relations were regulated by the moral and sacred norms and values of a code of honor.
The self was viewed as embedded in a nexus of social relations. Honor
depended on the fulfillment of obligations and responsibilities to those
with whom one was linked by ties of blood and locality.

Both the ricos and the caciques put gold before blood, violating social
obligations and acting as isolated individuals who were interested only
in power and wealth. By putting their individual interests before those
of family and community, the agents of "progress" and "order" transgressed the code of honor and violated the norms and values that oriented social reproduction. In effect, both the ricos and the caciques
stood in a profane and immoral relationship to the social whole. Thus,
capitalism and state centralization did not represent "progress" and
"order" but instead social, moral, and sacred chaos.

The serranos' vision of the social transformations generated by the
processes of state formation and economic development inverted the
logic of history advanced by the Porfirian state; as the Bachinivans affirmed, "Until now, there has been no progress; to the contrary, we are
heading towards the most frightful ruin."[48] The discourse of "order"
and "progress" rang false when compared to the serranos' everyday experience of the dislocations that change had engendered. Hence, official
discourse became construed as a pack of lies; as the Bachinivans put it,
the cacique's words "turn white into black, and vice versa."[49]

The epic frontier past rather than the fallen present became the locus
of order. The disjuncture between official and popular memory became

almost complete: for the dominant classes and the state, the past had to be transcended; for the serranos, it had to be recovered.

Scott has pointed to the need for a phenomenology of exploitation, since "objective" definitions that ignore "subjective" dimensions often fail to take into account that the effects of power are not always experienced as exploitative and can even be viewed as benign (1976). This point is clearly illustrated by the history of the Chihuahuan peasants' contrasting attitudes toward different forms of authority. When authority was exercised in accordance with the norms and values of honor, which sanctified power, and with the legal-rational prescriptions of electoral democracy, it was apprehended as legitimate. By endowing authority with virtue, the ideology of honor disguised asymmetries of power and made obedience a matter of just deference to a benign patriarch rather than forced servility to a tyrannical "stepfather." When rule relied on the symbolism of humiliation rather than of honor, domination was experienced as exploitative. It was then that asymmetries of power became viewed as the cause of moral and sacred disorder as well as of the personal and social degradation of subjects.

On the Chihuahuan frontier, forms of subjection-subjectivity advanced by the state were actively reproduced by the peasant-warriors, since these implied a relatively privileged class position and status situation. Moreover, frontier warriors, unlike most peasants elsewhere in Mexico, acquired an honorable social identity that gave them access to personal and social esteem as well as a relatively high degree of self-mastery and community sovereignty. By contrast, the forms of subjection-subjectivity advanced by economic development and state centralization entailed real reversals in the class position, status situation, and social identity of serrano peasants. "Order" and "progress" denied the serranos social honor and transformed them into barbarians, into representatives of a class likened to a disease in the social body, to a leprosy that had to be cured by force. Not surprisingly, these new forms of subjection-subjectivity were resisted rather than reproduced.

In order to understand resistance, we cannot simply focus on institutional politics but must also pay attention to the politics of everyday life, to the way in which power is experienced and negotiated outside formal contexts, to the effects of power on identities and bodies. Seemingly cryptic or senseless statements, such as one Namiquipan's assertion that his uncle had joined the revolutionary forces because the local cacique destroyed his flower garden, become meaningful if we keep in mind that the locus of power is not simply in an institution but also in everyday practice and that the effects of power are articulated in a variety of domains, including the construction of social personhood.

Serrano resistance was not just a question of autonomy from the state, as Alan Knight (1986) contends. Nor was it merely an effort to retain control over the means of production so as to conserve a measure of economic security from the uncertainties of the market. Instead, it was an attempt to resist the symbolic and material reversals entailed by the imposition of new forms of subjection-subjectivity that threatened the reproduction of a whole way of life, as well as of locally valued forms of social identity rooted in a frontier past.

Significantly, serrano peasant complaints against agrarian expropriation and caciquismo were articulated in the idiom of honor. The social transformations engendered by capitalism and state formation were apprehended and experienced as a collective and personal dishonoring. To be dishonored was to be in a liminal state; the actor's everyday status could not be recovered until honor was avenged. This had implications for serrano resistance because the avenging of honor often takes the form of violence against the agents of dishonor.

The competition for honor is one instance of the everyday negotiation of power. To be dishonored as a man was to be rendered powerless, was to be feminized, was to lose the respect of community and family, that is, the social esteem that accrued to those who embodied the ideals of masculinity. Moreover, to be likened to a social disease, to a backwards and insensate mass, to bandits and to other agents of disorder was to be dishonored as an ethnic group whose members perceived themselves as gente de razon, as transformers of nature and bearers of order.

For the serranos, economic development and state centralization were a threat not merely to their access to resources but, more significantly, to the reproduction of honorable forms of social identity and all that this implies. In this sense nineteenth-century serrano rebellion and twentieth-century revolutionary mobilization can be seen as a collective and personal avenging of honor, as an attempt to reaffirm locally valued forms of social being. And indeed, from the serrano point of view, the revolution was a form of vengeance. Recalling the abuses committed by the Porfirian caciques, the serrano Eligio Cisneros offered the following reflections:

> For those of us who were witnesses to those brutal acts— those that paved the way—[the revolution] was not a surprise.

And I, like all my countrymen,[50] think that without such cruel-
ties, maybe the "Bolt of Lighting of Warfare" — Francisco Villa —
would never have appeared. . . . Maybe those who proceeded
in that [brutal] manner ignored, surely, that each act of cruelty
engenders an act of vengeance, by virtue of a natural law. (In
Calzadíaz Barrera 1969:175; my translation)

For the serranos, armed struggle was also the reenactment of the
founding act of their communities — land and honor would go to those
who defended the family and the pueblo against the agents of disorder.
Clearly, resistance was oriented by a social memory and by a popular ideology of history that inverted the relationship between past and
present advanced by the official logic of "progress." The epic past became the locus of order and justice, but this past, although not wholly
invented, was constructed and reconstructed from the vantage point of
contemporaneous struggles.

CHAPTER EIGHT

Caciques at Home

One of the acts of resistance that contributed to the removal from power of the cacique who was municipal president of Namiquipa in early 1983 was organized by the *madres de familia* of the *cabecera*. They kidnapped the cacique, made him take his pants off, and held him for several hours. "What did you do with him all that time?" I asked some of the women. Laughing, they recalled that after a while the cacique began to complain of hunger; they took pity on him and gave him some frijolitos and tortillas, for which he was very grateful. Their laughter put the cacique's claim to honor-precedence into question. How could he be a man who knew how to *fajarse los pantalones* if a bunch of mothers could force him to take them off altogether? How could he have *muchos huevos* if he had begged these madres to feed him? That he had no honor-virtue was tacitly understood: "Debts were all he left," my friends told me. "Did he retaliate against you?" I asked. "How could he?" they responded, laughing some more. Emasculated and infantilized, he preferred not to publicize the incident; if he had proceeded against them, even more people would have heard about his humiliation.

In 1989, as my friends and I were on our way home from a women's party we'd had, we ran into Concepción, a man who was a good provider but who drank and beat his wife. ¡Pobrecita! She had become so thin and unhappy. Although she told the best dirty jokes and did wonderful imitations, portraying people's foibles and quirks so wryly and vividly that we could always guess who she was parodying, we'd had to urge her to make us laugh at the party. "Next time," Concepción slurred, "I may not let her go." "Oh, then we'll have to come for her," the women answered, laughing. Concepción said nothing and lurched off into the night. "Poor Irasema," one friend said, "she has such a sad life. Look at how thin she is! Concepción is very hard-working, but when he gets hold of the bottle, he loses his reason. He hits her, he abuses her."

I have discussed wife beating with some of these same women on other occasions. From their point of view, a man who beats his wife is engaged in a cowardly abuse of force; a husband should use his strength to protect and not to offend his wife, they maintain. Some of them have commented that wife beaters are machos—that is, they possess the natural qualities of masculinity that are the basis for honor-precedence—but they are not hombres—that is, they lack honor-virtue and are not fully socialized men. Such men's actions reflect badly on the honor of their family of origin and imperil the stability of their family of procreation, setting a bad example for their children and creating conflicts with their sons, and sometimes with their daughters, who try to protect their mothers. Like caciques, wife beaters lack legitimate authority because they abuse the power their masculinity confers on them: their conduct is *fuera de orden*, and the reasons they give for proceeding against people are unreasonable.

This chapter on serrano women's forms of resistance in the past opens with stories about women's resistance in the present because they have shaped the interpretation that is presented herein. Most serrano women were illiterate: their voices, insofar as they are inscribed in the archival record, are accessible to us only through the mediation of men's. Women's voices in the present cannot be assumed to be the same as those in the past, but they do provide an alternative ground for reading the archival record and for crafting telling tales from historical documents.

Because local constructions of gender confined Namiquipan women to the domestic sphere, the richest source of information about women's lives in the past is the judicial archive, particularly women's testimonies in cases of wife beating and marital conflict. These cases evince a range of responses to contradictions of gender and power, from covert negotiation[1] to more open defiance.

Asked to appear before the Namiquipan justice of the peace in 1909 to respond to her husband's complaint that she had abandoned the conjugal home for her parents', Isabel Antillón Molina sent word that she was too ill to present herself and that she had left her husband because of the "despotism and tyranny" with which he treated her.[2] Like her brothers, Juan María and José Angel, who became Maderistas in 1910, Isabel was contesting caciquismo; indeed, she used the same idiom to denounce what she saw as an illegitimate form of governing. But in her case the cacique was not the president of the Republic or the jefe municipal, but the jefe of her family.

Listening to women in the present has taught me to pay attention to the articulation of constructions of authority in the domestic and public spheres and to conceive of resistance as taking place not only outside but also inside the home. The functionaries of the liberal state who criminalized domestic violence as part of a project to undermine the link between the masculine capacity for violence and social authority understood that forms of governing are exercised in domestic and public spheres. So, too, did Namiquipans, both in the past and in the present. Cases concerning domestic violence, especially marital conflict, indicate that while the community as a whole was struggling against caciquismo in the public sphere, at least some women were contending with men who acted like caciques at home—who asserted their honor-precedence in ways that contravened the norms and values of honor-virtue. Men drew on the frontier discourse of honor, refracted through aspects of liberalism that grounded legitimate authority in the exercise of reason, ratified by popular consent rather than in rulers' capacity for force, to challenge patrimonial sultanism in the public sphere. Women also deployed this discourse to contest the exercise of masculine precedence without virtue in the domestic sphere.

Por las Buenas, Buena, Por las Malas, Al Juzgado

On September 10, 1891, Ignacio Ornelas notified the local justice of the peace that his sister-in-law, Angela Flores, had told him that her husband, José Ornelas, had hit and "abused [*estropeado*]" her.[3] He asked the judge to investigate and to punish his brother, who was quickly jailed. By defining his brother's actions as "abuse" meriting legal sanction, Ignacio Ornelas was construing the use of violence to enforce domestic patriarchy as an immoral act that dishonored his family.

Angela Flores, the abused wife, described herself as twenty-seven years old, married, and "under the respects of her husband." According to her testimony, she had found her husband near the river talking with Soledad Frías, a woman who, in the judge's paraphrase of Angela's words, "disturbs the peace of her married state with her immorality." After Angela called Soledad "an impudent abuser [*abusona atrevida*]," her husband beat her and took her home. In her testimony Angela Flores used the idiom of honor to construe herself as a virtuous woman whose sexuality, legitimately exercised within marriage, was exclusively her husband's. She characterized Soledad Frías as a so-called public woman (*mujer publica*) whose sexuality was immoral because it belonged to all men in general and no man in particular and was exercised so as to affront her honor as a wife and her right to domestic tranquility.

A twenty-nine-year-old peasant, her husband, José Ornelas, provided a different interpretation of these events. He insisted that he had had no illicit relations with Soledad Frías. He admitted hitting Angela but defended himself by impugning her morality: she had insulted both him and Soledad by saying "with insolent words, things that should not be said because they are immoral." According to one witness, Angela had called José a "*pasante desgraciado* [wretched passant]"[4] and Soledad "an imposer who didn't tire of taking advantage of her in her house and even went as far as the river to impose on her." José's version of events affirmed his moral innocence and put the blame on his wife: he merely disciplined her for her immorality, defending his honor-precedence as head of the family.

Soledad Frías, who was also jailed by the judge and who identified herself as single and thirty-four years old, had at least three children born out of wedlock (*hijos naturales*).[5] In the preceding month she had broken off "illicit relations [*relaciones ilicitas*]" with Ornelas. She made no attempt to defend the morality of their liaison or to justify Ornelas's abuse of his wife.

Angela Flores asked that her husband and his lover "be punished only in accordance with the offense committed on her person so that they recognize the duty of domestic respects." Although inflicting lesions was a criminal offense, it could only be prosecuted at the wronged party's request, unless the crime occurred in public.[6] Since her husband was "the only protector she can count on to provide for her and her children's subsistence"—and her children were still quite young—she asked the judge for clemency in sentencing him.

Like other women who denounced their husbands' abuses to the judge, Angela Flores was in a contradictory position. On the one hand, she considered her husband's adultery and violence to be dishonorable and a violation of her rights to respect as a wife. Moreover, if her husband's relationship with Soledad Frías continued, he might abandon her and their children. On the other hand, she and her offspring were wholly dependent on José economically, and a jail term would prevent him from giving them sustenance; furthermore, her accusation could provoke further violence from him. Also, if the judge imprisoned him, she would be without his protection and therefore vulnerable to the sexual rapacity and violence of other men. Her ambivalence is evident in her request for the judge's clemency, in her affirmation of being under her husband's respects, and in her placing much of the blame on Soledad Frías's immorality.

On September 14 the judge sentenced José Ornelas to fifteen days in jail and prohibited him from going to Soledad Frías's house again. In addition, the judge sought and obtained the conciliation of Angela Flores and her husband. Although ostensibly this was a criminal case against Ornelas for "lesions," the judge sentenced Soledad Frías to the same jail term. If the judge protected the limited rights of the married woman, he penalized the woman whose exercise of sexuality was outside the bounds of legitimate marriage and a threat to the stability of domestic patriarchy.

Just over a year later, Pedro Ramos, a fifty-year-old married peasant and scp member, reported to the municipal president of Namiquipa, who contacted the judge, that José Ornelas and Soledad Frías had hit Angela Flores the previous day.[7] Although a neighbor of the Ornelas-Flores family, Ramos bore no kinship relationship to them or to Soledad. He told the judge that he had left his house on Saturday morning and seen Isidoro Bustillos, another neighbor, wrestling with José Ornelas, trying to prevent him from hitting his wife, who was exchanging insults with Soledad Frías (*"se estaban dirigiendo personalidades"*).[8] Ramos rushed over, "begging them to abstain from that scandal," angering Ornelas, who shouted that "nobody bossed him in what was his, that he had to proceed against his wife" and tried to attack him with a hoe. Despite Ornelas's assertion of the autonomy of his patriarchal domain and his right to beat his wife, Ramos and Bustillos continued trying to restrain him. Two female neighbors, one of them related to Ornelas, took his wife to Bustillos's house to get her out of her husband's way.

Angela Flores told the judge that she had been "living in good harmony" with her husband until Soledad Frías came to her neighborhood and provoked her with her presence. Her husband slapped her twice "because of that woman with whom he has illicit relations and perhaps he would have struck her again if there hadn't been people to impede him." "For her part," Flores told the judge, "she had nothing to ask against her husband but she begged the authorities, in regard to justice and her right to live well in her married state . . . to exile Soledad Frías from this place or to impose on her the penalty she might deserve for the scandal." Her testimony provided sufficient basis for holding both Ornelas and Frías in the local jail while a judicial investigation took place.

Removed from jail in order to testify, Soledad Frías, pregnant once again, made a futile bid for feminine respectability by describing herself as married. Originally from Ciudad Guerrero, she was now working as a domestic servant in Namiquipa. That Saturday she had asked her mistress for permission to go fetch one of her daughters, and when she passed by Angela Flores's house, the woman came out "insulting and stoning me"—a biblical punishment for women who had committed sexual transgressions—with no provocation, since she had not had "relations in private life" with Ornelas for a year and three months. Ornelas, who was also jailed, denied hitting his wife or having sexual relations with Frías. By his account, Soledad grabbed his wife in order to stop her from stoning her, and he and Pedro Ramos separated them.

In contrast to the judge in the prior case, this judge declared that no crime had been committed, only violations of the Edict of Good Government. He did sentence Ornelas to eight days of reclusion, but for having broken out of jail to "protect" Soledad Frías, not for beating his wife. As in the prior case, Frías was penalized for her shamelessness (*falta de verguenza*), receiving the same sentence as Ornelas for having gone near Flores's house. Both were admonished not to repeat the "abuses" that Angela Flores accused them of committing. According to the Criminal Code of 1871, admonishment is a preventive measure consisting of "the paternal warning that the judge directs to the accused, making him/her see the consequences of the crime he/she committed, urging him/her to reform, and threatening that a greater punnishment will be imposed on him/her if he/she repeats the offense."[9] The judge concluded that his decision was based on the power the law gave him to "impede scandals and proceedings that perturb public tranquility and morality." What he sanctioned verbally was Ornelas's beating of his wife *in public*, implying that a man did have a right to do this in private.

For Angela Flores, her husband's ill treatment of her—his adultery and physical violence—breached the norms of masculine gender honor. Numerous cases in the judicial archive indicate that her perspective was shared by other women negotiating domesticity and gender. Some of these cases reveal additional foci of conflict between men and women contesting the distribution of power in the home and how that was to be enforced.

On March 3, 1898, María Dolores Delgado de Rivera, a fifty-one-year-old *originaria* of Namiquipa, complained to the local justice of the peace that

> it has been about sixty days since her husband has abandoned her and left her living in a state of greatest poverty, even though he makes a fairly good living; that in addition to having abandoned her, he disposessed her of the household furniture and equipment, leaving her without even a single utensil; that in addition, every day he comes to her house with the sole objective of atrociously insulting her, threatening her, and the like, so that she will leave her house, but that she has never wanted to abandon the conjugal home; to the contrary, in the past she has exhorted her husband to change his way of life, but far from agreeing to do so, he has responded with imperious and absurd words, and not even satisfied with insulting and abusing her in the most vile manner, he has slandered her reputation, saying that she has stolen money from him, it being the case that he has never given her even one cent to keep for him, let alone the keys. About eleven years ago they became united in illicit relations and she took care of his children, who were still young; the hard work and difficulties she had to endure to help maintain the family are notorious and public knowledge, for example, washing, grinding, and other tasks from which she obtained a small salary, which she invested in the well-being of the children, as the avarice of her husband is also very well known; it being public and notorious too that since then her husband's interests began to prosper due to her great economies, and that the proof of this is that, seeing that she helped him greatly, Señor Rivera proposed to her and they got married here under the current civil laws [on April 8, 1894]; that they spent the first months of their marriage more or less all right but that since then he has changed his manners in the most brusque and gross way, a change born of the unfounded hatred and rancor that he has for her, so that he has even reached the point of ordering his children to abuse her and disobey her in everything; and that lastly, taking advantage of her departure to visit a daughter, he was able to realize his harmful intention of

leaving her on the street, since in order to do so he used a key he possessed, entering and bolting the doors from the inside, leaving her without a home, without clothing, and without food, and in the most horrible misery; that for these reasons she is demanding that he submit to legal arbitration for insults/injuries and abuse.

María Dolores Delgado stated her willingness to abide by the terms of any legal pact that they might celebrate, but her husband, Longino Rivera, refused to submit to arbitration. Subsequently, María Dolores decided to pursue the criminal and civil aspects of her case in the Juzgado de Letras of Guerrero.[10]

The cases I have presented demonstrate that the negotiation of gender, domesticity, and power was conditioned by the degree to which wives were dependent on their husbands for economic support and protection. Factors such as the availability of moral and material support from relatives and community members, the number of children and their ages, the woman's place in the life cycle, and her opportunities for earning money all influenced the degree to which a woman had to defer to her husband while simultaneously decrying his ill treatment of her. Isabel Antillón Molina was able to denounce her husband's "despotism and tyranny" because she had the moral and material support of her family of origin. As a young woman with small children who was entirely dependent on her husband economically, Angela Flores was in a much more tenuous position than María Dolores Delgado, a woman in her fifties with grown children and a history of paid work. Hence, while Flores was careful to stress her deference to her husband and to deflect much of the conflict onto "the other woman," Delgado was much more critical of her husband's abuses. Indeed, Delgado's access to "a small salary" and lesser degree of economic dependence on her husband relative to other women may well have been one of the foci of conflict in her marriage: it is significant that her husband accused her of theft.

These cases also illuminate the contradictions entailed in the negotiation of gender, power, and domesticity. If home was a sphere of patriarchal power, it was also the domain of women's influence, responsibilities, work, and contribution. Colonial ideology imbued non-Indian women's domestic role with a moral authority and a civilizing mission that gave them a degree of informal power within the home and without. The cases presented above (and discussed more fully in the context of the general analysis of domestic violence below) show that in practice the lines of power and influence within the home were ambiguous and contested, even if official ideology endowed men with the exclusive right to govern.

Namiquipan wife-beating cases usually involved both violence and verbal insults: indeed, women did not draw a sharp distinction between these two forms of *ultraje* (offense). Women who were hit by men were generally married to them. In most cases blows were administered with the hand and resulted in bruises.[11] Although a few women specified that their husbands had hit them before, most did not state this. Moreover, most wife beaters who were prosecuted were not repeat offenders; José Ornelas was an exception.

Tensions between masculine honor-precedence and honor-virtue are key to understanding these cases. Patriarchal status is one of the prerequisites of fully adult masculinity in Namiquipa; yet men often feel that the responsibilities of the patriarchal role and the demands of conformity to honor-virtue involve a domestication of natural masculinity, which entails a loss of autonomy and a tempering of macho attributes. A conversation I had with one friend about religion helped me to understand this. "Religion for me is a brake," he said, "a brake one needs to avoid hell in this life." He proceeded to tell me that when he first got married, he would stay out drinking with his friends until all hours and do whatever he pleased. But his marriage turned into hell, and after speaking with a priest, he decided to change and act like a good family man. Yet, he hastened to assure me, "I could still do all those things I used to do if I wanted to." My friend, like many other Namiquipan men, resents the domestication entailed by domesticity even as he recognizes its necessity; this resentment is manifest in the ambivalence he feels for his wife's civilizing role and the influence this gives her over his conduct.

Angela Flores was hit by her husband because she exercised this civilizing role, contesting the morality of his adultery. María Dolores Delgado also tried to convince her husband to abide by the norms of honor-virtue, exhorting him to change his way of life, reproaching him for his "avarice," and hence implicitly challenging the way he managed household economic resources. Both José Ornelas and Longino Rivera responded to these perceived challenges to their authority with abuse, insisting on their absolute precedence in the domestic domain. Similarly, men prosecuted for wife beating used physical and verbal violence to assert their honor-precedence in the face of their wives' reproaches and to insist on their rights to commit adultery, have exclusive access to their wives' sexuality and generativity, have complete control over household economic resources and their wives' property, command their wives' domestic services whenever and however they wanted, and use violence to discipline their children, particularly sons. The first two were the most common motives for domestic violence cited by both men and women, although since the judicial archive is incomplete, surviving cases may not be fully representative of all the cases tried.

Many accused husbands denied hitting their wives. Others, like José Ornelas, admitted hitting them but challenged the law's criminalization of wife beating by representing it as a prerogative of patriarchal governance, as a legitimate form of correction of their wives' faults, particularly if exercised in the privacy of the home. Yet others claimed that they hit their wives in order to defend their honor because they suspected their wives were betraying them with other men. This defense of wife beating was at times invoked as a strategy to get a reduced penalty; according to Mexican law, defending one's honor could be construed as an attenuating circumstance.[12] Moreover, such a claim could destroy a wife's reputation and hence imperil her ability to obtain a favorable legal verdict, since the judge's decisions were based not just on the state's laws but also on community values, local accounts of the events of a case, and the reputation of the parties involved.

This tension between the law and community judgments could explain why, in a minority of domestic violence cases, there was no legal resolution. For example, when Jesus María Burciaga accused Margarito Ramírez of beating his sister, Isidora Burciaga, Ramírez countered that he had found his wife "sleeping" with Librado Delgado.[13] Isidora responded that her husband's allegations were false and that the real motive was that he wanted to sell two of her cows and she refused to let him do so. She asked for a separation from her husband because he was "out of his senses" and might murder her. Yet despite the seriousness of her allegations, this case, unlike most domestic violence cases, was not resolved.

But if some wife beaters defended their actions as the legitimate exercise of masculine precedence, others expressed more ambivalent attitudes. There were those who blamed their violence on drunkenness, thought to be a state marked by a temporary loss of reason and hence self-control and intentionality, as well as a regression into natural masculinity. Invoking inebriation as an alibi could lead to a reduced sentence;[14] however, it also implicitly denied the rationality and morality of wife beating. Moreover, the pledges made by some abusers to their wives betray ambivalence about the morality of domestic violence and male adultery; for example, one husband promised his wife that "in the future he would treat her with the decorum that a wife deserves, offering never again to put a foot in the house of his concubine."[15] Significantly, in those cases I found in the local judicial archive in which the couple was conciliated by the judge, husband and wife stayed together and no further legal complaints about domestic violence were presented.

Simply by denouncing their husbands' violence and mistreatment to the judge, the municipal president, or a male or, more rarely, female relative, who then reported it, women were contesting their men's exercise of a precedence untempered by reason and virtue, their definition of the home as an autonomous domain in which they had absolute authority, and their use of violence and insults to enforce patriarchy in defiance of the precepts of traditional and legal authority. They were affirming their right to "good treatment" (*buenos tratamientos*) and respect, which included their husbands' faithfulness, courtesy, trust, and economic maintenance.

Importantly, the serrano women's definitions of the identities of husband and wife and of the extent of men's domestic authority and obligations conflicted with those of their husbands. Women like Angela Flores questioned the morality of their husbands' adultery. María Dolores Delgado and other women contested their husbands' management of the household economy; at times women challenged the way their own property, as well as joint property, was administered by their husbands. One woman, for example, included in the motives for her husband's abuse her refusal to give permission to his sale of some land unless he paid her the value of the property she had brought into the marriage; she was worried that her family would become wholly destitute as the result of his "dissipated conduct."[16] Women also questioned the absoluteness of their hubands' claims to their domestic labor and services. Teresa Tena, for example, complained to the judge that her husband had beaten her on one occasion because the water she had heated for him to wash with had some rubbish in it; on another occasion he hit her because she would not mend a shirt for him.[17] Lastly, women contested their husbands' right to beat them because of jealousy (*celos*) and protested the implicit challenge men's policing of their sexuality posed to their own capacity to abide by the norms and values of *pudor*.

Many women characterized their husbands' violence and verbal abuse as an *ultraje* (in English, an outrage, offense, or insult, and a term also used as a gloss for rape), implying that malos tratamientos affronted their honor and dishonored the abuser. The rhetoric of honor, as Pitt-Rivers argues (1965), sacralizes persons and the ideal sphere surrounding them: for women, the forcible breaching of this sphere was both dishonoring and dishonorable.

The account that María Dolores Delgado gave to the judge of her husband's malos tratamientos illustrates women's use of the idiom of honor. This idiom frames her case—a demand for arbitration "for insults/injuries and abuse"—and is deployed throughout her testimony, evinced in such phrases as "atrociously insulting her," or "abusing her in the most vile manner." Delgado's testimony also exemplifies the confluence between the discourses of struggle in the public and domestic spheres. She calls her husband's form of domestic governance "imperious": like the cacique, Longino Rivera makes claims to precedence that violate the norms of reason and honor-virtue and abuse his authority, governing por las malas. Moreover, he, too, is a hoarder of wealth, a man whose avarice leads him to value gold more than blood. Indeed, he is so mean with his own children that María Dolores must work outside the home to help maintain them. Despite the fact that his prosperity owes a great deal to her hard work, sacrifices, and astute management of the household economy, he violates the logic of reciprocity, and instead of honoring her efforts, he accuses her of theft, slandering her reputation. Finally, he dispossesses her of her home and household furniture and equipment, leaving her "in the most horrible poverty," violating the traditional and legal norms that specified that a husband had an obligation to maintain his wife.

A notion of "companionate love" (Giddens 1992:43) is implicit in the idiom of honor that María Dolores and other women use in their testimonies: love is linked to the mutual responsibility of husbands and wives in the running of the household, a product of gender complementarity founded on reciprocity. Jefes' failures to abide by the norms of reciprocity, whether in the public or domestic sphere, delegitimated their authority and damaged their reputation. Although Longino Rivera was from Matachic, three of his sons—Blas, Isabel, and Federico (all born in the 1870s) were founding members of the scp; Blas, Isabel, and their brother Longino Jr. all fought in the revolution. Unfortunately, the archival record does not provide any information on their reactions to caciquismo at home, so I cannot make a firmer connection between their revolutionary mobilization and their experience with domestic sultanism.

Isabel Antillon, Angela Flores, María Dolores Delgado, and other women used the idiom of honor and the legal system to denounce men's failure to embody both honor-precedence and honor-virtue. Yet in order to do so successfully, they had to establish their own honor; in effect, they had to affirm their general submission to domestic patriarchy in order to challenge some of its particular manifestations. Angela Flores demonstrated her embodiment of the dominant gender ideology by contrasting her actions with those of Soledad Frías, a "public woman" — one of the community's internal "others" — and by deferentially asserting that she was "under the respects of her husband." María Dolores was in a more ambiguous position because her relationship with Longino Rivera had begun as an "illicit" union. Yet the persona she constructed in her testimony exemplified wifely virtues, such as the maternal instinct, self-sacrifice, economy, and hard work, thereby fulfilling the feminine role of civilizer of men.

Departure from the conventions of gender honor significantly decreased women's chances of a favorable legal verdict. In one case in which the woman was in a consensual union rather than a legal marriage, the man who beat her was not penalized. In another case in which the woman assumed the masculine prerogative of self-defense and hit her husband back rather than penalizing him, the judge admonished her for her lack of respect toward her elderly and weak spouse.[18]

Reputation was also key to women's ability to obtain support from kin and neighbors. Not only did this support have an impact on legal verdicts, but it also tempered women's dependency on their husbands and enabled them to leave abusive marriages. Although spouses were conciliated in the majority of domestic violence and marital conflict cases, some women affirmed that they could no longer bear their husbands' ill treatment and asked for a divorce,[19] economic maintenance, and custody of the children. Although some of these women went to live with members of their family of origin, others remained as heads of their own families. I have not found a single case in which the woman was forcibly returned to the conjugal home, even when her husband demanded it.

Although constructions of gender motivated the struggles against caciques in the public and domestic spheres, men and women's involvement in these struggles did not simply follow lines of gender dualism. Men's violence pitted women against each other. As Angela Flores's actions illustrate, if a wife felt that the immediate cause of a beating was her challenging the morality of her husband's adultery, she would frequently lay at least equal, if not more, blame on "the other woman." Indeed, the few cases of violence between women in the judicial archives involve wives and concubines. But wife abuse also provided bases for solidarity among women. In some cases mothers and sisters of beaten wives supported them against their husbands. In other cases female neighbors or relatives of the abuser lent support to the victim.

Although many, if not all, of the men accused in domestic violence cases affirmed their right to "correct" their wives, not all men shared this view. Given that men's honor depended on that of their close female kin, it is not surprising that fathers and brothers of abused wives would formally accuse husbands. Although one could argue that abused women's male kin were defending their own status rather than questioning a husband's right to discipline his wife, the support of men not related to abused wives suggests that a different interpretation of men's motivations is called for. Men who were neighbors or kin of either party often risked the wrath of the abuser by intervening to stop the beating. Accusations of wife beating were brought before the judge by such men as Ignacio Ornelas, who were relatives of the abuser—fathers or brothers—or by male neighbors like Pedro Ramos. In addition, local male judges, who were community members—as opposed to legal professionals—and had a great deal of leeway in the interpretation of laws, generally censured wife abuse.

Most of the legal complaints of domestic violence were followed up, and the accused was arrested as soon as possible and kept in jail until a verdict was reached. A guilty verdict was reached in most of these criminal cases, and even when wives pardoned their husbands or asked judges for clemency, husbands were generally sentenced to between eight and thirty days in the local jail. In cases in which male adultery was an issue, judges frequently prohibited the husband from seeing his concubine again.

Some judges censured wife beating in very strong terms, regardless of the class position of the perpetrator. For example, one judge condemned "the scandal with which this individual is accustomed to outrage or insult his poor family in a fairly cowardly and vile manner."[20] The "individual" in question was a hacienda worker. In another case a wealthy merchant's defender argued that the woman had brought the violence upon herself and "that he only did it to maintain the legitimate right that he who commands has to repress in the home and in private the faults of his wife." To which the judge responded that the husband was not "authorized to offend his wife for any reason with legal right"[21] and sentenced the merchant to fifteen days in jail.

Overall, local judges promoted the stability of domestic patriarchy by serving as arbiters in marital conflict, using the clout their position afforded to conciliate the couple and encourage the good functioning of the family. The women who were most likely to obtain a favorable verdict were those who abided by the norms and values of honorable femininity. Like the state's laws, the judges' verdicts did not represent a critique of women's subordination to men, but instead support for a form of patriarchy based more on "civilized" reason than "barbaric" force.

Although Namiquipans contested certain aspects of the liberal and Porfirian state projects, they implemented others. Legislation criminalizing wife beating was applied in Namiquipa only because it resonated with some dimensions of local ideology and gender constructions. The feminine was a crucial signifier of the stakes in the struggle for territory on the frontier, of what had to be "protected." Men's treatment of women was one of the indexes of the capacity to reason, the key mark of civility and privileged ethnic status in Namiquipa. From the serranos' point of view, Apache men, who lacked reason and were the epitome of unruly natural masculine instincts and passions, mistreated their women, making them do all the work and correcting faults like adultery with "barbaric" punishments such as cutting off the nose of the woman. As the policies of the Porfirian regime increasingly jeopardized peasants' claims to land, Namiquipans' assertion of civility played a key role in their attempt to retain corporate agrarian rights. Inflected by the frontier idiom of honor as well as a popular recension of liberalism, the discourse of resistance against caciquismo also privileged reason and opposed it to force. Governing por las malas, both the cacique and the abusive husband contravened the community norms and values that legitimated traditional as well as legal-rational authority.

But the boundaries between reasonable leadership and abuse of force, between honor-virtue and honor-precedence, between private and public spheres, between protection and discipline, obedience and defiance, were contested. Constructing themselves as "beautiful souls" deserving masculine protection, abused Namiquipan wives paradoxically challenged the extent of their husbands' power while affirming their own submission and reproducing hegemonic constructions of femininity. By contrast, abusive husbands construed their wives' actions as disobedience meriting legitimate discipline. But surviving cases indicate that the law was applied more often than not, and that many men and women in the community censured domestic violence as an abuse of force and an offense to community and family honor and morality. Yet by construing domestic violence as a practice of deviant men, of machos rather than hombres, both men and women reproduced patriarchy—albeit a form of patriarchy based more on "civilized reason" than "barbaric force." The notion of governance por las buenas that serranos were struggling for conflated honorable masculinity and formal political authority in the public and domestic spheres and endowed femininity with a moral authority that sustained only limited forms of empowerment for women.

Women's role as "beautiful souls" inflected and contained their struggles against caciques inside and outside their homes. Just as they had not fought in the Apache wars, serrano women did not fight in the revolution. Nevertheless, they were perceived as contributing to the struggle, but their role was as an icon of the Virgin Mary. For serrano men, armed struggle was an opportunity to reactualize themselves as "just warriors," as macho destroyers but also as patriarchal life givers, self-sacrificing Christs who redeemed the existence of others by offering up their own lives.

Such a construction of men and women's roles is articulated in a diary written between 1910 and 1911 by the Namiquipan revolutionary Pedro Rascón y Tena:

> It is not only on the battlefields—where the deafening explosions of the canons resound and where the earth is fecundated with the sweat and the tears and the blood of our brothers who fight and who raise altars to the patria—it is not only there where heroism, that sacred virtue, is exercised; in each humble hut, in each home, there are beings who suffer and who irrigate [*riegan*] with their tears the bloody altar. The breasts of these beings don't harbor hatreds or bastard ambitions, and it is love that leads them to sacrifice. Women! Here are the martyrs of all the bloody epics of history.
>
> When he takes his leave, the warrior rends the soul of his mother, fills the heart of his wife or fiancée [*novia*] with bile, and marches to battle—sad and tearful, yes . . . but soon enough, [the warrior] dissipates [his sorrow] with triumph or death. [But]

those ones [those novias, wives, and mothers], each time they wish to console themselves with the idea that the beloved man for whom they cry marched to the post that duty assigned him feel—through and through—something terrible, something in-explicable, which rebels in their entrails and seems to kill them.

Sometimes that sentiment triumphs in them, and crazed [with it], they ask who, and with what right, has torn from their arms the beloved being. At other times, the most frequent, the senti-ment of duty triumphs and they contribute with their tears to the holocaust; but always, their hearts shed bitter tears.

When the widow contemplates the son who, stammering, asks for his father, she tells him with pride that he died for the patria, but these words do not leave her mouth without knotting them-selves in her throat and without moving her heart. It is glory or it is pain that produces these emotions. Blessed be the Marías who in the valor/value [*valor*] of life cry for their loves at the foot of the cross.

In this text women are heroized as Marías who put patriotic duty above maternal instinct and contribute their suffering to the cause. Women's contribution to the struggle is a source of social esteem. But the value of their contribution is mediated through men's actions. Their bravery consists in knowing how to let their men kill and die.

Men in this text are presented as both destroyers and reproducers of life. The battlefield is not just a space of death; like the agricultural field, it is also a space of fecundation and renewal, a site where life is reproduced at the same time that it is destroyed. In fighting, men are not just destroyers but also engenderers, warrior Christs who create life for others, who redeem the community by sacrificing themselves on the altar that is the battlefield.

Serrano insurrection contested certain effects of power. Indeed, what the rich bodily symbolism of discourses of serrano resistance demon-strates is that "the social skin" (Turner 1980) is a site of political contes-tation, that there is a somatics of rule and of resistance to rule.

Serrano discourses of resistance cannot be dismissed as "prepoliti-cal." These discourses did not merely reproduce but rather contested the inscription of the effects of hegemony in bodies and selves. However, while certain forms of subjectivity-subjection implemented by state cen-tralization and capitalist development became an object of serrano criticism and contestation, other effects of power continued to be construed as natural.

As a reaffirmation of patriarchal forms of gendered being, serrano insurrection reproduced forms of subjectivity that perpetuated the oppression of women by men. Forms of domination, as O'Malley avers,

> emasculated lower-class men, who recovered their manhood during the revolution by assaulting the socioeconomic structures that had oppressed them. They then took their places, at least in theory, as equals in the post-revolutionary society. As they conceived it, equal manhood included the prerogatives of the patriarch. That entailed the continued oppression of women as women, although women shared in the improved status of their classes. (1986:136–37)

Ironically, although the serranos were fighting against state control of subjectivities, the very forms of identity they construed as natural and valorized as honorable had been advanced by an earlier state project and inflected by official liberalism.

Eric Wolf has observed that "ideology not only represents class relations, and not only naturalizes social relationships, but it anchors itself in concepts and symbols of . . . the orectic [sic] pole, in blood and sex and other primordial constructs" (in Ghani 1987:361). In blood and sex, in gender and ethnicity, power finds alibis that are very difficult to expose.

Class, gender, and ethnicity were complexly concatenated in serrano subjectivities. Serrano discourses of resistance attest to the centrality of gender in the inscription of power and powerlessness. An analysis of such discourses confirms that gender is not only the social construction of distinctions between male and female but also a primary site for the production of more general effects of power and meaning. This implies that gender should be as important a category in the analysis of domination and resistance as ethnicity and class have been. What should be at issue is not conflating one form of oppression with another but instead uncovering the mutually supporting as well as contradictory relations among them.

Ya no hay Valientes

The Re-Presentation of the Past

Every oppressed group needs to imagine through the help of history and mythology a world where our oppression did not seem the pre-ordained order.

Moraga 1986:188

From 1983 to 1985, while Daniel Nugent and I were living in
Namiquipa, local political discourse centered around a collective perception that *ya no hay valientes*, that is, "now there are no more brave
men."

Central to this discourse was a conception of the local community, or
patria chica, as a motherland, as an eternal place and source of being.
Like the nation, the patria chica is *ideally* sovereign: her spatial boundaries are as impermeable as the bodily margins of the Virgin Mary and
of the flesh-and-blood women who are her icons. She is hermetic and
hence wholly the patrimony of the corporate local group and of the men
who are its guardians and representatives.

In contrast to the nation and the patria chica, which are feminine,
for Namiquipans the state is a masculine entity. Ideally, the state is the
padre of the nation, the patria chica, and the people. But from 1983 to
1985, as the political and economic crisis in Mexico became more acute,
the state was increasingly being construed as the padrastro.

The state-as-padre is the government as the good, wise, and beneficent father who protects and respects the sovereignty of the patria chica
and the honor of her "sons." The state-as-padrastro is the government as
the bad father who encroaches upon local sovereignty, penetrating and
redrawing the boundaries that should ideally subsist between state and
community. State penetration is seen as both the cause and the effect
of Namiquipan men's increasing difficulties in enacting the ideals of
masculine valor and consequently in maintaining the proper boundaries
between the community and the state.

Today state-organized forms of subjection-subjectivity continue to be perceived as emasculating and dishonoring. Although the Namiquipans recovered their corporate landholdings after the revolution, they do not see the armed struggle of 1910–20 as having brought about a victory for *them*. They point out that since the revolution, the state has managed to gain even more control over the forms of reproduction of local life and over the Namiquipans themselves.

Namiquipans see many of the benefits of "progress" as forms of state control. Characterizing the credit policies of rural banks as a means by which the state regulates agricultural production, one Namiquipan said, "During the Porfiriato we were the peons of the hacendados. Today we are the peons of the bank."

"The problem is that there are no more brave men." But what if there were? Namiquipan women often argue that if today's men were like the "brave" patriarchs of yesteryear, the community would be better able to negotiate the terms of its subjection to the state. Namiquipans would have more control over their lives, forms of activity, and being, and the patria chica would be a sovereign domain.

Namiquipan women have no critique of patriarchy as such (although they do criticize men). Paradoxically, in arguing that men should once again be *valientes*, they are reproducing gendered forms of personhood that have made them the subjects of masculine control and have confined them to the domestic sphere. Ironically, women are at times the ones who argue most forcibly for the emulation of the patriarchs of yesteryear. The state would be a padre if the men of today were like the valientes of old. They knew how to *hacerse valer* and *respetar*. They knew how to make the authorities exercise their mandate *por las buenas*.

Today the "corrupt" present continues to be contrasted with the "primordial society,"[1] that time when "brave" patriarchs protected the pueblo and when the state was a beneficent padre. The primordial society is located in the time of community origins, the frontier past. Although situated in historical time, however, this past is epic and remote, simultaneously remembered and beyond memory. The outlines of the primordial society are nebulous, eluding sharp delineation precisely because they are the contours of an idealized past, a past from which the effects of power and traces of pain have been effaced so as to conjure up a memory of a time in which oppression was not preordained.

Carlos Fuentes once commented that "no Mexican time has as yet been fulfilled" because the history of Mexico consists of a "series of 'subverted Edens' which . . . we would finally like to return to or forget"

(1978:10; my translation). Clearly, the Namiquipans' vision of the past is motivated by the periodizations of Catholic mythology, as well as by the Catholic notion of historical experience as a falling-away from an initial state of perfection. Moreover, the transferral of utopia to an epic time is also an effect produced by a "traditional" hermeneutic mode that makes the past a source of legitimacy and authority. But Namiquipan social memory is also a product of historical practice and of the frontier experience.

Significantly, descendants of the frontier Mexicans who were con-quered by the Anglos in 1848 periodize their history in ways very similar to the Namiquipans'. In his analysis of Americo Paredes's vision of the past, Renato Rosaldo writes:

> Consider initially the primordial terrain and its coherent social order. The latter establishes certain standards against which more contemporary social life can be judged. Then comes "The Fall," the disruption and alteration of "The Primordial Society." Through American conquest, the primordial homeland is torn asunder, becoming the border. No longer dominant, but domi-nated, the Mexican people enter into "The Conflict" with Anglo-Texans. . . . Throughout these three episodes, Mexican resistance to domination is guided by patriarchs embodying a distinctive version of manhood. (1987a:68)

With just a few modifications, this paragraph could depict the Namiquipans' memory of historical experience as well as it does that of the Norteños' from "the other side." "The Fall" for the Namiquipans is likewise the transformation of the frontier into the border, but the agent of this change is not the American but the Mexican state. "The Conflict" is the period of resistance and revolution, also a struggle for empowerment, but one conducted against the ruling classes and groups of Mexico rather than the United States. Finally, for the Namiquipans, the patriarchal order of "The Primordial Society" also "establishes the terms for constructing a figure of resistance," for developing "a concep-tion of manhood mythically endowed with the rhetorical capacity to combat" (Rosaldo 1987a:71)—not Anglo hegemony and anti-Mexican prejudice but new forms of subjectivity-subjection implemented by pro-cesses of Mexican state formation and capitalist development.

For Rosaldo, Paredes's inscription of memory is more a "myth" than a description of the "historical past" (1987a:71). However, I find that this distinction between myth and history is characterized by considerable slippage and hence is difficult to maintain.

My own research has established that the Namiquipans' construction of the past and vision of frontier society is rooted in concrete historical experience. At the same time it is a fiction, an idealization, a symbolic elaboration of lived history. Neither a myth nor a history that is only a mimetic description, a mirroring of experience, the Namiquipans' construction of the past is more like what Freud called a screen memory. Writing about such screen memories, Taussig has observed that "an oppressive present sparks fantasies of hope that become conscious in an image of the past as a 'memory.' Based on something which really occurred, this memory fictionalizes that occurrence. The product, as a memory, is a finely wrought symbolic construction bringing together past, present and desired future. There is *something* in the past to which this memory corresponds" (1987:245).

The primordial society of the Chihuahuan frontier *was* characterized by a distinct form of patriarchy; men were valientes. The patria chica *was* a more sovereign social domain. And the state *was* more like a padre than like a padrastro. It had to be. The pueblo had the guns. "The Fall," that is, the transformation of the frontier into the border, *did* entail radical reversals and dislocations. Change engendered new forms of terror and suffering. And "The Conflict," which should have introduced a new episode, "The Redemption"—yes, it became another "Fall." The benefits of "progress" have provided new alibis for power, for state penetration and regulation of peasants' lives and forms of being, knowing, and doing.

Raymond Aron has written, "The past is never definitively fixed except when it has no future" (cited in Stoianovich 1976:35). Re-presentations of history blur the lines between fiction and fact because they are the product of a dialectics between present and past, engagement and distance.

"A Dialectics of Engagement and Distance"

Rosaldo argues that "exploring the dynamic interplay of culture and power" as "embedded more in social processes than in static structures" entails a "dialectics of engagement and distance" (1987b). I fully agree with these remarks, as well as with Rosaldo's suggestion that we explore "social criticism done from subordinate social positions" (1987b).

For me a dialectics of engagement and distance has involved simultaneously writing within and against the point of view of the subaltern group I have lived and worked with—the serranos of Namiquipa. In some ways I have articulated their perspectives. Obviously, the structure of this book replicates the periodizations of Namiquipan historical memory. But my theoretical orientation and my analysis have also been shaped by their insights.

My concern with the concatenation of power and meaning certainly antedates my years in Namiquipa. But Namiquipans' exposures of the alibis of power have helped me to understand many things, including the role of the state in the construction of forms of subjectivity-subjection. My interpretations of the past have been greatly enhanced by theirs. For it is all too easy to naturalize the inscriptions of administrative routine, to accept at face value the alibis that render innocent the discourses and technologies of power, and to miss the culturally constituted character of official documents written in the bland idiom of bureaucratic practice. Although this book is set in the past, my engagement with Namiquipans in the present has substantially informed my understanding of their history.

Writing this book has also involved a taking of distance in two senses. First, I have written in a style that is distanced, in that it does not fully convey the *felt* dimension of the suffering that has marked serrano history and is relived in the act of remembering past experience. But in talking with people about the past, I had to engage the pain I have largely effaced from my prose.

When I went to see the daughter of a Villista general from Namiquipa, I asked her if she had any memories (*recuerdos*) of her father's involvement in the revolution. In response, she opened her clenched fist. "Do you see this?" she asked. Close to tears, she showed me a hand missing its little finger, "This is the memento [*recuerdo*] that my father left me."

Her father, Candelario Cervantes of Namiquipa, and his companion-in-arms, José Bencomo of Cruces, had died trying to drive the Americans from Mexican soil in 1916. The revolutionary Teodosio Duarte Morales, who identified General Cervantes's body, recalled:

> My cousin Candelario's body and face were black because they [the Americans] had lassoed and dragged him from their horses for over one and a half kilometers. . . . Moments after [his death in battle with the Americans], a cavalry squad had arrived and lassoed Candelario and José by their feet, dragging them off. . . .

An invading soldier of Mexican origin told me that when they dragged Candelario, he was still alive. This was the tragic end of one of the famous Dorados of Pancho Villa, who with José Bencomo was loyal to Villa until his death, fighting for a cause they thought just. (Duarte Morales n.d.:75–76; my translation)

A bullet from her father's gun cost my friend her little finger. Don Candelario had accidentally fired the gun he was cleaning. For his daughter, this physical dismemberment became a sign of a life fractured and dislocated by revolution. After her father died, she and her family became the object of vengeances carried out by members of the *defensa social* of Namiquipa. "We lost everything," she recalled; "the *sociales* came to the house and took everything, even the furniture. Later my mother lost the land."

The last time I talked with my friend Don Ciriaco[2] about the revolution, he was recovering from a stroke that had partially paralyzed him. Don Ciriaco is the son of a Villista from Cruces, and like his father he has fought against caciquismo. He has also disputed the caciques' monopolization of the best lands of Cruces. Shortly before I saw him last, he had gone out to the common lands to cut pasture for the family milk cow. There he had been beaten with his own hoe by two young toughs who claimed that he was trespassing on their private property. His wife told me, "It was the anger [*coraje*] that made him have the stroke." Don Ciriaco was in his eighties. There was little he could do to avenge this humiliation.

One day a friend from Namiquipa took Daniel and me to "interview" Don Gabriel, a Villista who had gone on the Columbus raid. Initially he was afraid to talk to us. Since our friend told him we were from "the other side," Don Gabriel thought we were coming to exact reprisals for his part in Villa's attack on the United States. "No, all that is over with now," our friend told him; "you have nothing to fear from these people." Lying on a sagging bed, ill, nearly blind, too weak to swat the flies buzzing about his body, Don Gabriel said, "What's the point in talking about the revolution? My general [Pancho Villa] is dead." After a while he began to reconsider. "Come back tomorrow morning," he said, "and bring some mariachis who can sing Villista *corridos*. Maybe I'll be better. Maybe we can talk about the revolution."

For one Villista kinswoman, recalling the past entailed re-experiencing a grief that more than six decades had not effaced. Through her tears she narrated how her Villista kinsman had been captured, imprisoned, tortured, castrated, and subsequently killed by members of the defensa social. The sociales left his dismembered body for the wild animals to eat.

A historical anthropology, as Bernard Cohn points out, must "deal with the fact that events have consequences for those people who are our 'subjects'" (1981:252). Cohn argues that we can no longer persist in producing our own versions of the primordial society, that we cannot continue to separate meaning and power, culture and process, past and present, that we must situate the people we study in historical terms and analyze the consequences that colonialism, imperialism, patriarchy, state formation, and capitalism have had on their ways of knowing, being, and doing.

These consequences are not just cognized—they are felt. I have largely effaced emotion from my prose because I cannot envision a form of writing that would allow me to capture the pain of these consequences. A style that is distanced from felt experience has characterized much anthropological writing. This is a form of distance that I think we should try to overcome.

But I have also taken distance in a second sense, one that I think is necessary to a historically situated cultural analysis that has as its goal the unraveling of nexuses of power and meaning. As Stuart Hall points out, in order to understand the dialectics of cultural struggle, we must dispense with that "heroic" view of popular discourses and practices which presumes an autonomous subaltern domain, which represents subordinated groups and classes as the victims but never the accomplices of effects of power that are construed as wholly external (1981).

If popular culture is not wholly determined by dominant discursive forms, neither is it wholly autonomous. One of the main goals of this book has been to demonstrate that power is not just external but also internal, not just repressive but also productive—of forms of being, knowing, and doing. Power inserts itself into bodies and selves and finds its alibi in the very "natures" it configures. Hegemony is the process of constructing subjectivities: the subaltern domain is a site for the inscription and contestation of effects of power in identities.

On the whole, while the Namiquipans' point of view advances a critique of some hegemonic forms, it reproduces others. For example, their epic re-presentation of the frontier past naturalizes the effects of power inscribed in gender and ethnicity—effects of power that were advanced by state forms of control and regulation and reproduced by the serranos. Taking distance, then, has involved exposing the alibis inscribed not only in state but also in subaltern discourses.

A dialectics of engagement and distance involves a blurring of the lines between *self* and *other*, *fact* and *fiction*, *power* and *meaning*, *past* and *present*. It also entails a crossing and a redrawing of the boundaries that have constituted and institutionalized interrelated forms of knowledge as distinct "disciplines." As forms of understanding sociocultural practice, history and anthropology shade into each other: "Given a theoretical approach that views society as a process in time, structured by principles that are historically constituted, reproduced and transformed, it is evident that history and social science cease to be distinguishable" (Smith 1984:27).

Clearly, the antinomies that have plagued our understanding of society are encoded in the very ways in which knowledge is disciplined. In order to deconstruct these antinomies, we must subvert the distinctions that have policed intellectual practice in our own well-ordered polity.

NOTES

Part I: Introduction

1. The North encompasses that portion of Mexico north of the Tropic of Cancer and includes Baja California, Sonora, Coahuila, Chihuahua, and the greater part of Sinaloa, Durango, Nuevo León, and Tamaulipas (Carr 1973:321n). Prior to the Mexican-American War of 1846–48, it also included Alta California, Arizona, New Mexico, and Texas.

2. A chilango (pejorative term for central or southern Mexican) asked a norteño for advice on sneaking across the international bridge to the United States. "Just say 'American citizen' and you'll have no problem," the norteño counseled. A short while later the chilango returned. "What happened?" asked the norteño, "Didn't you follow my advice?" "Yes," replied the chilango. "I said 'American citizen, *patroncito*,' and they sent me back." *Patroncito*, literally the diminutive for "boss," is rarely used by norteños.

3. Barry Carr's seminal article (1973) paved the way for such an analysis. However, Carr does not deal with norteño ideology.

4. The Turner thesis relies on the same metaphor; see Weber 1988:33–54.

5. "Military settlement colony" is used here in an analytical sense to designate a particular form of militarized peasant community that developed on the frontier. It should not be taken literally; that is, it is not used to refer to settlements the Mexican state specifically labeled military colonies.

Chapter 1

1. The analysis of the ideology of frontier warfare has been almost completely neglected in published sources. Moreover, scholarly accounts of the social organization of warfare have largely ignored the role of civilians, particularly members of subaltern groups and classes, in the conquest of the frontier. While there are books and articles that are valuable sources on the frontier army in the

colonial period, these have been overly concerned with the analysis of the legal regulations passed by the state rather than the practical conduct of warfare. In addition, almost nothing has been written on the social organization and ideological construction of warfare after independence.

2. I use *Hispanic* to encompass both Spanish and Mexican.

3. Prior to 1776 what is today the state of Chihuahua was one of two provinces included in the Gobernación of Nueva Vizcaya. In 1776, Nueva Vizcaya (Chihuahua, Durango, and the jurisdictions of Saltillo and Parras, Coahuila) and the provinces of Nuevo México, Sonora, Sinaloa, Coahuila, Texas, and the Californias were incorporated into a new administrative unit, the Provincias Internas, independent of the viceroyalty and under the authority of a military governor directly responsible to the Spanish Crown; however, each province retained its distinctive jurisdiction within this larger unit. From 1786 to the end of the colonial period, the Provincias Internas underwent multiple administrative reorganizations, being combined and recombined into different commands that were repeatedly accorded and denied a jurisdiction independent of the viceroyalty. In 1824, after independence, the state of Chihuahua was formed (Lister and Lister 1979:18; Barnes, Naylor and Polzer 1981:61–65).

4. This was the perception of Spanish military strategists experienced in frontier warfare. See Bernardo de Gálvez (1786) in Worcester, ed. 1951:98–100; and circa 1790, "Noticias y reflexiones sobre la guerra que se tiene con los indios Apaches en las Provincias de la Nueva España," University of Arizona microfilm no. 71; no author appears on the original manuscript, but Martínez Caraza 1983:76ff cites portions of the same text and attributes it to Bernardo de Gálvez. See also Cordero (1796) in Matson and Schroeder, eds. 1957:335–56.

5. Thomas comments that in the early eighteenth century, the Comanche emerged from the Rocky Mountains, sweeping down across the Texas plains by mid-century and driving the Apache before them (1941:6). The intensification of Apache raiding in Chihuahua in 1748 may be related to Comanche displacement of Apache groups.

6. "Razón individual de los insultos, muertes, cautivos y heridos, robo de ganado y demás bienes; hechos por los indios enemigos bárbaros, en la propiedad del Valle de Basúchil, en los años 1782 y 1783," June 30, 1783, reproduced in Chávez 1939; my translation.

7. Primary sources on colonial policy toward the Apache include Gálvez in Worcester 1951 and "Noticias y reflexiones"; Croix in Thomas 1941; O'Conor in González Flores and Almada 1952; and Escudero 1834:236–48. Secondary sources include Moorhead 1968:115–42.

8. Namiquipa, January 9, 1908, Francisco Vásquez to the *comandante general* of the Second Flying Company; copy provided by José Muñoz.

9. For contemporary observers' reports on the frontier military, see Gálvez in Worcester 1951 and "Noticias y reflexiones"; Lafora in Kinnaird 1958; Croix

in Thomas 1941; O'Conor in González Flores and Almada 1952; Pike in Coues 1895; Lt. José Cortés, "Memorias sobre las Provincias Internas del Norte de Nueva España," 1799, University of Arizona Ms. no. 40. The Archivo General de la Nación (AGN), Ramos Provincias Internas and Presidios y Cárceles contain muster lists, letters, and reports.

10. Gálvez, "Noticias y reflexiones"; my translation.

11. For a lengthy comparison of the Apache's fighting style with that of colonial frontier forces, see ibid. After independence settler warriors continued to fight like Apaches; see Terrazas 1905.

12. However, on the frontier, charismatic authority was generally routinized because warfare became a part of everyday life. The distinction between charismatic and traditional authority became blurred. See chapter 3 for a discussion of this point.

13. Gálvez, "Noticias y reflexiones."

14. Although Pike as well as many scholars have taken the preponderance of bows, arrows, and lances over firearms to indicate that frontier settlers were poorly armed, another interpretation suggests itself. As Gálvez reiterates, in Apache warfare, bows and arrows were much more efficient than firearms (in Worcester 1951:passim). This continued to be true until after independence, when the Apache themselves began to rely more on firearms than on bows and lances.

15. "Bando de Teodoro de Croix," November 15, 1778 (copy furnished by José Muñoz of Namiquipa) establishes these five *villas* and details the obligations and privileges of prospective colonists.

16. The mission was established in 1662 and abandoned by the Franciscans in 1763 (Gerhard 1982:187–89).

17. This ideal type was developed by Eric Wolf in order to characterize the Indian communities of central Mexico and to contrast them to the "open" communities of non-Indian peasants (1967). Paradoxically, however, the agricultural pueblos of Chihuahuan Apache fighters approximate the ideal type developed for Indian as opposed to non-Indian communities in Mexico.

18. "Bando de Teodoro de Croix," November 15, 1778, and letter, January 9, 1808, Francisco Vásquez to the *comandante general*.

19. April 25, 1796, Felipe González de Cossio, administrator Hacienda de Encinillas, to Miguel González de Cossio, in Barri Jr. 1942.

20. This assumption is largely based on the work of Chevalier (1963), which focuses on the *tierra de paz*, that is Durango and Zacatecas, rather than on the *tierra de guerra*. The situation of hacendados in Chihuahua was quite different from that of landed proprietors in the tierra de paz. Chihuahuan haciendas were much more impoverished, since their livestock was constantly being appropriated by the raiding Apache. Their owners simply lacked the resources to maintain large private armies. Not surprisingly, contemporary reports by agents

of the state commissioned to evaluate frontier defenses rarely mention the existence of armed nuclei on Chihuahuan haciendas. I have found only one such reference–to a group of thirty-five men armed with guns, bows, and arrows on the Hacienda del Carmen (Lafora in Kinnaird 1958:96).

21. Indeed, the 1783 request for more effective state aid against the Apache from the desperate hacendados and ranchers of the Basúchil Valley (in Chávez 1939) indicates that landed proprietors relied on the state for protection.

22. AGN, Provincias Internas, vol. 193, pp. 165–66, "Noticia de los enemigos muertos y apresados por las Armas del Rey en las Provincias Internas de N.E. y de los Vasallos sacados de Cautiverio . . ." Chihuagua, May 29, 1789, Jacobo Ugarte y Loyola.

23. Ibid.

24. E.g., Documentary Relations of the Southwest (DRSW) 041-01184, 1767.

25. E.g., DRSW 041-04313, July 16, 1790, to August 12, 1790.

26. E.g., DRSW 041-02458, 1771.

27. DRSW 041-02458, April 30, 1763, letter from auditor de guerra to Muñoz.

28. Eighteenth-century baptismal records for El Valle de San Buenaventura and the presidio of Janos suggest that similar forms of incorporating Apache children who were captives may have also been taking place in these sites (see data in Griffen 1979:86–87, 92–94).

29. Bando Colonial, March 12, 1728, Durango, signed Don Ignacio Francisco de Barrutia, governor and *capitán general* of Nueva Vizcaya, reproduced in *Boletín de la Sociedad Chihuahuense de Estudios Históricos* (BSCEH) I(12):395–423, May 1939.

30. E.g., DRSW 041-02317, March 16, 1771; DRSW 041-03746, September 10, 1772, to July 17, 1790.

31. On illness of prisoners and treatment of the sick, dying, and dead, see, e.g., DRSW 041-03505, April 16, 1794, to June 23, 1794; 041-03532, March 27, 1792, to January 30, 1793; 041-03751, December 11, 1779, to February 23, 1790; 041-04600, November 14, 1797, to February 15, 1798; 041-05280, November 27, 1794, to April 1, 1802.

32. DRSW 041-03751, December 11, 1779, to February 23, 1790.

33. Ibid.

34. DRSW 041-03531, March 20, 1792, to May 26, 1792.

35. DRSW 041-05280, November 27, 1794, to April 1, 1802.

36. E.g., DRSW 041-01541, March 4, 1793, to March 6, 1793; DRSW 041-03758, July 1782 to March 17, 1789; DRSW 041-04518, November 9, 1788; DRSW 041-05280, November 21, 1794, to April 1, 1802.

37. Ibid.

38. DRSW 041-03745, September 7, 1780, to October 27, 1789.

39. Ibid.

40. DRSW 275-00577, December 6, 1732, to February 5, 1733.

41. Archivo Municipal Ciudad Guerrero (AMCG), box 2 file 25, February 25, 1833, Chihuahuan Congress to the vice-president of the Republic; Escudero 1834:56–58.

42. AMCG, box 2 file 24, January 9, 1832, organization of "public security forces" for defense against "internal or external factions" in certain localities, with officers appointed by the Chihuahuan government; box 3 file 32, July 7, 1836, organization of militias in pueblos, haciendas, and ranchos; box 3 file 49, December 18, 1847, box 5 file 55, December 18, 1847, and December 29, 1849, organization of men eighteen to fifty years of age from Bachíniva and Namiquipa into "National Guard" according to circular of November 1, 1847; box 3 file 55, March 9, 1848, officers of National Guard to be elected by members; box 7 file 78, April 25, 1851, details of organization of National Guard, lower-ranking officers to be appointed by municipal authorities, and higher-ranking ones by district authorities; box 5 file 63, May 30, 1851, and June 13, 1851, organization of men of Bachíniva and Namiquipa into militia squadrons in accordance with law of April 22, 1851, lower-ranking officers elected by men, and higher-ranking ones appointed by Chihuahuan government; box 6 file 72, September 6, 1855, military census of men eighteen to fifty years of age in Namiquipa, and October 8, 1855, list of members of the National Guard in Namiquipa, organized according to the law of July 19, 1848; box 8 file 93, July 23, 1863, military census of men in Namiquipa; scattered references to the National Guard occur through the end of the 1870s.

43. AMCG, box 7 file 78, April 25, 1851; box 5 file 63, June 13, 1851.

44. AMCG, box 6 file 74, February 16, 1865; box 7 file 78, April 8, 1856; file 86, February 25, 1861; box 9 file 108, May 18, 1865. *Secretaría de reforma agraria*, Archivo Histórico, Sección Terrenos Nacionales (ATN), 121(06) file 516, December 24, 1869.

45. A fifth type could be added—the American military entrepreneur who, with a group of mercenaries, waged warfare for profit. Entrepreneurs such as Santiago Kirker were contracted by the Chihuahuan government in the 1830s and 1840s and remunerated with rights to captured booty and cash payments for scalps; however, these mercenaries' use of force could not be controlled effectively by the Mexican state. By 1850, American mercenaries were scalping more Mexicans than Indians and had to be driven from Mexico by force (Smith 1965).

46. E.g., AMCG, box 6 file 74, June 21, 1855; box 7 file 78, April 21, 1856, Chihuahua; file 82, September 10, 1858, Chihuahua; October 26, 1858, Chihuahua; October 12, 1858, Mátachic; file 89, March 5, 1862, Chihuahua; box 9 file 109, November 14, 1869, Namiquipa; file 112, April 18, 1869, Chihuahua, and December 17, 1869, Namiquipa; box 10 file 122, March 13, 1871, Chihuahua; March 17, 1871, Namiquipa; April 15, 1871, Chihuahua; November 27, 1871, Chihuahua; December 4, 1871, Chihuahua.

47. Joaquín Terrazas's memoirs are a rich source on the organization of war-

fare as well as on the "career" of one key military leader (1905). The AMCG is full of reports on campaigns organized by regional leaders in the Guerrero District. These include box 5 file 66, March 31, 1852, April 5, 1852, July 15, 1852; box 6 file 73, May 14, 1855; box 7 file 81, April 1, 1857; box 12 file 151, October 8, 1878; box 13 file 154, November 13, 1879; file 159, August 24, 1880, September 3, 1880, September 16, 1880, September 21, 1880, September 28, 1880; box 14 file 171, February 7, 1882; box 16, December 1885.

48. AMCG, box 15 file 175, July 31, 1883, Chihuahua, *secretaría de estado* to *jefe politico*, Guerrero (JPG).

49. AMCG, box 7 file 83, July 18, 1859, C. Guerrero, rebels' "plan."

50. AMCG contains hundreds of documents that provide information on the role of municipal and district authorities in warfare. For some examples, see box 3 file 32, July 7, 1836; box 5 file 59, July 1850; file 66, June 3, 1852; box 6 file 73, May 14, 1855, September 10, 1855, September 17, 1855; box 7 file 78, April 25, 1851, March 11, 1856; file 81, February 14, 1857; file 82, March 29, 1858; box 8 file 94, May 16, 1863; box 9 file 105, February 15, 1867, September 4, 1867; file 112, December 28, 1869; file 117, January 8, 1870; box 10 file 128, February 26, 1872; box 13 file 158, September 6, 1880; file 159, August 24, 1880; box 14 file 164, September 14, 1881; file 165, September 9, 1881; file 170, June 18, 1882; box 15 file 183, November 15, 1884.

51. Whereas in Namiquipa eighty-nine men owned their own firearms, in the neighboring town of Bachíniva only forty-one men had weapons; AMCG, box 5 file 56, September 29, 1849. However, even those who owned their own weapons were constantly short of ammunition.

52. On state exactions of financial subsidies for warfare from the elite, see Almada 1955:195, 201–2 and passim. Also, AMCG, box 2 file 25, November 25, 1832; file 26, December 17, 1833; box 3 file 32, May 18, 1838; box 4 file 49, December 18, 1847; box 6 file 73, May 14, 1855.

53. AMCG, box 3 file 32, July 7, 1836, armed forces organized on haciendas to be at the disposition of state functionaries when necessary; box 4 file 47, March 4, 1845, no worker or peasant could go to the fields unarmed, and all were obliged to defend themselves if attacked; box 3 file 31, December 29, 1835, armed men from haciendas requested by neighboring pueblos for aid against raiding Apaches.

54. AMCG, box 7 file 81, March 2, 1857, secretaría de estado to JPG.

55. BSCEH vii:509–13.

56. Biblioteca Nacional (BN) ms. 1283, "Educación Social" by Cuilty, *El Chasco*, February 3, 1842.

57. See Weber 1978 for a discussion of charismatic, patrimonial, and legal-rational forms of provisioning and rewarding followers.

58. This is a common phrase in documents dealing with the Center's lack of

support for frontier warfare after independence; the legitimacy of patrimonial authorities was compromised by their neglect of frontier defense.

Chapter 2

1. For discussions of the construction of race and of social stratification in colonial Mexico, see Morner 1967, 1970; Rosenblat 1954; McAlister 1963; Warman 1977; Chance 1978; Todorov 1984; Gutiérrez 1980, 1991; Nash 1980. Humboldt 1966 is a rich "primary source."

2. Ethnicity continued to affect access to the means of production because it determined the types of rights that persons were given to land. In Chihuahua, "Indians" who redefined their ethnic identity through acculturation and separation from indigenous society could receive the same rights to land as other Hispanicized settlers, even in the colonial period; as members of a community with a property title to corporate holdings, they had derechos de posesión to their own plots and were free to buy or sell land as well as to transmit it to their heirs (e.g., "Bando de Teodoro de Croix," November 15, 1778). Indian communities also held title to land as corporate groups but their members had usufruct rather than posesión rights in particular plots. In the colonial period Indians who were members of such communities had the legal status of minors and were unable to buy, sell, or contract. As a result, they were legally unable to acquire more land than what the Crown allotted them; the repeal of discriminatory legislation after independence did not substantially alter the situation (Warman 1977). Access to land, despite these limitations, enabled Indians to survive as subsistence peasants until the implementation of the liberal Reform Laws after the mid-nineteenth century. In Chihuahua the massive proletarianization of Indians began in the 1860s but did not gain momentum until the 1880s.

3. Attempts had been made to christianize both "wild" and "pacified" frontier indigenes. However, efforts to convert the Apache failed; neither Jesuit nor Franciscan missionaries were very successful in "reducing" the Tarahumara to the "true religion" (Nugent 1982). By the eighteenth century the conversion of the frontier's heathen Indians was not a priority for the state.

4. The first is an account entitled "Quality [*Calidad*] of Indians who Harass the Frontier," part of a long report to the Spanish monarch covering the years 1771-76 and written by Hugo O'Conor, commandant of the Provincias Internas (reproduced in González Flores and Almada 1952; all translations mine). The second is a text entitled "Notes about the Apache nation composed in the Year 1796 by Lieutenant Colonel Don Antonio Cordero by Order of the Commandant General Field Marshal Don Pedro de Nava," which was reproduced in full in 1864 in Manuel Orozco y Barra's *Geography of the Languages and Ethnographic Map of Mexico* (English translation in Matson and Schroeder 1957). Cor-

dero served from early youth in the frontier military, spoke the language of the Apache, and had had extensive dealings with them. That Cordero's account was reproduced almost one century later attests to its perceived "authoritativeness" as well as to the continuity between colonial and postcolonial constructions of the Apache. Orozco y Barra's book is not the only place where Cordero's text is reproduced; the latter seems to have informed several other accounts of the Apache, for example, "The Apache Indians," an article published in the Chihuahuan newspaper *El Correo de Chihuahua*, February 22, 1902. The third is a report dated September 27, 1851, written by General Emilio Lamberg, inspector of the military colonies of the state of Chihuahua and addressed to the minister of war in Mexico City, General Manuel Robles Pezuela (reproduced in Lozano 1949; all translations mine).

5. Jones 1979 points out that on the Mexican frontier, unlike the American frontier, settlement was planned by the state and the movements of colonists were regulated and authorized by the state. Nugent 1982 demonstrates the importance accorded by the colonial state to the settlement of seminomadic Indians in pueblos and the centrality that the fixing of the Indians in space had in the civilizing mission. A colonial edict drawn up in 1728 by the governor and captain general of Nueva Vizcaya contains several clauses designed to limit and regulate the mobility of reduced Indians (partially reproduced in Hernández Rodríguez 1939).

6. *Gente política* is used by O'Conor to contrast the civilized with the savage when writing about styles of warfare (in González Flores and Almada 1952:103).

7. In the twentieth century, indigenes became regarded as "natural resources" to be "developed"; significantly, in his book on Chihuahua, the former Porfirian governor Enrique C. Creel included a description of the Tarahumara in the section on geography rather than in that on history (1928:77–78). Discussed after some paragraphs on railroads, the Tarahumara are characterized as a "primitive," "inferior race," given over to "sloth" and "drunkenness" and resistant to "civilization."

8. Cf. the analysis in Taussig 1987 of Putamayo colonists' constructions of nature and their fear of the "deconstructing tropicality" of the jungle.

9. The Spanish term is *intereses*, which means both interests in general and economic interests in particular, as in intereses de campo, which includes diverse forms of rural property.

10. Significantly, the word here is *encarnizamiento*, from *encarnizar*-"to be greedy for flesh (said of animals)"; Williams 1963.

11. Preconquest indigenous rights to land went unrecognized. Those lands legally held by Indian communities were conferred by the Crown.

12. For supporting discussions of ethnicity on the frontier in the eighteenth and nineteenth centuries, see Jones 1979; Tjarks 1979; Weber 1982; Vigil 1973; Servín 1979; Jordán 1981; Lister and Lister 1979.

13. These terms are prevalent in colonial documents. After independence, gente de razón becomes less common in administrative documents, although the distinction between the "civilized" and the "barbaric" continues to be articulated. In day-to-day life, gente de razón continued to be used in the Chihuahuan sierra and is still used today.

14. Taussig 1987 reports a similar blurring of distinctions between whites and the castas in the Putamayo.

15. DRSW 041-02435, Julimes, June 7, 1763 through July 20, 1768, correspondence between Captain Manuel Muñoz and viceroy regarding the administration of the presidios of Junta de los Ríos and Julimes.

16. The consumption of wheat rather than corn tortillas is still an important sign of "whiteness" in the North and is regularly evoked by norteños to distinguish themselves from the "more Indian" chilangos. Although corn tortillas are eaten in the North, white wheat tortillas are preferred and their preparation is one of the privileged signs of a fully socialized femininity.

17. See Vigil 1973 for this "myth of Spanish settlement" in California.

18. Benigna, or its masculine form, Benigno, meaning benign, was a name commonly given to Christianized Apaches in the nineteenth century. The baptism of Lino Leyba, son of Leonardo Leyba and Beningna Arvizo, is registered in the Archivo de la Iglesia de Namiquipa (AIN).

19. For an oral history of Juh, as told by his son, Asa Daklugie, to Eve Ball, see Ball 1980; Doña Aurora's information about Juh is different from Asa Daklugie's.

20. AGN, Provincias Internas, vol. 21, pp. 268–72.

21. The characterization of Apaches as cruel is prevalent in reports by state functionaries and settlers; many examples can be found in AMCG.

Chapter 3

1. This story is told by Don Jesús's descendants and was related to me by one of his granddaughters. Don Jesús is not his real name. In order to protect people's identities, real names are only used here when they appear in documents or published sources.

2. Leach 1959 makes the point that hair is a symbol for sexual states and qualities.

3. AMCG, box 39 file 359, April 9, 1888, Santana Pérez to the JPG.

4. The interpolation, part of the sentence that immediately precedes this quote, is what "this other kind of subject" refers back to.

5. Since the 1980s, writing on difference has tried to explore the links between gender, ethnicity, and class as forms of oppression. Brittan and Maynard 1984 provide a critical discussion of various positions on ethnicity, gender, and class and their interrelations. Literature on gender, sexuality, ethnicity, nation-

alism, and the state includes Chatarjee 1993; Das 1994; Davin 1978; Enloe 1989; Mohanty, Russo, and Torres 1991; Mosse 1985; Ong 1990; Parker, Russo, Sommer, and Yaeger 1992; Yuval-Davis and Anthias 1989. Nakano Glenn 1985 attempts to integrate the Marxist-feminist and internal colonialism models. For approaches influenced by Lacan, see Henriques et al. 1984. Other works I have found useful include Abelove, Barale, and Halperin 1993; Anzaldúa 1987, 1990; Butler and Scott 1992; Carby 1985; Davis 1981; di Leonardo 1991; Franco 1989; Gutiérrez 1980, 1991; Gilman 1985; hooks 1990; Lewis 1983; Lowenhaupt-Tsing 1993; Minh-ha 1989; Moraga 1986; Mullings 1986; O'Neale 1986; Radcliffe and Westwood 1993; Spivak 1985, 1987; Stoler 1989. Although the interrelations among gender, ethnicity, and class began to garner widespread attention as "a new topic" in the 1980s, these issues have been explored before. The work of R. T. Smith (1967, 1970, 1982a, 1982b) and V. Martínez-Alier (1974) in the Caribbean are just two examples.

6. For those not familiar with Peircean terminology, an icon is a sign that represents its object by virtue of some resemblance to it. An index is a sign that "points" to its object, that is, refers to the object it denotes by virtue of some connection to it (a weather vane, a pointing finger). A symbol is a sign whose relation to its object is wholly arbitrary. See Singer 1984:44.

7. Works that make masculinity central include Brittan 1989; Connell 1987; Herdt 1982; Herzfeld 1985; Theweleit 1987.

8. For a feminist critique of Lévi-Strauss's argument, see Brooke-Rose 1986.

9. The discussion of masculine and feminine honor that follows (this and the next two subsections) is based on ethnographic fieldwork, archival documents, newspapers, and oral histories. The numerous records of disputes of honor found in the Archivo Judicial del Municipio de Namiquipa (AJMN) were particularly rich sources. The many exhortatory articles and editorials in the Chihuahuan newspaper *El Correo de Chihuahua*, 1899–1908, were also an important source attesting to the centrality of gender in Chihuahuan society. I have also consulted Gutiérrez 1980, 1991; Anzaldúa 1987, 1990; Franco 1989; Radcliffe and Westwood 1993; Seed 1988; Paz 1985; Ramos 1938; Alegría 1978; Wolf 1959; Wolf and Hansen 1967; Stevens 1965, 1973; Romanucci-Ross 1973; essays in Naranjo 1981; essays in Ramos Escándon 1987; Moraga 1986; Lecompte 1981; Boxer 1975; Martínez-Alier 1974; Fox 1973; and Lauria 1963 for gender and honor in Mexico and Latin America. I have also looked at the literature on honor for the Mediterranean, e.g., Pitt-Rivers 1961, 1965; Schneider 1971; Ortner 1978; Blok 1984; essays in Peristiany 1965; essays in Dubisch 1986; and essays in Gilmore 1987.

10. In Spanish, the unmarked meaning of *huevos* is "eggs"; in Chihuahua, however, the marked sense has become primary, and unless one wants to be the object of ridicule, one is careful to refer to eggs as *blanquillos*.

11. As Mirande 1985 points out, the ambiguous and contradictory character

of masculinity is often flattened or suppressed in the literature. Hispanic masculinity is presented in wholly negative terms as a form of cultural pathology. Mirande argues that this interpretation of machismo (by which he means both "natural" and culturalized masculinity) is itself an effect of power, a technology of Anglo hegemony. Certainly, many Anglo reviews of the film *La Bamba* evince such a reading (as do representations of Latinos and Chicanos in other Anglo films, as well as newspapers, judicial cases, etc.). However, it is not just Anglo writers who have advanced this negative characterization of Hispanic masculinity (e.g., Ramos 1938). Apart from Anglo ethnocentrism, I would argue that since masculinity is a contradictory unity, it is as difficult to write about as it is to enact; one has to think and write dialectically, not digitally.

12. In serrano communities such as Namiquipa, the construction of the *cacique* and of *caciquismo* is wholly negative: the cacique has "power" but lacks "legitimate authority" (in Weber's sense of these terms). Caciquismo will be discussed in Part II. In other areas of Mexico, caciquismo is differently construed and appears to be much more ambiguous; see Friedrich 1965, 1981, 1986; Wolf 1977.

13. AIN, records of marriages, baptisms, and deaths from 1780 on.

14. "Denaturalized Mother," an article from *El Correo de Chihuahua*, June 18, 1902, reports the discovery of the body of a newborn boy outside Chihuahua City and adds that the judge was not able to determine the identity of "the denaturalized mother, who knew how to place herself very much below the beasts"; my translation.

15. Paz 1985 argues that the chingada is identified with la Malinche, the Indian woman who became Cortés's guide and concubine. In the North, however, la Malinche is not a significant cultural symbol, since the dynamics of conquest and colonization were completely different.

16. Although Western medical ideology has led to the decline of this practice, some women from rural areas continue to observe these interdictions, and as a rule, when pregnancy becomes evident, women try to conceal their state from the public gaze, wearing clothes that dissimulate their condition, confining themselves to the home, and avoiding public contexts and gatherings.

17. Mexican women remained disenfranchised until 1953. See Soto 1986.

18. AJMN, July 30, 1894, Criminal contra Cleofas Ramos por escandalo.

19. In the North this expression does not have the same connotations that Paz claims it has in the rest of Mexico (1985). Since in the North the chingada is not identified with la Malinche, to call a man an *hijo de la chingada* is not to say that he is the fruit of an ur-violation, the bastard offspring of a white conqueror and a violated Indian woman who betrayed her people by allowing her body to be possessed by the alien aggressor. Indeed, since the Namiquipans identified themselves as conquerors, they would hardly have shared in this legend of colonization.

20. State claims on peasants' economic surplus and labor power were diminished while claims on fighting power were at their height, especially since warfare forced peasants to invest part of their surplus in arms, horses, and munitions. In the colonial and postcolonial periods, the state explicitly exempted peasant communities located in zones of warfare from the payment of taxes on the condition that they fight the Apache; e.g., see "Bando de Teodoro de Croix," November 15, 1778; AMCG, box 2 file 25, Chihuahua, August 29, 1832; box 4 file 47, Chihuahua, June 9, 1845.

21. The adjective here is *estólidos*, which the dictionary (Williams 1963) translates as "stupid" or "imbecile" and which I have rendered as "irrational" to stress that it is not so much a lack of intelligence that is at issue but a lack of reason.

22. The Spanish is *abatir la cerviz*, literally, "to lower or humble the nape of the neck/base of the brain" (Williams 1963).

23. Clearly, a mistake was made in the original in the estimate of the population of Chihuahua.

24. AMCG, box 2 file 26, Chihuahua, December 17, 1833, José S. Pareha, vice-governor of Chihuahua, to the inhabitants; my translation and emphasis.

25. AMCG, box 3 file 32, May 18, 1838, the governor and military commander of Chihuahua to the inhabitants.

26. Documents in AMCG commonly use these terms; some examples can also be found in AGN, Provincias Internas, e.g., vol. 252, pp. 233–34, January 30, 1820, José Gaspar de Ochoa to Alexo García Conde.

27. *Jarras* usually means "pitchers"; in this context, however, it may signify the poisoned arrows of the Apache, which Elías says were prepared by Apache women.

28. Bernardo de Gálvez, circa 1790, "Noticias y reflexiones sobre la guerra que se tiene con los indios Apaches en las Provincias de la Nueva España," University of Arizona microfilm no. 71; no author appears on the original manuscript, but Mártinez Caraza 1983:76ff cites portions of the same text and attributes it to Bernardo de Gálvez; my translation.

29. Ibid.

30. I am not sure when this term began to be used to characterize the serranos. I know it was in use by the time of the Revolution of 1910–20, since serranos and other Villistas often referred to themselves and were frequently characterized as centaurs.

31. AMCG, box 7 file 81, March 2, 1857, *secretaría de estado* to the *juez politico de Guerrero* (JPG); prisoners taken in campaign were given to officers who distinguished themselves in action, with the stipulation that they were "to civilize, educate, and inspire them with horror of the savage life."

32. Lafora's text is reproduced in English in Kinnaird 1958; this quote is my translation from the Spanish as cited in Jordán 1981:180.

33. AMCG, box 4 file 49, September 28, 1847, *prefecto* Chihuahua District to *subprefecto* Concepción; my translation and interpolation.

34. AMCG, box 3 file 32, Chihuahua, 1836, "from an inhabitant of Chihuahua to his fellow citizens"; my translation. Numerous other examples in which the rhetoric of patriotism frames the struggle with the Apache can be found in the same archive.

35. AMCG, box 7 file 78, November 25, 1856, Juan B. Escudero to the JPG; my translation.

36. AMCG, box 7 file 81, 1857, speech given by the governor of Chihuahua, Bernardo Devilla, upon the installation of the congress; my translation.

37. AMCG, box 4 file 47, Chihuahua, September 9, 1845, prefecto Chihuahua District to subprefecto Concepción.

38. AMCG, box 7 file 78, Chihuahua, November 25, 1856, secretaría de estado to the JPG.

39. Gálvez, "Noticias y reflexiones."

40. AMCG, box 4 file 49, Chihuahua, September 28, 1847, prefecto Chihuahua District to subprefecto Concepción; my translation.

41. Note the parallel here to the notion of the ghiyata of eastern Morocco that "horsemen are the fence of the land."

42. The oral histories taken by Ball (1970, 1980) on the Mescalero Reservation clearly demonstrate the centrality of these values in Apache constructions of gender.

43. ATN, 1.71(06)E75669, November 14, 1885, "Deslinde practicado por la Cia. Jesús E. Valenzuela en el Cantón Guerrero."

Chapter 4

1. The analysis presented here is based on oral histories, archival documents, and ethnographic fieldwork.

2. However, "tame" Indians who lived in communities of gente de razón like Namiquipa, instead of the mission pueblos, were given the same land rights as other settlers. Many of them redefined their ethnic identity over time and lost their "Indianess."

3. AMCG, box 5 file 55, November 25, 1848, Namiquipa, Registro de Vagos (Register of Vagrants).

4. Ibid.

5. For example, this characterization of wage labor occurs in AJMN, November 18, 1888, Criminal por abigeato y otros delitos contra Ramon Ornelas y Ventura Pérez.

6. For anecdotes that affirm hacienda cowboys' embodiment of the frontier code of honor, see Romero 1939.

7. AJMN, November 18, 1888, Criminal por abigeato y otros delitos contra

Ramon Ornelas y Ventura Pérez. Other such cases can be found in the same archive, e.g., October 11, 1888, Criminal contra Mariano Márquez y Eligio Salcido por lesiones; June 4, 1909, Querella, Adolfo Stayer contra Pedro Castro por injurias y calumnia; see also the description of a dispute between the administrator of the Hacienda de Providencia and several of his workers, AMCG, box 11 file 144, February 24, 1876.

8. As John Coatsworth points out, per capita and total income levels fell in postindependence Mexico until the 1860s and did not surpass colonial income levels until the Porfiriato (1877–1910), when capitalist development took off (1978:81).

Chapter 5

1. Article 22, Constitución política de la República Mexicana, February 12, 1857, published in *Código de la Reforma o Colección de Leyes, Decretos y Supremas Ordenes Expedidas desde 1856 hasta 1861*. Mexico: Imprenta Literaria; Código Penal para el Distritio Federal y la Baja California Sobre Delitos de Fuero Comun y Para Toda la República Sobre Delitos Contra la Federación, December 7, 1871, reproduced in Dublan and Lozano, vol. XI, pp. 567ff.

2. *Código de la Reforma*.

3. 1871 Código Penal; see Arrom 1985:310, note 110.

4. Código de Reforma no. 52, July 23, 1859, in *Código de la Reforma*; all quotes my translations.

5. Art. 30, art. 34, Constitución, in *Código de la Reforma*.

6. Art. 201, Código Civil para el Distrito Federal y la Baja California, December 13, 1870, reproduced in Dublan and Lozano, vol. XI, pp. 201ff; my translation.

7. Art. 206, art. 212, Código Civil, December 13, 1870.

8. Art. 205, Código Civil, December 13, 1870.

9. Legislation on divorce appears in arts. 239–76, Código Civil, December 13, 1870.

10. Discussions of Porfirian state centralization and economic development that I have used in this section include de la Garza et al. 1986; Cardoso, ed. 1980; Knight 1986:1–36 and passim, vol. 1; Katz 1981:passim; Katz 1986; Coatsworth 1978; Hamilton 1982:44–56; Córdova 1973:39–79; Meyer and Sherman 1979: 431–79; Vanderwood 1981; and Wolf 1971.

11. According to Weber, sultanism is an extreme case of traditional domination characterized by a broadening of the range of the ruler's arbitrary power at the expense of traditional limitations on authority. Sultanism arises when traditional domination develops an administration and a military force that are purely personal instruments of the master; the primary military support of the ruler is an army of conscripted subjects and mercenaries (Weber 1978:231–32).

12. According to one source, about 25 percent of the economically active rural

population was absolutely without access to land (Garciadiego 1986:24); how-ever, another writer affirms that 90 to 95 percent of the rural population was landless (Hamilton 1982:55).

13. "Economic miracle" is used to draw attention to the similarities between Porfirian and post-1940s economic policies.

14. As Nugent points out, the ideology of force is what makes today's Judi-ciales—the equivalent of the Porfirian Rurales—effective (pers. comm.).

15. This section is based on archival documentation, especially from AMCG and ATN, as well as on oral history and ethnographic fieldwork. I have also re-lied on the following secondary sources: Lister and Lister 1979; Almada 1955, 1964, 1980; and Wasserman 1984.

16. The term is taken from Lomnitz and Pérez-Lizaur 1984; these are three-generation descent groups.

17. AMCG, box 7 file 78, Chihuahua, February 20, 1856, secretaría de estado to JPG; file 81, Chihuahua, February 11, 1857, secretaría de estado to JPG; file 82, Chihuahua, November 29, 1857, secretaría de estado to JPG.

18. ATN 1.21(06) file 77214.

19. AMCG, box 10 file 122, Chihuahua, secretaría de estado to JPG, April 20, 1871; June 10, 1871; June 26, 1871; August 8, 1871; August 9, 1871.

20. Archivo General del Cuerpo Consultativo Agrario (AGCCA), file 24/434.

21. ATN 1.21(06) file 137; AMCG, box 9 file 112, December 18, 1869; file 117, December 4, 1871.

22. Numerous documents on this invasion of pueblo lands by the Guerre-rense elite can be found in AMCG. ATN also contains extensive documentation on these land sales; for some examples, see 1.21(06): file 142, 17,555 hs. to Manuel Herrera, municipality of Temósachi; file 235/191, 10,533 hs. to Jesús María Casa-vantes, municipality of Temósachi; both from the year 1865.

23. In 1865, Ignacio Legarreta, judge for the Guerrero District, bought lands, a spring, and a mill that the indigenes and settlers had constructed with their "personal labor"; ATN, 1.21(06) exps. 175 and 194. He subsequently sold it to Tomás Dozal y Hermosillo, who had taken possession by 1869; ATN, 1.21(06) file 516.

24. Ibid.; also 1.21(06) file 520, April 1870.

25. Ibid. Moreover, in February of 1863, Terrazas sold some Yepomerans, in-cluding Santana Pérez, 1,755.5 hectares of so-called baldíos to the north of the ejidos; ATN, 1.21(06) file 970.

26. AMCG, box 7 file 82, Chihuahua, June 27, 1859, secretaría de estado to JPG; file 89, Chihuahua, January 3, 1862, secretaría de estado to JPG; box 8 file 92, C. Guerrero, n.d. 1862; file 93, Chihuahua, January 30, 1863, secretaría de estado to JPG.

27. Numerous documents can be found in AMCG, Archivo Municipal de Namiquipa (AMN), and Archivo Seccional de Cruces (ASC).

28. Dissatisfaction with state control of the socialization of children is still

evident in Namiquipa today, despite the partial internalization of an ideology of education advanced by the state in which schooling is viewed as necessary for the personal and social "progress" of the individual. Moreover, schoolteachers are resented as outsiders, as agents of the state, and as agents of the ruling PRI. In the 1930s, when a "socialist" curriculum, at odds with local ideology, was imposed by the Cárdenas regime, some schoolteachers were almost killed in Namiquipa's El Terrero neighborhood.

29. His denunciation of this and other Reform Laws is documented in AMCG as well as in the Archivo General de Notarías, Chihuahua (ANC); Vásquez was eventually arrested by the Chihuahuan government for his opposition to the liberals' policies.

30. In Namiquipa today people comply with the law, but civil marriage is considered a formality. One is not "really married" unless one has undergone the religious rite of passage that sacralizes sexual unions. Women who do not get married by the church are dishonored, as are their offspring, who are classified and stigmatized as *hijos naturales*; their fathers and brothers are also dishonored for their failure to protect the sexual purity of their female relatives.

31. Significantly, when Calles decreed the closing of the churches in the 1920s, Namiquipan women successfully resisted efforts by local and provincial level functionaries to impose the order. This was related to me by a female friend from Cruces who used the anecdote to exemplify the clout of Namiquipan women.

32. These remarks are taken from an oral history related to Alberto Calzadíaz Barrera by Eligio Cisneros, who lived in Namiquipa during the 1860s (1969:21; my translation).

33. Almada 1955:316; also documents in AMCG attest the order was carried out.

34. AMCG, box 11 file 144, November 15, 1876, from the people of Santo Tomás to the Chihuahuan state legislature; "work in our fields" is rendered as *labores*, a term which for the serranos means both fields and agricultural work on one's lands.

35. Numerous documents in AMCG attest to this revaluation of serrano identity by the state and the elite. Moreover, this redefinition of the subjectivity of frontier warriors appears to have parallels elsewhere in Latin America. Baretta and Markoff (1978) demonstrate that as the processes of state centralization and capitalist development began to transform Latin American cattle frontiers in Venezuela, Argentina, and elsewhere, the part-time military specialists who had helped to conquer these territories became redefined as "barbarians" in the discourses of the state and the elite.

36. Local archives such as AMN, ASC, and AMCG are full of these arms permits.

37. AMCG contains many complaints against the *leva*. As documents in AMCG and AMN attest, peasants would sometimes hide in the sierra or leave their pueblos for days in order to avoid forced conscription; district and municipal functionaries had trouble filling their quota of men for the federal army.

38. ATN, 1.71(06) file 75669; 1.24(06) file 17.

39. ATN, 1.71(06) file 75669.

40. AGCCA, file 24/434.

41. Ibid.

42. AMCG, box 19, May 20, 1889.

43. AMCG, box 23, July 23, 1891.

44. The same logic is evoked in Mexico today by PRI functionaries to justify electoral fraud. As one loyal PRIsta asked a friend, "How can the peasants vote when they can't even brush their teeth?"

45. AMCG contains many complaints against caciquismo that detail the abuses of these sultanistic strongmen.

46. Creel was a naturalized Mexican of American origins, son of a former U.S. consul in Chihuahua. He was the son-in-law and business partner of Luis Terrazas and the second-in-command of the Terrazas grand-family. After Luis Terrazas retired in 1903, Creel assumed the day-to-day supervision of the group's economic interests. Creel had excellent connections to the national oligarchy; he was a member of the Científicos, Díaz's coterie of "scientific" advisers. See Wasserman 1984:29–30.

47. Today elections serve much the same function; they are rituals designed to legitimate authority rather than the means of succession to office. Caciquismo is still alive and well in Chihuahua. Popular discontent with the electoral process has been particularly salient since the 1980s.

48. The historical reconstruction presented in the preceding paragraphs is based on numerous documents from AMN; AJMN; AIN; ANC; Registro Publico de la Propiedad, Ciudad Chihuahua (RPPC); Registro Publico de la Propiedad, Ciudad Guerrero (RPPG); AMCG; and AGCCA, as well as on oral history and ethnographic fieldwork. Information on household composition was obtained from local censuses. Much of the data on plot size were culled from tax records; because these are not wholly reliable, the average size of plots is a rough estimate.

49. The extension claimed by Santa Clara y Anexas is given in Enrique Müller's will, filed in RPPG, vol. VIII, no. 5, ff. p. 152, April 8, 1909.

50. I have extensive, in-depth documentation on Namiquipa's agrarian history. The information presented here comes from the following archives: AMCG, AMN, AJMN, ATN, RPPG, ANC, and AGCCA.

51. Bando de Teodoro de Croix, November 15, 1778, and letter, July 8, 1808, Francisco Vásquez to comandante general.

52. For example, see AMN, Namiquipa, May 15, 1903, José de la Luz Morales to municipal council.

53. This information was obtained from many documents, including peasant requests for land from the municipal council found in AMN.

54. Ibid.

55. Ibid.

56. Information on these conflicts comes from documents found in AMCG, AMN, and AJMN.

57. Torres was an outsider who had immigrated to Namiquipa after the end of the Apache wars. In 1889 the municipal council of Namiquipa accused Torres of embezzlement and forcibly removed him from his posts as municipal treasurer and schoolteacher. In 1892 the district judge sentenced him to two years of public works for insulting the justice of the peace of Namiquipa. From 1896 to 1897, Torres was municipal president, a post to which he was probably appointed by the Chihuahuan government. A group of Namiquipan peasants, many of them future revolutionaries, tried to depose him by getting the justice of the peace to arrest him on a charge of cattle rustling. Since Torres had the support of higher-level functionaries, the justice of the peace, Cornelio Espinosa, leader of Namiquipan resistance, was removed from office instead. Torres ran for municipal president in 1903 and lost the election to Reyes Ortiz. In 1904 the Creel administration forcibly removed Ortiz and replaced him with Torres.

58. AMN.

59. AMN, box 2, 1906 and 1907, lists of persons paying rent for municipal lands in Namiquipa.

60. AMCG, box 73 file 625, May 17, 1911, from Cenobio Varela, *jefe municipal* of Namiquipa (JMN) to JPG; AMN, box 3, October 8, 1907, unsigned letter, and April 28, 1906, JMN to JPG.

61. ATN, July 28, 1908, complaint from the peasants of Namiquipa to Porfirio Díaz, and report by Chihuahuan governor Enrique Creel, July 9, 1909; AMN, box 2-bis, December 27, 1904, complaint from the peasants of Namiquipa, transcribed to the JMN by the JPG.

62. Anuario Estadistico del Estado de Chihuahua, 1905–9.

63. AMN, box 4, land claim of Pedro Loya, adjudicated October 26, 1905; land claim of Victoriano Torres and partners, adjudicated August 22, 1906; land claim of José Casavantes, adjudicated December 24, 1906.

64. Anuario Estadistico.

65. For example, see AMN, box 3-bis, January 25, 1907, letter from the JPG to the JMN notifying the latter of the Chihuahuan government's approval of a contract between the municipal council of Namiquipa and José Casavantes for the cutting of timber in común repartimiento lands; for protest against this, see AMCG, box 56 file 508, November 22, 1906, JMN to JPG.

66. AMCG, box 59, October 8, 1907; my translation.

67. Both of these quotes are taken from an account written by Heriberto Frías, one of the federal officers who fought against the serrano rebels of Tomochi in 1892.

Chapter 6

1. Magonismo was a revolutionary movement with anarcho-syndicalist and radical liberal tendencies. Its main leaders, the middle-class Flores Magón brothers, began to publish their journal, *Regeneración*, in 1900, and by 1903 they had galvanized some popular support. In 1906 and 1908 the Magonistas tried to organize a general uprising in Mexico from their bases in the United States (where the movement's leaders had been exiled). However, they were unable to generate and coordinate sufficient popular support in Mexico. Moreover, their attempts to organize a revolution in Mexico were subverted by the repressive actions of the United States government, which collaborated with the Mexican regime to "decapitate" the movement. Since the Mexican Constitution of 1917 replicated and coopted many of the positions of the Magonista Liberal Party's 1906 platform, Magonismo has always been the object of historical attention. Its radical potential has been circumscribed through discursive strategies that have defined it as a "precursor" movement. In addition, the ideology of Magonismo is overtly "political" and has therefore been more readily intelligible to many investigators; the rhetoric of popular protest often (though not always) deploys a symbolic repertoire that is more removed from the experience and understanding of middle-class intellectuals.

2. This section is largely based on documents from AMCG.

3. AMCG, box 9 file 117, November 4, 1871.

4. The municipal president (PM) of Bachíniva writes in 1864 that he has not been able to organize the National Guard to fight against the French because the people have fled the pueblo (AMCG, box 8 file 99, June 17, 1864). According to Eligio Cisneros, who lived in Namiquipa in the 1860s, military recruiters were sent to the town to raise men to fight the French; the *vecinos* fled to the sierra in order to evade military service (Calzadíaz Barrera 1969:20–21). The Chihuahuan government had to resort to coercion in order to recruit serrano "volunteers" to fight the Porfirista rebels in 1876. See AMCG, box 11 file 144, December 2–5, 1876, for information on the failure to recruit "volunteers" in Namiquipa, Bachíniva, Temósachi, and Basúchil.

5. AMCG, box 10 file 122, August 4, 1871, secretaría de estado to JPG.

6. The documentation for this section is drawn from AMCG.

7. AMCG, box 7 file 82, April 25, 1858, PM Bachíniva to JPG.

8. AMCG, box 8 file 100, April 1866, "Colección de Actas de Adhesión al Supremo Gobierno del Estado de los Pueblos que se Habían Separado de la Obediencia de su Legítimo Gobierno."

9. AMCG, box 11 files 142, 144, contain documentation on serrano support for the Porfirista rebels.

10. AMCG, box 13 file 154, various documents.

11. AMCG, box 17 file 195, various documents.

12. This section is based on oral history and documents from AMCG, AMN, ASC, ATN, and AJMN.

13. Chávez was the cacique of San Isidro, as well as the head of the armed forces in charge of guarding the transport of precious metals in the sierra. Recall that Chávez had insulted and harassed the men of Tomochi and that his false reports to the government influenced the decision to send the federal army against the Tomochis. Chávez was known and hated by the majority of the serrano peasants.

14. *El Correo de Chihuahua*, February 26, 1908.

15. ANC, Protocolos de Namiquipa, 1896–1919, May 26, 1906.

16. AMN, May 29, 1908, F. M. Logan, administrator of the Hacienda de Santa Ana, to JMN. Ironically, the peasants' resistance was successful partly because in this instance they received the support of the cacique; the petty bourgeoisie was as interested as the peasantry in preventing hacendados from encroaching on community lands. Torres's ties of clientage to higher-level functionaries helped to secure an order directing Logan to move the fence back to its original position; AMN, November 4, 1908, JPG to JMN.

17. The discussion of serrano resistance between 1887 and 1910 is based on hundreds of documents from AMCG, AMN, ASC, and AGN, Ramo Manuel González Ramírez. For a narrative history of serrano armed struggle in the 1880s and 1890s, see Almada 1938. The synopsis of serrano involvement in the Revolution of 1910–20 is based on even more documents culled from AMCG; AMN; ASC; AJMN; AGN (various *ramos*); Biblioteca Nacional, Archivo Madero (BNAM); *secretaría de relaciones exteriores*, Archivo Histórico (SRE); Archivo Venustiano Carranza (AVC); United States National Archives (NA); on oral histories obtained in Namiquipa, from the Archivo de la Palabra (IAP), and from Rubén Osorio's collection; and on the written testimonies of serrano revolutionaries.

18. AGN, Ramo Manuel González Ramírez, vol. 8, pp. 124–27, November 1893.

19. Almada claims that rebels received support from Luis Terrazas and his allies from 1889 to 1892 (1938:12–20).

20. Colección Porfirio Díaz (CPD) l.41-c.7.16-d.339, f.154, September 5, 1889, Díaz to the governor of Oaxaca; translation A. Alonso and D. Nugent.

21. Ibid.

22. Bancroft Library, Silvestre Terrazas Collection (ST), MB-18, box 26 folder 8-C, Namiquipa, October 13, 1905.

23. ASC, box 6, December 4, 1910.

24. Although the records of the SCP were destroyed after the revolution, copies of the "certificates of possession" given out to peasants by this agrarian society can be found in AJN.

Chapter 7

1. This is not her real name. In order to protect people's identities, I have used real names only when these appear in archival documents or published sources.

2. For us these narratives require interpretation. That is, their symbolic content has to be unpacked, contextualized, and rearticulated in a scholarly idiom. I was unable to get any "exegesis" from Doña Aurora; that is, she was both unwilling and unable to restate the significance of her stories in my idiom. The meaning was clear to her, as it would be to any "native" listener. Doña Aurora was always impatient with stupidity. When I asked her what the story of the fetus meant, she asked me whether I knew what *obrar* (to defecate) signified.

3. As I found out from documents subsequently discovered in AMN, Victoriano Torres's allies did indeed appropriate the hoard of gold and silver objects and coins contained in the church's colonial altar.

4. Note that in this story it is the woman who mediates between this world and the next; her husband's dependence on her is tied to her ability as a woman to negotiate the relationship between the temporal and the otherworldly.

5. Indeed, as Gudeman points out, the church did not begin to permit marriage between co-parents until 1918 (1971:53).

6. The Spanish term is *lacra*, a sore or scab that is an index of illness; to be dishonored is to be diseased and to bear the signs of sickness.

7. Tax complaints in AMCG frequently cite this as a reason why peasants could not pay their "quotas."

8. According to Pitt-Rivers, the rebellion of the campesinos of Andalusía, Spain, was also prompted by a popular vision of the dominant classes' dishonorableness: "The term of respect towards a member of the ruling class became extended in *señoritismo* to mean the rule of corruption and social injustice" (1965: 72–73).

9. AGN, Ramo Manuel González Ramírez, vol. 8, pp. 123–25; my translation.

10. Native histories also recount this defilement and dishonoring of women. See Calzadíaz Barrera 1969; Duarte Morales 1968.

11. The Spanish is *riqueza almacenada*. An *almacén* is a storehouse. The verb *almacenar* means both to store and to hoard (Williams 1963). *Riqueza almacenada* evokes an image of crops produced by hacienda workers stored for sale as commodities; what workers produce through activity and sweat is appropriated and transformed into riqueza almacenada by the patron.

12. ATN, 1.24(06) file 3, March 17, 1865, peasants of Galeana complain about the alienation of their lands as baldíos to Enrique Müller; 1.21(06) file 516, December 24, 1869, and 1.21(06) file 520, complaints from peasants of Yepómera and Temósachi whose lands are being sold as baldíos; 1.29(06) file 48, February 8, 1900, Namiquipans ask that the Müllers respect the boundaries of their colonial land grant; 1.24(06) file 23, March 20, 1901, agrarian representative of

Namiquipa complains that foráneos are acquiring rights in the común repartimiento lands; July 28, 1908, peasants of Namiquipa complain that their lands are being sold under the umbrella of the 1905 Municipal Land Law; 1.29(06) file 45, peasants of Cruces complain that their lands are being sold to outsiders as baldíos; Janos file, complaints 1908 and May 5, 1910, by Porfirio Talamantes and peasants that land is being sold to strangers under rubric of 1905 Municipal Land Law. AMN, box 1-D, May 1, 1894, from municipal council of Namiquipa to Chihuahuan government, complaining about the alienation of the community's lands to the Müllers; March 21, 1895, statement on land question by municipal council. All subsequent quotes from these ocursos are my translations. Other agrarian complaints can be found in AMCG.

13. AMN, March 21, 1895, "Agreement" (Acuerdo) of the municipal council of Namiquipa.

14. Significantly, the agrarian complaints of peasants from the one-time military colony of Fronteras, Sonora, deploy the same idiom as those from Chihuahua; moreover, members of a rural petty bourgeoisie were also key agents in the expropriation of the lands of the peasants of Fronteras; see, e.g., AGN, Ramo Manuel González Ramírez, October 14, 1893, vol. 8, pp. 110–11. Not surprisingly, Fronteras was also a revolutionary pueblo.

15. The Spanish term is *vecino*, which means both an inhabitant of a locality, a neighbor, as well as a member of a community of persons. *Vecino* has the same double sense as *pueblo*, which conflates the locality with the corporate group; *pueblo* means both town and people.

16. ATN, 1.24(06) file 3, March 17, 1865.

17. ATN, July 28, 1908.

18. AMN, May 1, 1894; my emphasis.

19. ATN, 1.24(06) file 3, March 17, 1865.

20. ATN, 1.24(06) file 23, Namiquipa, March 20, 1901.

21. ATN, July 28, 1908.

22. ATN, file de Janos, May 5, 1910; the peasants of Janos, Galeana District, protest against the municipal administration's charging of rent for use of ejido land and for use of water, pasture, and timber.

23. ATN, July 28, 1908.

24. ATN, 1908 Namiquipa file, Chihuahua, July 9, 1909, Enrique C. Creel's response to a request by the *secretaría de fomento* of Mexico to inform on the agrarian history and rights of Namiquipa; the adjective "monstrous" originally appears in an 1893 report of the Chihuahuan *secretaría de gobierno*, which Creel transcribes in full.

25. These can be found in AMCG.

26. Disputes in which *mantenido* is used to defame a man's honor can be found in AJMN.

27. There has been very little research on Chihuahuan haciendas, and information on the relations of workers with administrators and owners is negligible; I base these remarks on the documentation I have encountered.

28. This story was told to us by his nephew.

29. AJMN, May 30, 1907, Criminal contra Valerio y Abraham Ontiveros por lesiones.

30. AMN, June 1, 1909, from the administrator of Santa Clara to the JMN.

31. Bernardo de Gálvez, circa 1790, "Noticias y reflexiones sobre la guerra que se tiene con los indios Apaches en las Provincias de la Nueva España," University of Arizona microfilm no. 71; no author appears on the original manuscript, but Mártinez Caraza 1983:76ff cites portions of the same text and attributes it to Bernardo de Gálvez; my translation.

32. This and the following quotes are my translations of Torres's remarks to the JPG, formulated in response to the Namiquipans' complaints against him; AMCG, box 53 file 487, March 4, 1905.

33. AMCG, box 39 file 361, December 27, 1898, secretaría de estado to JPG, transcription of two complaints against caciquismo from the Bachinivans; my translation.

34. See Olea Arias 1961 for his account of his collaboration with the Magonistas and of his subsequent arrest, imprisonment, and "martyrdom." Information on the trial of the Magonista revolutionaries can be found in *El Correo de Chihuahua*, January 8 and 14, 1907; the Magonistas were defined as bandits by the regime, and their defense hinged precisely on establishing that they were not bandits but patriots with a political plan that would lead to the real progress of Mexico.

35. The information presented here and in the paragraphs that follow was taken from numerous complaints presented in writing to the JPG, Urbano Zea, in 1907 by the Bachinivense men who were the privileged objects of Barray's and Galaviz's tactics of terror and torture; Galaviz's self-justification is also included; AMCG, box 58 file 529, March 1907.

36. AMN, February 24, 1905, transcription of a December 30, 1904, complaint sent by the JPG to the JMN.

37. AMCG, box 39 file 361, December 27, 1898.

38. AMCG, box 58 file 529, March 1907.

39. Ibid.

40. AMN, February 24, 1905.

41. These symbolic correspondences are clearly established in the political poetry of the Bachinivense revolutionary leader Heliodoro Olea Arias; for an analysis of the poetic structure of one of these poems, see Alonso 1982.

42. AMN, February 24, 1905.

43. AMCG, box 39 file 361, December 27, 1898.

44. Torres's marriage to María Gutiérrez is not registered in the ecclesiastical records of Namiquipa; he either found a cooperative priest elsewhere or he legitimated his union with his co-mother purely through civil law.

45. It is difficult to gauge from state archives exactly what this charismatic folk Catholicism was like because, as Chávez points out, official sources misrepresented and distorted the Tomochis' ideology. Why were Urrea's teachings assimilated by the Tomochis and not other serranos? Contingent factors appear to have played a key role: (1) Tomochi did not have a resident priest for many years, and a folk Catholicism that differed from official doctrine had already developed; (2) the priests who visited Tomochi from time to time were corrupt, and instead of inspiring local respect for the clergy, they alienated the people; for the Tomochis, the priests became identified with the caciques.

46. Heriberto Frías, it will be recalled, was one of the federal officers who fought against the Tomochi rebels in 1892. This quote is taken from his own account of his experiences.

47. Nellie Campobello was a Chihuahuan woman who experienced the events of 1910–20 as a child. This quote is taken from her account of the Villista movement in Chihuahua.

48. AMCG, box 39 file 361, December 27, 1898.

49. Ibid.

50. The word is *paisanos*, and Cisneros is using it to refer to serranos only, not Mexicans as a whole.

Chapter 8

1. The use of *negotiate* "in the sense of 'tackle successfully' (a fence or other obstacle or difficulty) originated in the hunting field," and was first cited in 1862; in Fowler's opinion, *negotiate* "implies a special need for skill and care" (1965: 386).

2. AJMN, box 6, October 15, 1909, Pedro García demands that his wife return home or that she be subjected to judicial deposit.

3. AJMN, box 2, September 10, 1891, Criminal contra José Ornelas.

4. *Pasante* or *passant* is used in Mexico to signify someone who has not yet received their university degree. Raquel Rubio Goldsmith has told me that *pasante* can have a pejorative sense, signifying someone who is not worth much, who tries to pass him or herself off as the professional he or she is not. In the context of this case, *pasante* is insulting because it signifies that Ornelas is not really an hombre. This was also Raquel Rubio Goldsmith's interpretation of the meaning of *pasante* in this context; I thank her for her input.

5. Information on her hijos naturales comes from AIN records and AMN censuses.

6. Art. 509, Código Penal para el Distrito Federal y la Baja California Sobre

Delitos de Fuero Comun y Para Toda la República Sobre Delitos Contra la Federación, December 7, 1871, reproduced in Dublan and Lozano, vol. XI, p. 567.

7. AJMN, October 24, 1892, Criminal contra José Ornelas y Soledad Frías por Lesiones.

8. This is a localism unusual elsewhere in Latin America.

9. Art. 168 of the 1871 Código Penal.

10. AJMN, conciliaciones, March 3, 1898. I was unable to find any archival records in the Juzgado de Letras, so I do not know what the outcome was.

11. I have found no cases in which women were permanently injured or killed. However, a few women stated that their husbands threatened to kill them, and in one instance a drunken husband shot at his wife and missed.

12. See Arts. 39–43 and 534–35, 1871 Código Penal.

13. AJMN, box 3, April 19, 1897, Criminal contra Margarito Ramírez por Golpes a Su Esposa, Isidora Burciaga.

14. See Art. 41, 1871 Código Penal.

15. Isabel Iturrales against Trinindad Flores for adultery with her husband, Blas Camarena.

16. June 8, 1897, Conciliación, María de la Luz Dominguez de Rivera.

17. AJMN, February 28, 1907, Criminal contra Calixtro Marquez por lesiones.

18. AJMN, box 6, July 20, 1910, Criminal contra Romulo Trillo por lesiones a su esposa, Manuela Cano.

19. Divorce did not suspend the marriage tie, only some of its obligations, and in practice was a separation of bed and board; see arts. 239–76, Código Civil para el Distrito Federal y la Baja California, December 13, 1870, reproduced in Dublan and Lozano, vol. XI, p. 201.

20. Box 1, April 7, 1890, case involving María Luisa Ivarra de Ivarra, forwarded by the Juez Rural de la Hacienda de Providencia.

21. July 3, 1904, Criminal contra Jesús M. Gutierrez por lesiones.

Afterword

1. The term is Renato Rosaldo's (1987a).

2. This is not his real name. In order to protect people's identities, I have used their real names only when these appear in archival or published sources.

BIBLIOGRAPHY

A Note on Sources

This book is based on knowledge acquired through ethnographic fieldwork, the collection of oral histories, archival research, and work with other primary sources such as newspapers, published documents, and contemporaneous accounts. Fieldwork and archival research in Mexico were conducted in collaboration with Daniel Nugent between June 1983 and October 1985. The bulk of this period was spent in the pueblo of Namiquipa, Chihuahua, Mexico. In addition, I did follow-up research in Namiquipa in July and August 1986 and during the summer of 1989.

The Archivo Municipal of Namiquipa had been partially organized by archivists from the Archivo General de la Nación. Daniel Nugent and I finished putting it into order with the help of local high school students, whose participation in the project of archival rescue was authorized by the director of the local high school and supervised by Professor Colmenero. The Archivo Judicial and the Archivo Ejidal of Namiquipa were completely organized by us with the aid of local high school students. With the cooperation and assistance of the municipal president of Namiquipa, Rafael Ruiz Barrera, room was found for these archives in a municipal office.

Archival research in the United States was conducted in December 1985, and archival sources available on microfilm were also examined in subsequent months. I list all the archives we worked in, although not all of them are cited in the text, since the arguments advanced here are informed by all the sources consulted.

In the text I have cited individual sources where this is warranted—because the source is of exceptional interest or because there are few sources on the topic or because the point being documented is particularly contentious. I have also provided more general references to particular archives or collections of documents. I have done this because the information for many points is actually spread out over numerous documents, and citing them all would have resulted in an exceptionally cumbersome text.

The extracts of archival material appearing in the text have been translated by me unless otherwise stated in a note.

Archives and Collections of Primary Sources
Mexico

Chihuahua, Chihuahua
  Archivo General de Notarías (ANC)
  Centro de Investigación y Documentación del Estado de Chihuahua (CIDECH)
  Registro Público de la Propiedad (RPPC)
Cruces, Namiquipa
  Archivo Seccional (ASC)
Guerrero City, Chihuahua
  Archivo Municipal (AMCG)
  Registro Público de la Propiedad (RPPG)
Namiquipa, Chihuahua
  Archivo de la Brigada de Educación Tecnológica Agropecuaria #331 (Secretaría de Educación Pública)
  Archivo de la Iglesia (AIN)
  Archivo Ejidal
  Archivo Judicial (AJMN)
  Archivo Municipal (AMN)
Parral, Chihuahua
  Archivo de Parral
Gómez Palacio, Durango
  Archivo General del Cuerpo Consultativo Agrario (AGCCA)
Mexico City
  Archivo de la Palabra, Instituto de Investigaciones Dr. José María Luis Mora (IAP)
  Archivo General de la Nación (AGN)
    Comisión Nacional Agraria
    Gobernación
    Incorporados
    Manuel González Ramírez
    Presidentes
    Presidios y Cárceles
    Provincias Internas
    Resoluciones Presidenciales
    Revolución
  Archivo Venustiano Carranza, CONDUMEX (AVC)

Biblioteca de la Secretaría de Hacienda y Crédito Público (Lerdo de Tejada)
Biblioteca e Hemeroteca Nacional, UNAM
   Archivo Jacinto B. Treviño
   Newspaper Collection
   Rare Book Collection
Biblioteca Nacional
   Archivo Franciscano
   Archivo Francisco I. Madero (BNAM)
   Fondo Reservado
Colección Porfirio Díaz, Ibero-Americana (CPD)
Secretaría de Reforma Agraria
   Archivo General
   Archivo Histórico, Sección Terrenos Nacionales (ATN)
Secretaría de Relaciones Exteriores
   Archivo Histórico (SRE)

United States

Berkeley, California
   Silvestre Terrazas Collection, Bancroft Library, University of California (courtesy of F. Katz)
Carlisle, Pennsylvania
   U.S. Military History Institute Collections
Deming, New Mexico
   Luna County Courthouse Records
El Paso, Texas
   El Paso Public Library
   Special Collections, University of Texas
Suitland, Maryland
   Washington National Records Center
     Records of the Mexican and American Claims Commission
Tucson, Arizona
   Arizona Pioneer Historical Society Collection
   Documentary Relations of the Southwest, Arizona State Museum
   Special Collections, University of Arizona
Washington, D.C.
   United States National Archives
     Military Reference Branch
     State Department 812 Files
   Pershing Papers, Library of Congress

Other Unpublished Documents and Texts

"Bando de Teodoro de Croix," November 15, 1778, and accompanying letters. Courtesy of José Muñoz, Namiquipa, Chihuahua.
"Diary of Ignacio Licano." Courtesy of a Namiquipan who does not wish to be identified.
"Diary of Pedro Rascón y Tena." Courtesy of his relatives in Sonora.
"Grito de Dolores!" Play by José María Espinosa. Courtesy of Felix Sotelo, Ana Maldonado, and José María Espinosa, Jr., Namiquipa, Chihuahua.

Published Primary Sources Cited

Alessio Robles, Vito (ed.)
   1937   *Demostración del Vastísimo Obispado de la Nueva Vizacaya—1765,* Pedro Tamarón y Romeral. Mexico: Antigua Librería Robredo.
Barri, León, Jr., ed.
   1942   "Correspondencia Colonial." *Boletín de la Sociedad Chihuahuense de Estudios Históricos* 4(4):149–55.
Chávez Calderón, Plácido
   1964   *La Defensa de Tomochi.* Mexico: Editorial Jus.
Chávez, Carlos (ed.)
   1939   "Clamor de los Papigochis del Siglo XVIII por los Constantes Ataques de los Apaches." *Boletín de la Sociedad Chihuahuense de Estudios Históricos* 1(12):399–405.
Codigo de la Reforma o Colección de Leyes, Decretos y Supremas Ordenes Expedidas desde 1856 hasta 1861. Mexico, Imprenta Literaria, 1861.
Coues, Elliot (ed.)
   1895   *The Expeditions of Zebulon M. Pike,* vol. 2. New York: Francis P. Harper; London: Simkin, Marshall, Hamilton, Kent and Co.
El Correo de Chihuahua, 1899–1908. Chihuahua, Mexico.
Duarte Morales, Teodosio
   1968   *El Rugir del Cañón.* Juárez, Chihuahua.
   n.d. *Villa y Pershing: Memorias de la Revolución.* Juárez, Chihuahua.
Dublan, Manuel, and José María Lozano
   1879   *Legislación Mexicana o Colección Completa de las Disposiciones Legislativas Expedidas Desde la Independencia de la Republica.* Mexico: Imprenta del Comercio.
Escudero, José Agustín
   1834   *Noticias Estadisticas del Estado de Chihuahua.* Mexico: Imprenta del Puente del Palacio y Flamencos #1.
   1839   *Observaciones Sobre el Estado Actual del Departamento de Chihuahua y los Medios de Ponerlo al Cubierto de las Incursiones de los Bárbaros.* Mexico: Impreso por Juan Ojeda.

Florescano, Enrique, and Isabel Gil Sánchez
  1976   *Descripciones Económicas de Nueva España: Provincias del Norte, 1790–1814.* Mexico: SEP-INAH
Frías, Heriberto
  1983   *Tomochic.* Mexico: Editorial Porrua.
González Flores, Enrique, and Francisco R. Almada (eds.)
  1952   *Informe de Hugo de O'Conor Sobre el Estado de las Provincias Internas del Norte, 1771–1776.* Mexico: Editorial Cultura.
Hernández Rodríguez, Pedro (ed.)
  1939   "Bando Colonial 1728." *Boletín de la Sociedad Chihuahuense de Estudios Históricos* 1(12): 395ff.
Humboldt, Alejandro de
  1966   *Ensayo Político Sobre el Reino de la Nueva España.* Mexico: Editorial Porrua.
Kinnaird, Lawrence (ed.)
  1958   *The Frontiers of New Spain: Nicolás de Lafora's Description, 1766–1768.* Berkeley: The Quivira Society.
Lozano, Jesús J. (ed.)
  1949   "Vida y costumbres de los Indios Salvajes que Habitaban el Estado de Chihuahua a Mediados del Siglo XIX" (General Emilio Lamberg's report, September 27, 1851). *Boletín de la Sociedad Chihuahuense de Estudios Históricos* 6: 272–81.
Memoria del Secretario de Estado y del Despacho de Guerra y Marina. Mexico, 1851.
Matson, Daniel S., and Albert H. Schroeder (eds.)
  1957   "Cordero's Description of the Apache." *New Mexico Historical Review* 32(3): 335–56.
Olea Arias, Heleodoro
  1961   *Apuntes Históricos de la Revolución de 1910–1911.* Chihuahua: Impresora AIFFER.
Reed, John
  1969   *Insurgent Mexico.* New York: International Publishers.
Terrazas, Joaquin
  1905   *Memorias del Señor Coronel Don Joaquín Terrazas.* Juárez, Chihuahua: Imprenta de "El Agricultor Mexicano."
Thomas, Alfred B. (ed.)
  1941   *Teodoro de Croix and the Northern Frontier of New Spain, 1776–1783.*
Worcester, Donald F. (ed.)
  1951   *Instructions for Governing the Interior Provinces of New Spain, 1786, by Bernardo de Gálvez.* Berkeley: The Quivira Society.

Published Oral Histories Cited

Ball, Eve
   1970   *In the Days of Victorio*. Tucson: University of Arizona Press.
   1980   *Indeh*. Provo, Utah: Brigham Young University Press.
Calzadíaz Barrera, Alberto
   1969   *Víspera de la Revolución: (Abuelo Cisneros)*. Mexico: Editorial Patria.

Secondary Sources Cited

Abelove, Henry, M. A. Barale, and D. M. Halperin (eds.)
   1993   *The Lesbian and Gay Studies Reader*. New York: Routledge.
Abrams, Philip
   1982   *Historical Sociology*. Ithaca, N.Y.: Cornell UniversityPress.
   1988   "Notes on the Difficulty of Studying the State." *Journal of Historical Sociology* 1(1):58–89.
Aguilar Camín, Héctor
   1979   *La Frontera Nómada*. Mexico: Siglo XXI.
Alegría, Juana A.
   1978   *Sicología de las Mexicanas*. Mexico: Editorial Diana.
Almada, Francisco
   1938   *La Rebelión de Tomochi*. Chihuahua.
   1939   "Los Apaches." *Boletín de la Sociedad Chihuahuense de Estudios Históricos* 2(1):5–15.
   1955   *Resumen de la Historia del Estado de Chihuahua*. Mexico: Libros Mexicanos.
   1964   *La Revolución en el Estado de Chihuahua*. 2 vols. Chihuahua: Biblioteca del Instituto Nacional de Estudios Históricos de la Revolución Mexicana.
   1980   *Gobernadores del Estado de Chihuahua*. Chihuahua: Centro Librero La Prensa.
   1982   *Diccionario de Historia, Geografía y Biografía de Chihuahua*. Chihuahua: Gobierno del Estado.
Alonso, Ana María
   1982   "Return to a Subverted Eden: An Analysis of an Invocation to the Fathers of the *Patria*." Manuscript.
   1986   "The Hermeneutics of History: Class Struggle and Revolution in the Chihuahuan *Sierra*." Manuscript.
   1988   "Gender, Ethnicity and the Constitution of Subjects: Accommodation, Resistance and Revolution on the Chihuahuan Frontier." Ph.D. dissertation, University of Chicago.
   1988a "The Effects of Truth: Re-presentations of the Past and the Imagining of Community." *Journal of Historical Sociology* 1(1):33–57.

1988b "'Progress' as Disorder and Dishonor: Discourses of *Serrano* Resistance." *Critique of Anthropology* 8(1):13-33.

1988c "U.S. Military Intervention, Revolutionary Mobilization and Popular Ideology in the Chihuahuan *Sierra*, 1916-1917." In *Rural Revolt in Mexico and U.S. Intervention*. Daniel Nugent, ed. La Jolla: Center for U.S.-Mexican Studies.

1992a "Work and *Gusto*: Gender and Re-Creation in a North Mexican Pueblo." In *Workers' Expressions: Beyond Accommodation and Resistance*. John Calagione, Doris Francis, and Daniel Nugent, eds. Albany: SUNY Press.

1992b "Gender, Power and Historical Memory: Discourses of *Serrano* Resistance." In *Feminists Theorize the Political*. Judith Butler and Joan Scott, eds. New York: Routledge.

1994 "The Politics of Space, Time and Substance: State Formation, Nationalism and Ethnicity." *Annual Review of Anthropology* 23:379-406.

Anderson, Benedict

1983 *Imagined Communities*. London: Verso/NLB.

Anuario Estadistico del Estado de Chihuahua, 1905-1909. Chihuahua: Imprenta del Gobierno, 1906, 1908, 1909, 1910, 1913.

Anzaldúa, Gloria

1987 *Borderlands/La Frontera: The New Mestiza*. San Francisco: Spinsters/Aunt Lute.

Anzaldúa, Gloria (ed.)

1990 *Making Face, Making Soul/Haciendo Caras: Creative and Critical Perspectives by Women of Color*. San Francisco: Aunt Lute.

Appadurai, Arjun

1986 "Theory in Anthropology." *Comparative Studies in Society and History* 28(2):356-61.

Appiah, K. A.

1990 "Racisms." In *Anatomy of Racism*. David T. Goldberg, ed. Minneapolis: University of Minnesota Press.

Arrom, Silvia M.

1985 *The Women of Mexico City, 1790-1857*. Stanford: Stanford University Press.

Bailey, David C.

1978 "Revisionism and the Recent Historiography of the Mexican Revolution." *Hispanic American Historical Review* 58(1): 62-79.

Bakhtin, M. M.

1981 *The Dialogic Imagination*. Michael Holquist, ed. Austin: University of Texas Press.

Bannon, John Francis

1970 *The Spanish Borderlands Frontier, 1513-1821*. New York: Holt, Rinehart, and Winston.

Barnes, Thomas, Thomas Naylor, and Charles Polzer
  1981   *Northern New Spain: A Research Guide.* Tucson: University of Arizona Press.
Barretta, Silvio, R. Duncan, and John Markoff
  1978   "Civilization and Barbarism: Cattle Frontiers in Latin America." *Comparative Studies in Society and History* 20(4):587–620.
Barth, Fredrik
  1969   "Introduction." In *Ethnic Groups and Boundaries: The Social Organization of Culture Difference.* F. Barth, ed. Boston: Little, Brown.
Barthes, Roland
  1972   *Mythologies.* New York: Hill and Wang.
Benjamin, Thomas, and Mark Wasserman (eds.)
  1990   *Provinces of the Revolution: Essays on Regional Mexican History, 1910–1929.* Albuquerque: University of New Mexico Press.
Blok, Anton
  1984   "Rams and Billy-Goats: A Key to the Mediterranean Code of Honour." In *Religion, Power and Protest in Local Communities.* Eric R. Wolf and Hubert H. Lehmann, eds. New York: Mouton Publishers.
Bommes, Michael and Patrick Wright
  1982   " 'Charms of Residence': The Public and the Past." In *Making Histories.* Centre for Contemporary Cultural Studies. Minneapolis: University of Minnesota Press.
Boxer, Charles R.
  1975   *Mary and Misogyny: Women in Iberian Expansion Overseas, 1415–1815.* London: Duckworth.
Brading, D. A. (ed.)
  1980   *Caudillo and Peasant in the Mexican Revolution.* New York: Cambridge University Press.
Brittan, Arthur
  1989   *Masculinity and Power.* Oxford: Basil Blackwell.
Brittan, Arthur, and Mary Maynnard
  1984   *Sexism, Racism and Oppression.* Oxford: Basil Blackwell.
Brooke-Rose, Christine
  1986   "Woman as a Semiotic Object." In *The Female Body in Western Culture.* Susan Rubin Suleiman, ed. Cambridge, Mass.: Harvard University Press.
Butler, Judith, and Joan W. Scott (eds.)
  1992   *Feminists Theorize the Political.* New York: Routledge.
Cain, M.
  1983   "Gramsci, the State and the Place of Law." In *Legality, Ideology and the State.* D. Sugarman, ed. London: Academic Press.
Calzadíaz Barrera, Alberto
  1967   *Hechos Reales de la Revolución,* vol. 2. Mexico: Editorial Patria.

1972   *Hechos Reales de la Revolución: (El Fin de la División del Norte)*, vol. 3. Mexico: Editorial Patria.

1977   *Hechos Reales de la Revolución: Por Que Villa Ataco Columbus? Intriga Internacional*, vol. 6. Mexico: Editorial Patria.

1979   *Hechos Reales de la Revolución*, vol. 1. Mexico: Editorial Patria.

1980   *Hechos Reales de la Revolución: Muerte del Centauro: Villa Contra Todo y Contra Todos: El Fin del Centauro*, vol. 7. Mexico: Editorial Patria.

1982   *Hechos Reales de la Revolución: (General Felipe Angeles)*, vol. 8. Mexico: Editorial Patria.

Campbell, Federico

1985   "Villa, El Gran Desconocido; Su Estilo de Lucha Rompió Moldes Convencionales." *Proceso* 472:6ff.

Campobello, Nellie

1940   *Apuntes Sobre la Vida Militar de Francisco Villa*. Mexico: E.D.I.A.P.S.A.

Carby, Hazel V.

1985   " 'On the Threshold of Woman's Era': Lynching, Empire, and Sexuality in Black Feminist Theory." *Critical Inquiry* 12(1):262-77.

Cardoso, Ciro (ed.)

1980   *México en el Siglo XIX (1821-1910)*. Mexico: Editorial Nueva Imagen.

Carr, Barry

1973   "Las Peculiaridades del Norte Mexicano: Ensayo de Interpretación." *Historia Mexicana* 22(3):321-46.

1980   "Recent Regional Studies of the Mexican Revolution." *Latin American Research Review* 15(1):3-15.

Chance, John K.

1978   *Raza y Clases de la Oaxaca Colonial*. Mexico: Instituto Nacional Indigenista.

Chatarjee, Partha

1993   *The Nation and Its Fragments: Colonial and Postcolonial Histories*. Princeton, N.J.: Princeton University Press.

Chávez, José Carlos

1939   "Extinción de los Apaches—Victorio." *Boletín de la Sociedad Chihuahuense de Estudios Históricos* 1(10):336ff.

Chevalier, François

1963   "The North Mexican Hacienda." In *The New World Looks at Its History*. Archibald Lewis and Thomas McGann, eds. Austin: University of Texas Press.

Coatsworth, John

1978   "Obstacles to Economic Growth in Nineteenth Century Mexico." *American Historical Review* 83(1):80-100.

Cockcroft, James D.

1968   *Intellectual Precursors of the Mexican Revolution 1900-1913*. Austin: University of Texas Press.

Cohn, Bernard
  1981   "Anthropology and History in the 1980s." *The Journal of Interdisciplinary History* 12(1):227-52.
Cohn, Bernard, and Nicholas Dirks
  1987   "Beyond the Fringe: The Nation State, Colonialism and the Technologies of Power." Manuscript.
Collier, Jane, and Sylvia Junko Yanagisako (eds.)
  1987   *Gender and Kinship: Essays Toward a Unified Analysis.* Stanford: Stanford University Press.
Comaroff, Jean
  1983   "Bodily Reform as Historical Practice: The Semantics of Resistance in Modern South Africa." Manuscript prepared for *International Journal of Psychology* 18(2).
  1985   *Body of Power, Spirit of Resistance: The Culture and History of a South African People.* Chicago: University of Chicago Press.
Comaroff, John L.
  1992   "Of Totemism and Ethnicity." In *Ethnography and the Historical Imagination.* John and Jean Comaroff. Boulder, Colo.: Westview Press.
Comaroff, John L., and Jean Comaroff
  1987   "The Madman and the Migrant: Work and Labor in the Historical Consciousness of a South African People." *American Ethnologist* 14(2): 191-209.
Connell, R. W.
  1987   *Gender and Power.* Stanford: Stanford University Press.
  1990   "The State, Gender and Sexual Politics: Theory and Appraisal." Manuscript accepted for publication by *Theory and Society.*
Córdova, Arnaldo
  1973   *La Ideología de la Revolución Mexicana.* Mexico: Siglo XXI.
Corrigan, Philip
  n.d. "State Formation (Entry)" Manuscript.
Corrigan, Philip and Derek Sayer
  1985   *The Great Arch: English State Formation as Cultural Revolution.* Oxford: Basil Blackwell.
Craig, Ann
  1983   *The First Agraristas.* Berkeley: University of California Press.
Creel, Enrique C.
  1928   *El Estado de Chihuahua.* Mexico: Tip. El Progreso.
Das, Veena
  1994   *Critical Events.* Delhi: Oxford University Press.
Davin, Anna
  1978   "Imperialism and Motherhood." *History Workshop* 5:9-66.
Davis, Angela Y.
  1981   *Women, Race and Class.* New York: Vintage Books.

Deal, D.
  1975   "Peasant Revolts and Resistance in the Modern World: A Comparative View." *Journal of Contemporary Asia* 5(4):414-45.
de la Garza, Luis Alberto, et al.
  1986   *Evolución del Estado Mexicano*, vol. 1. Mexico: Ediciones el Caballito.
de La Peña, Guillermo
  1980   *Herederos de Promesas: Agricultura, Política y Ritual en Los Altos de Morelos*. Mexico: Ediciones de la Casa Chata.
de Lauretis, Teresa
  1986   "Feminist Studies/Critical Studies: Issues, Terms, and Contexts." In *Feminist Studies/Critical Studies*. Teresa de Lauretis, ed. Bloomington: Indiana University Press.
  1987   *Technologies of Gender*. Bloomington: Indiana University Press.
DePalo, William, Jr.
  1973   "The Establisment of the Nueva Vizcaya Militia During the Administration of Teodoro de Croix, 1776-1782." *New Mexico Historical Review* 48(3):223-49.
di Leonardo, Micaela (ed.)
  1991   *Gender at the Crossroads of Knowledge: Anthropology in the Postmodern Era*. Berkeley: University of California Press.
Douglas, Mary
  1966   *Purity and Danger*. Harmondsworth: Penguin Books.
Dubisch, Jill (ed.)
  1986   *Gender and Power in Rural Greece*. Princeton, N.J.: Princeton University Press.
Eagleton, Terry
  1991   *Ideology: An Introduction*. London: Verso.
Elías, Emilio, Ing.
  1950   "El Terrible Veneno, Táctica Guerrera de los Indios Apaches." *Boletín de la Sociedad Chihuahuense de Estudios Históricos* 7(2):392-93.
Elshtain, Jean
  1987   *Women and War*. New York: Basic Books.
Enloe, Cynthia
  1989   *Bananas, Beaches and Bases: Making Feminist Sense of International Politics*. Berkeley: University of California Press.
Falcón, Romana
  1984   *Revolución y Caciquismo: San Luis Potosí, 1910-1938*. Mexico: El Colegio de México.
Faulk, Odie B.
  1979   "The Presidio: Fortress or Farce?" In *New Spain's Far Northern Frontier*. David Weber, ed. Albuquerque: University of New Mexico Press.
Florescano, Enrique
  1969   "Colonización, Ocupación del Suelo y 'Frontera' en el Norte de

la Nueva España, 1521-1750." In *Tierras Nuevas*. Alvaro Jara, ed. Mexico: El Colegio de México.

Foucault, Michel

1977   *Discipline and Punish: The Birth of the Prison*. New York: Vintage Books, Random House.

1978   *The History of Sexuality*. New York: Vintage Books, Random House.

1980   *Power/Knowledge: Selected Interviews and Other Writings, 1972-1977*. Colin Gordon, ed. New York: Pantheon Books.

1982   "The Subject and Power." In *Michel Foucault: Beyond Structuralism and Hermeneutics*. Hubert L. Dreyfus and Paul Rabinow, eds. Chicago: University of Chicago Press.

1986   *The Use of Pleasure*. New York: Vintage Books, Random House.

Fowler, H. W.

1965   *A Dictionary of Modern English Usage*. New York: Oxford University Press.

Fowler-Salamini, Heather

1978   *Agrarian Radicalism in Veracruz, 1920-1938*. Lincoln: University of Nebraska Press.

1993   "The Boom in Regional Studies of the Mexican Revolution: Where Is It Leading?" *Latin American Research Review* 28(2):175-90.

Fox, Geoffrey

1973   "Honor, Shame and Women's Liberation in Cuba." In *Female and Male in Latin America*. Ann Pescatello, ed. Pittsburgh: University of Pittsburgh Press.

Franco, Jean

1989   *Plotting Women: Gender and Representation in Mexico*. New York: Columbia University Press.

Freud, Sigmund

1963   *Studies in Parapsychology*. Philip Rieff, ed. New York: Collier Books.

Friedrich, Paul

1965   "A Mexican Cacicazgo." *Ethnology* 4(2):190-209.

1977   *Agrarian Revolt in a Mexican Village*. Chicago: University of Chicago Press.

1981   *Agrarian Leadership and Violence in Mexico*. Chicago: Center for Latin-American Studies.

1986   *The Princes of Naranja*. Austin: University of Texas Press.

Fuentes, Carlos

1978   *Tiempo Mexicano*. Mexico: Cuadernos de Joaquín Mortiz.

Garciadiego, Javier

1986   "El Estado Moderno y la Revolución Mexicana (1910-1920)." In *Evolución del Estado Mexicano*, vol 2. Javier Garciadiego et al., eds. Mexico: Ediciones el Caballito.

Gerhard, Peter
   1982   *The North Frontier of New Spain.* Princeton, N.J.: Princeton University Press.
Ghani, Ashraf
   1987   "A Conversation With Eric Wolf." *American Ethnologist* 14(2):346–66.
Giddens, Anthony
   1992   *The Transformation of Intimacy: Sexuality, Love and Eroticism in Modern Societies.* Stanford: Stanford University Press.
Gilliam, Angela
   1988   "Telltale Language: Race, Class, and Inequality in Two Latin American Towns." In *Anthropology for the Nineties: Introductory Readings.* Johnetta B. Cole, ed. New York: The Free Press.
Gilly, Adolfo
   1971   *La Revolución Interrumpida.* Mexico: Ediciones el Caballito.
Gilman, Sander L.
   1985   "Black Bodies, White Bodies: Toward an Iconography of Female Sexuality in Late Nineteenth-Century Art, Medicine, and Literature." *Critical Inquiry* 12(1): 204–42.
Gilmore, David (ed.)
   1987   *Honor and Shame and the Unity of the Mediterranean.* Washington: American Anthropological Association, special publication 22.
González, Carlos
   1988   "El Villismo Frente al Problema Agrario." *Cuadernos del Norte* 1(3): 18–25.
González, Luis
   1974   *San José de Gracia, Mexican Village in Transition.* Austin: University of Texas Press.
Gramsci, Antonio
   1971   *Selections from the Prison Notebooks.* Quintin Hoare and Geoffrey Nowell-Smith, eds. New York: International Publishers.
Griffen, William B.
   1979   *Indian Assimilation in the Franciscan Area of Nueva Vizcaya.* Tucson: University of Arizona Press.
Gudeman, Stephen
   1971   "The *Compadrazgo* as a Reflection of the Natural and Spiritual Person." *Proceedings of the Royal Anthropological Institute of Great Britain and Ireland for 1971,* 45–71.
Guha, Ranajit
   1982   "On Some Aspects of the Historiography of Colonial India." In *Subaltern Studies I.* Ranajit Guha, ed. Delhi: Oxford University Press.
   1983   *Elementary Aspects of Peasant Insurgency in Colonial India.* Delhi: Oxford University Press.

Gutiérrez, Ramón

1980   "Marriage, Sex and the Family: Social Change in Colonial New Mexico, 1690–1846." Ph.D. dissertation, University of Wisconsin.

1991   *When Jesus Came, the Corn Mothers Went Away: Marriage, Sexuality and Power in New Mexico, 1500–1846.* Stanford: Stanford University Press.

Hall, Stuart

1981   "Notes on Deconstructing 'the Popular.'" In *People's History and Socialist Theory.* Raphael Samuel, ed. London: Routledge and Kegan Paul.

1988   "The Toad in the Garden: Thatcherism Among the Theorists." In *Marxism and the Interpretation of Culture.* Cary Nelson and Lawrence Grossberg, eds. Urbana: University of Illinois Press.

Hamilton, Nora

1982   *The Limits of State Autonomy.* Berkeley: University of California Press.

Haraway, Donna

1986   "Primatology is Politics by Other Means." In *Feminist Approaches to Science.* Ruth Bleier, ed. New York: Pergamon Press.

1991   *Simians, Cyborgs and Women: The Reinvention of Nature.* New York: Routledge.

Hartmann, Heidi

1983   "Capitalism, Patriarchy, and Job-Segregation by Sex." In *The Signs Reader.* Elizabeth Abel and Emily K. Abel, eds. Chicago: University of Chicago Press.

Harvey, David

1989   *The Condition of Postmodernity.* Oxford: Basil Blackwell.

Henriques, Julian et al.

1984   *Changing the Subject: Psychology, Social Regulation and Subjectivities.* London: Methuen.

Herdt, Gilbert

1982   *Rituals of Manhood: Male Initiation in Papua New Guinea.* Berkeley: University of California Press.

Herzfeld, Michael

1985   *The Poetics of Manhood: Contest and Identity in a Cretan Mountain Village.* Princeton, N.J.: Princeton University Press.

Hobsbawm, Eric J.

1959   *Primitive Rebels.* New York: W. W. Norton.

Hobsbawm, Eric J., and Terrence Ranger (eds.)

1984   *The Invention of Tradition.* Cambridge: Cambridge University Press.

Holden, Robert

1984   "Warfare, Settlers and Settlement on the Northern Frontier of New Spain and Mexico." Manuscript.

hooks, bell
  1990   *Yearning: Race, Gender and Cultural Politics*. Boston: South End Press.
Hughes, Anne E.
  1935   *The Beginnings of Spanish Settlement in the El Paso District*. El Paso: El
          Paso Public Schools.
Huston, Nancy
  1986   "The Matrix of War: Mothers and Heroes." In *The Female Body in
          Western Culture*. Susan Rubin Suleiman, ed. Cambridge, Mass.: Har-
          vard University Press.
Jacobs, Ian
  1983   *Ranchero Revolt: The Mexican Revolution in Guerrero*. Austin: Univer-
          sity of Texas Press.
Jones, Okah L.
  1979   *Los Paisanos*. Norman: University of Oklahoma Press.
Jordán, Fernando
  1981   *Crónica de un País Bárbaro*. Chihuahua: Centro Librero La Prensa.
Joseph, Gilbert
  1980   "Caciquismo and the Revolution: Carillo Puerto in Yucatan." In *Cau-
          dillo and Peasant in the Mexican Revolution*. D. A. Brading, ed. New
          York: Cambridge University Press.
  1982   *Revolution From Without*. New York: Cambridge University Press.
  1988   "The United States, Feuding Elites and Rural Revolt in Yucatan." In
          Rural Revolt in Mexico and U.S. Intervention. Daniel Nugent, ed. La
          Jolla: Center for U.S.-Mexican Studies.
Joseph, Gilbert, and Daniel Nugent
  1994   "Popular Culture and State Formation in Revolutionary Mexico." In
          Everyday Forms of State Formation. G. Joseph and D. Nugent, eds.
          Durham, N.C.: Duke University Press.
Joseph, Gilbert, and Daniel Nugent (eds.)
  1994   *Everyday Forms of State Formation: Revolution and the Negotiation of
          Rule in Modern Mexico*. Durham, N.C.: Duke University Press.
Katz, Friedrich
  1974   "Labour Conditions on Porfirian Haciendas: Some Trends and Ten-
          dencies." *Hispanic American Historical Review* 54(1):1-47.
  1976a   *La Servidumbre Agraria en México en la Epoca Porfiriana*. Mexico:
          Era.
  1976b   "Peasants and the Mexican Revolution of 1910." In *Forging Nations: A
          Comparative View of Rural Ferment and Revolt*. Joseph Spielberg and
          Scott Whiteford, eds. East Lansing: Michigan State University Press.
  1977   *Pancho Villa y El Ataque a Columbus Nuevo Mexico*. Chihuahua:
          Regma.
  1979   "Pancho Villa: Reform Governor of Chihuahua." In *Essays on the*

Mexican Revolution: Revisionist Views of the Leaders. George W. Wolf-skill and Douglas W. Richmond, eds. Austin: University of Texas Press.

1980   "Pancho Villa, Peasant Movements and Agrarian Rebellion in Northern Mexico." In *Peasant and Caudillo in the Mexican Revolution.* D. A. Brading, ed. New York: Cambridge University Press.

1981   *The Secret War in Mexico.* Chicago: University of Chicago Press.

1986   "The Porfiriato." In *The Cambridge History of Latin America*, vol. 5. Leslie Bethell, ed. Cambridge: Cambridge University Press.

1988   "Rebellion and Revolution in Rural Mexico: Patterns of Victory and Defeat Since Pre-Colonial Times." In *Riot, Rebellion and Revolution: Rural Social Conflict in Mexico.* Friedrich Katz, ed. Princeton, N.J.: Princeton University Press.

Knight, Alan

1980   "Peasant and Caudillo in Revolutionary Mexico, 1910–1917." In *Caudillo and Peasant in the Mexican Revolution.* D. A. Brading, ed. New York: Cambridge University Press.

1986   *The Mexican Revolution.* 2 vols. Cambridge: Cambridge University Press.

Koreck, Maria Teresa

1986a   "The Fetishism of the Written Word: On Historical Monologues." Manuscript.

1986b   "Social Organization and Land Tenure in a Revolutionary Community in Northern Mexico: Cuchillo Parado, Chihuahua, 1865–1910." Manuscript.

1988   "Space and Revolution in Northeastern Chihuahua." In *Rural Revolt in Mexico and U.S. Intervention.* Daniel Nugent, ed. La Jolla: Center for U.S.-Mexican Studies.

Krauze, Enrique

1986   "Chihuahua, Ida y Vuelta." *Vuelta* 115.

Kristeva, Julia

1982   "Women's Time." In *Feminist Theory: A Critique of Ideology.* Nannerl O. Keohane et al., eds. Chicago: University of Chicago Press.

Kundera, Milan

1981   *The Book of Laughter and Forgetting.* Harmondsworth: Penguin Books.

Laclau, Ernesto, and Chantal Mouffe

1982   "Recasting Marxism: Hegemony and New Political Movements." *Socialist Review* 12(6):91–113.

Lattimore, Owen

1968   "The Frontier in History." In *Theory in Anthropology.* Robert Manners and David Kaplan, eds. Chicago: Aldine Publishing Co.

Lauria, Anthony

1963   " 'Respeto,' 'Relajo' and Inter-personal Relations in Puerto Rico." *Anthropological Quarterly* 37:53–67.

Leach, Edmund
  1959   "Magical Hair." *Journal of the Royal Anthropological Institute of Great Britain and Ireland* 88(2):147–64.
  1966   "Virgin Birth." *Proceedings of the Royal Anthropological Institute of Great Britain and Ireland for 1966, 39–49.*

Lecompte, Janet
  1981   "The Independent Women of Hispanic New Mexico, 1821–1846." *Western Historical Quarterly* 12(1):17–36.

León-Portilla, Miguel
  1972   "The Norteño Variety of Mexican Culture: An Ethno-Historical Approach." In *Plural Society in the Southwest.* Edward Spicer and Raymond Thompson, eds. Albuquerque: University of New Mexico Press.

Lévi-Strauss, Claude
  1963   "Language and the Analysis of Social Laws." In *Structural Anthropology.* New York: Basic Books.

Lewis, Diane K.
  1983   "A Response to Inequality: Black Women, Racism and Sexism." In *The Signs Reader.* Elizabeth Abel and Emily K. Abel, eds. Chicago: University of Chicago Press.

Lister, Florence, and Robert Lister
  1979   *Chihuahua: Alamacén de Tempestades.* Chihuahua: Gobierno del Estado de Chihuahua.

Lloyd, Jane-Dale
  1983   "La Crisis Económica de 1905 a 1907 en el Noroeste de Chihuahua." *Humanidades Anuario VII.* Mexico: Iberoamericana.
  1988   "Rancheros and Rebellion: The Case of Northwestern Chihuahua, 1905–1909." In *Rural Revolt in Mexico and U.S. Intervention.* Daniel Nugent, ed. La Jolla: Center for U.S.-Mexican Studies.

Lomnitz, Larissa A., and Pérez-Lizaur, Marisol
  1984   "Dynastic Growth and Survival Strategies: The Solidarity of Mexican Grand-Families." In *Kinship Ideology and Practice in Latin America.* Raymond T. Smith, ed. Chapel Hill: University of North Carolina Press.

Lowenhaupt-Tsing, Anna
  1993   *In the Realm of the Diamond Queen.* Princeton, N.J.: Princeton University Press.

Ludlow, Leonor
  1986   "La Etapa Formativa del Estado Mexicano." In *Evolución del Estado Mexicano,* vol. 1. Luis Alberto de la Garza et al., eds. Mexico: Ediciones el Caballito.

MacCormack, Carol P., and Marilyn Strathern (eds.)
  1980   *Nature, Culture and Gender.* Cambridge: Cambridge University Press.

Machiavelli, Niccolo
  1950   *The Prince and the Discourses.* New York: The Modern Library.
MacKinnon, Catharine A.
  1983   "Feminism, Marxism, Method, and the State: An Agenda for Theory."
         In *The Signs Reader.* Elizabeth Abel and Emily K. Abel, eds. Chicago:
         University of Chicago Press.
Mallon, Florencia E.
  1988   "Peasants and State Formation in Nineteenth-Century Mexico: More-
         los, 1848–1858." *Political Power and Social Theory* 7:1–54.
Márquez Padilla, Paz Consuelo
  1986   "Dos Obstaculos Para la Consolidación del Estado en el Siglo XIX."
         In *Evolución del Estado Mexicano,* vol. 1. Luis Alberto de la Garza
         et al., eds. Mexico: Ediciones el Caballito.
Márquez Sterling, Manuel
  1958   *Los Ultimos Días del Presidente Madero.* Mexico: Editorial Porrua.
Martínez-Alier, Verena
  1974   *Marriage, Class and Colour in Nineteenth Century Cuba.* Cambridge:
         Cambridge University Press.
Martínez Caraza, Leopoldo
  1983   *El Norte Bárbaro de México.* Mexico: Panorama Editorial.
Mauss, Marcel
  1973   "Techniques of the Body." *Economy and Society* 2(1):70–88.
McAlister, L. N.
  1963   "Social Structure and Social Change in New Spain." *Hispanic Ameri-
         can Historical Review* 43(3):349–70.
McCaa, Robert
  1984   "*Calidad, Clase,* and Marriage in Colonial Mexico: The Case of Parral,
         1788–1790." *Hispanic American Historical Review* 64(3):477–501.
Meyer, Michael
  1967   *Mexican Rebel: Pascual Orozco and the Mexican Revolution 1910–1915.*
         Lincoln: University of Nebraska Press.
Meyer, Michael, and William Sherman
  1979   *The Course of Mexican History.* New York: Oxford University Press.
Miller, David, and Jerome Steffen (eds.)
  1977   *The Frontier.* Norman: University of Oklahoma Press.
Miller, Simon
  1988   "Revisionism in Recent Mexican Historiography." *Bulletin of Latin
         American Research* 4(1):77–88.
Minh-ha, Trinh T.
  1989   *Woman, Native, Other: Writing Postcoloniality and Feminism.* Bloom-
         ington: Indiana University Press.
Mirande, Alfredo
  1985   *The Chicano Experience.* Notre Dame: University of Notre Dame Press.

Mohanty, Chandra T., Ann Russo, and Lourdes Torres (eds.)
  1991   *Third World Women and the Politics of Feminism.* Bloomington: Indiana University Press.
Moorhead, Max L.
  1968   *The Apache Frontier.* Norman: University of Oklahoma Press.
  1975   *The Presidio.* Norman: University of Oklahoma Press.
Moraga, Cherrie
  1986   "From a Long Line of Vendidas: Chicanas and Feminism." In *Feminist Studies/Critical Studies.* Teresa de Lauretis, ed. Bloomington: University of Indiana Press.
Morner, Magnus
  1967   *Race Mixture in the History of Latin America.* Boston: Little, Brown.
  1970   "Introduction." In *Race and Class in Latin America.* Magnus Morner, ed. New York: Columbia University Press.
Mosse, George
  1985   *Nationalism and Sexuality: Middle-Class Morality and Sexual Norms in Modern Europe.* Madison: University of Wisconsin Press.
Muldoon, James
  1975   "The Indian as Irishman." *Essex Institute Historical Collections* 111: 267–89.
Mullings, Leith
  1984   "Minority Women, Work and Health." In *Double Exposure: Women and Health Hazards on the Job and at Home.* W. Chavkin, ed. New York: Monthly Review Press.
  1986   "Uneven Development: Class, Race and Gender in the United States Before 1900." In *Women's Work: Development and the Division of Labor by Gender.* Eleanor Leacock and Helen Safa, eds. South Hadley, Mass.: Bergin and Harvey.
Myres, Sandra L.
  1979   "The Ranching Frontier: Spanish Institutional Backgrounds of the Plains Cattle Industry." In *New Spain's Far Northern Frontier.* David Weber, ed. Albuquerque: University of New Mexico Press.
Nakano Glenn, Evelyn
  1985   "Racial Ethnic Women's Labor: The Intersection of Race, Gender and Class Oppression." *Review of Radical Political Economics* 17(3):86–108.
Namias, June
  1993   *White Captives: Gender and Domesticity on the American Frontier.* Chapel Hill: University of North Carolina Press.
Naranjo, Carmen (ed.)
  1981   *La Mujer y la Cultura: Antología.* Mexico: UNICEF, SEP Diana.
Nash, June
  1980   "Aztec Women: The Transition from Status to Class in Empire and

Colony." In *Women and Colonization: Anthropological Perspectives*. Mona Etienne and Eleanor Leacock, eds. New York: Praeger, J. F. Bergin Publishers.

Nugent, Daniel

  1982   "Ideology and Social Change in the Sierra Tarahumara." Manuscript.

  1987   Mexico's Rural Populations and La Crisis: Economic Crisis or Legitimation Crisis?" *Critique of Anthropology* 7(3):93-112.

  1989   " 'Are We Not [Civilized] Men?': The Formation and Devolution of Community in Northern Mexico." *Journal of Historical Sociology* 2(3): 206-39.

  1990   "Paradojas en el Desarollo de 'la Cuestión Agraria en Chihuahua, 1885-1935." In *Actas del Primer Congreso de Historia Regional Comparada, 1989*. Rubén Lau Rojo and Carlos González, eds. Juárez, Chihuahua: Universidad Autonoma de Ciudad Juárez.

  1991   Revolutionary Posturing, Bourgeois Land 'Reform': Reflections on the Agrarian Question in Northern Mexico. *Labour, Capital and Society* 24(1):90-108.

  1993   *Spent Cartridges of Revolution: An Anthropological History of Namiquipa, Chihuahua*. Chicago: University of Chicago Press.

Nugent, Daniel (ed.)

  1988   (ed.)*Rural Revolt in Mexico and U.S. Intervention*. La Jolla: Center for U.S.-Mexican Studies.

Nugent, Daniel, and Ana María Alonso

  1994   "Multiple Selective Traditions in Agrarian Reform and Agrarian Struggle: Popular Culture and State Formation in the Ejido of Namiquipa, Chihuahua." In *Everyday Forms of State Formation: Revolution and the Negotiation of Rule in Modern Mexico*. Gilbert Joseph and Daniel Nugent, eds. Durham, N.C.: Duke University Press.

Ollman, Bertell

  1971   *Alienation: Marx's Conception of Man in Capitalist Society*. Cambridge: Cambridge University Press.

O'Malley, Ilene

  1986   *The Myth of the Revolution: Hero Cults and the Institutionalization of the Mexican State 1920-1940*. London: Greenwood Press.

O'Neale, Sondra

  1986   "Inhibiting Midwives, Usurping Creators: The Struggling Emergence of Black Women in American Fiction." In *Feminist Studies/Critical Studies*.Teresa de Lauretis, ed. Bloomington: University of Indiana Press.

Ong, Aihwa

  1990   "State Versus Islam: Malay Families, Women's Bodies and the Body Politic in Malaysia." *American Ethnologist* 17(2):258-76.

Orozco, Victor
   1992   *Las Guerras Indias en la Historia de Chihuahua.* Juárez, Chihuahua: Universidad Autónoma de Ciudad Juárez, Instituto Chihuahuense de la Cultura.
Ortner, Sherry B.
   1974   "Is Female to Male as Nature is to Culture?" In *Woman, Culture and Society.* Michelle Z. Rosaldo and Louise Lamphere, eds. Stanford: Stanford University Press.
   1978   "The Virgin and the State." *Feminist Studies* 4:19–33.
Ortner, Sherry B., and Harriet Whitehead (eds.)
   1981   *Sexual Meanings: The Cultural Construction of Gender and Sexuality.* Cambridge: Cambridge University Press.
Osorio, Rubén
   1988   "Villismo From the Perspective of Villistas." In *Rural Revolt in Mexico and U.S. Intervention.* Daniel Nugent, ed. La Jolla: Center for U.S.-Mexican Studies.
   1990   *Pancho Villa, Ese Desconocido: Entrevistas en Chihuahua a Favor y en su Contra.* Chihuahua: Ediciones del Gobierno del Estado de Chihuahua.
Paige, Jeremy
   1975   *Agrarian Revolution.* New York: The Free Press.
Parker, Andrew, Mary Russo, Doris Sommer, and P. Yaeger (eds.)
   1992   *Nationalisms and Sexualities.* New York: Routledge.
Paz, Octavio
   1985   *The Labyrinth of Solitude and The Other Mexico, Return to the Labyrinth of Solitude, Mexico and the United States, The Philanthropic Ogre.* New York: Grove Press.
Peristiany, J. G. (ed.)
   1965   *Honour and Shame: The Values of Mediterranean Society.* Chicago: University of Chicago Press.
Pitt-Rivers, Julian
   1961   *The People of the Sierra.* Chicago: University of Chicago Press.
   1965   "Honour and Social Status." In *Honour and Shame: The Values of Mediterranean Society.* J. G. Peristiany, ed. Chicago: University of Chicago Press.
Rabinow, Paul (ed.)
   1984   *The Foucault Reader.* New York: Pantheon Books.
Radcliffe, Sarah, and Sallie Westwood (eds.)
   1993   *'Viva': Women and Popular Protest in Latin America.* New York: Routledge.
Ramos, Samuel
   1938   *El Perfil del Hombre y la Cultura en México.* Mexico: Editorial Pedro Robredo.

Ramos Escandón, Carmen, et al.

    1987   *Presencia y Transparencia: La Mujer en la Historia de México.* Mexico: El Colegio de México.

Ricoeur, Paul

    1978   "Can There Be a Scientific Concept of Ideology?" In *Phenomenology and the Social Sciences: A Dialogue.* J. Bier, ed. The Hague: Martinus Nijiioff.

Romanucci-Ross, Lola

    1973   *Conflict, Violence and Morality in a Mexican Village.* Palo Alto: National Press.

Romero, Manuel

    1939   "Anécdotas Rancheras de Antaño." *Boletín de la Sociedad Chihuahuense de Estudios Históricos* 2(3):110-14.

Rosaldo, Renato

    1987a "Politics, Patriarchs, and Laughter." *Cultural Critique* 6:65-86.

    1987b "Insubordinations." Manuscript.

    1989   *Culture and Truth: The Remaking of Social Analysis.* Boston: Beacon Press.

Roseberry, William

    1994   "Hegemony and the Language of Contention." In *Everyday Forms of State Formation: Revolution and the Negotiation of Rule in Modern Mexico.* Gilbert Joseph and Daniel Nugent, eds. Durham, N.C.: Duke University Press.

Rosenblatt, Angel

    1954   *La Población Indígena y el Mestizaje en America,* vol. 2. Buenos Aires: Editorial Nova.

Schneider, David

    1968   *American Kinship: A Cultural Account.* Englewood Cliffs, N.J.: Prentice-Hall.

Schneider, Jane

    1971   "Of Vigilance and Virgins: Honor, Shame and Access to Resources in Mediterranean Societies." *Ethnology* 10(1):1-24.

Schryer, Frans J.

    1980   *The Rancheros of Pisaflores: The History of a Peasant Bourgeoisie in Mexico.* Toronto: Univeristy of Toronto Press.

Scott, James C.

    1976   *The Moral Economy of the Peasant: Rebellion and Subsistence in Southeast Asia.* New Haven, Conn.: Yale University Press.

    1977a "Hegemony and the Peasantry." *Politics and Society* 7(3):267-96.

    1977b "Protest and Profanation: Agrarian Revolt and the Little Tradition." *Theory and Society* 4(1):1-38 and 4(2):211-46.

    1985   *Weapons of the Weak: Everyday Forms of Peasant Resistance.* New Haven, Conn.: Yale University Press.

Scott, Joan W.

1986   "Gender: A Useful Category of Historical Analysis." *American Historical Review* 91(5):1053-75.

1987   "On Language, Gender and Working Class History." *International Labor and Working Class History* 31:1-13.

Seed, Patricia

1988   *To Love, Honor and Obey in Colonial Mexico: Conflicts over Marriage Choice, 1574-1821.* Stanford: Stanford University Press.

Sepúlveda, Ximena

1975   "La Revolución en Bachiniva." Mexico: DEAS-INAH Serie de Estudios 7.

Servín, Manuel Patricio

1979   "California's Hispanic Heritage: A View into the Spanish Myth." In *New Spain's Far Northern Frontier.* David Weber, ed. Albuquerque: University of New Mexico Press.

Shanklin, E.

1994   *Anthropology and Race.* Belmont, Cal.: Wadsworth Press.

Singer, Milton

1984   *Man's Glassy Essence: Explorations in Semiotic Anthropology.* Bloomington: Indiana University.Press.

Smith, Gavin

1989   *Livelihood and Resistance: Peasants and the Politics of Land in Peru.* Berkeley: University of California Press.

Smith, Ralph

1962   "Apache Plunder Trails Southward, 1831-1840." *New Mexico Historical Review* 37(1):20-42.

1963   "Indians in American-Mexican Relations Before the War of 1846." *Hispanic American Historical Review* 43:34-64.

1965   "The Scalp Hunt in Chihuahua-1849." *New Mexico Historical Review* 40(2):116-40.

Smith, Raymond T.

1967   "Social Stratification, Cultural Pluralism and Integration in West Indian Societies." In *Caribbean Integration.* S. Lewis and T. G. Mathews, eds. Rio Pedras, Puerto Rico: Institute of Caribbean Studies.

1970   "Social Stratification in the Caribbean." In *Essays in Comparative Social Stratification.* L. Plotnicov and A. Tuden, eds. Pittsburgh: University of Pittsburgh Press.

1982a "Race and Class in the Post-Emancipation Caribbean." In *Racism and Colonialism.* Robert Ross, ed. The Hague: Martinus Nijiioff Publishers/Leiden University Press.

1982b "Family, Social Change, and Social Policy." Manuscript.

1984   "Introduction." In *Kinship Ideology and Practice in Latin America.* Raymond T. Smith, ed. Chapel Hill: University of North Carolina Press.

1993   "On the Disutility of the Notion of 'Ethnic Group' for Understanding
        Status Struggles in the Modern World." Paper presented at a Univer-
        sity of Guadalajara conference, Jalisco.

Socolow, Susan M.

1992   "Spanish Captives in Indian Societies: Cultural Contact Along the
        Argentine Frontier, 1600–1835." *Hispanic American Historical Review*
        72(1):73–100.

Soto, Shirlene

1986   "Women in the Revolution." In *Twentieth Century Mexico.* W. Dirk
        Raat and William H. Beezley, eds. Lincoln: University of Nebraska
        Press.

Spivak, Gayatri Chakravorty

1985   "Three Women's Texts and a Critique of Imperialism." *Critical In-
        quiry* 12(1):243–61.

1987   *In Other Worlds: Essays in Cultural Politics.* New York: Routledge.

Stanley, F.

1962   *The Apaches of New Mexico, 1540-1940.* Pampa, Tex.: Pampa Print
        Shop.

Stern, Steve J. (ed.)

1987   *Resistance, Rebellion and Consciousness in the Andean World: 18th to
        20th Centuries.* Madison: University of Wisconsin Press.

Stevens, Evelyn P.

1965   "Mexican *Machismo*: Politics and Value Orientations." *Western Politi-
        cal Quarterly* 18(4):848–57.

1973   "*Marianismo*: The Other Face of *Machismo* in Latin America." In
        Female and Male in Latin America. Ann Pescatello, ed. Pittsburgh:
        University of Pittsburgh Press.

Stoianovich, Traian

1976   *French Historical Method: The Annales Paradigm.* Ithaca, N.Y.: Cor-
        nell University Press.

Stoller, Ann

1989   "Making Empire Respectable: The Politics of Race and Sexual Mo-
        rality in Twentieth-Century Colonial Cultures." *American Ethnologist*
        16(4):634–60.

Suleiman, Susan Rubin

1986   *The Female Body in Western Culture: Contemporary Perspectives.* Cam-
        bridge, Mass.: Harvard University Press.

Taussig, Michael

1980   *The Devil and Commodity Fettishism.* Chapel Hill: University of North
        Carolina Press.

1987   *Shamanism, Colonialism and the Wild Man: A Study in Terror and Heal-
        ing.* Chicago: University of Chicago Press.

Terrazas Sánchez, Filiberto
   1973   *La Guerra Apache en México*. Mexico: B. Costa-Amic.
Terrell, John Upton
   1972   *Apache Chronicle*. New York: World Publishing.
Theweleit, Klaus
   1987   *Male Fantasies*. Minneapolis: University of Minnesota Press.
Thomas, Alfred B.
   1941   "Introduction." In *Teodoro de Croix and the Northern Frontier of New Spain, 1776-1783*. Alfred B. Thomas, ed. Norman: University of Oklahoma Press.
Tjarks, Alicia V.
   1979   "Comparative Demographic Analysis of Texas, 1777-1793." In *New Spain's Far Northern Frontier*. David Weber, ed. Albuquerque: University of New Mexico Press.
Todorov, Tzvetan
   1985   *The Conquest of America*. New York: Harper and Row.
Turner, Terrence
   1980   "The Social Skin." In *Not Work Alone*. J. Cherfas and R. Lewin, eds. London: Temple Smith.
Turner, Victor
   1967   *The Forest of Symbols*. Ithaca, N.Y.: Cornell University Press.
   1969   *The Ritual Process: Structure and Anti-Structure*. Ithaca, N.Y.: Cornell University Press.
Tutino, John
   1986   *From Insurrection to Revolution in Mexico*. Princeton, N.J.: Princeton University Press.
Vanderwood, Paul
   1981   *Disorder and Progress: Bandits, Police and Mexican Development*. Lincoln: University of Nebraska Press.
Van Gennep, Arnold
   1960   *The Rites of Passage*. Chicago: University of Chicago Press.
Vélez-Ibañez, Carlos G.
   1983   *Rituals of Marginality: Politics, Process and Change in Urban Central Mexico, 1969-1974*. Berkeley: University of California Press.
Vickers, Nancy J.
   1986   "This Heraldry in Lucrece's Face." In *The Female Body in Western Culture*. Susan Rubin Suleiman, ed. Cambridge, Mass.: Harvard University Press.
Vigil, Ralph H.
   1973   "The Hispanic Heritage and the Borderlands." *The Journal of San Diego History* 19(3):32-39.

Wagner, Roy
   1981 *The Invention of Culture*. Chicago: University of Chicago Press.
Warman, Arturo
   1977 "The Historical Framework of Inter-ethnic Relations."" In *Race and Class in Post-Colonial Society*. UNESCO. Paris: UNESCO.
   1980 *"We Come to Object": The Peasants of Morelos and the National State*. Baltimore: Johns Hopkins University Press.
Wasserman, Mark
   1980 "The Social Origins of the 1910 Revolution in Chihuahua." *Latin American Research Review* 15(1):15–38.
   1984 *Capitalists, Caciques and Revolution*. Chapel Hill: University of North Carolina Press.
Waterbury, Ronald
   1975 "Non-Revolutionary Peasants, Oaxaca Compared to Morelos." *Comparative Studies in Society and History* 17(4):410–42.
Weber, David
   1982 *The Mexican Frontier, 1821-1846*. Albuquerque: University of New Mexico Press.
   1988 *Myth and the History of the Hispanic Southwest*. Albuquerque: University of New Mexico Press.
Weber, Max
   1978 *Economy and Society*. 2 vols. Berkeley: University of California Press.
West, Robert
   1949 "The Mining Community in Northern New Spain: The Parral Mining District." *Ibero-Americana* 30.
Williams, Brackette F.
   1989 "A Class Act: Anthropology and the Race to Nation Across Ethnic Terrain." *Annual Review of Anthropology* 18:401–44.
Williams, Edwin
   1963 *The Williams Spanish and English Dictionary*. New York: Charles Scribner's Sons.
Williams, Raymond
   1983 *Keywords: A Vocabulary of Culture and Society*. Rev. ed. New York: Oxford University Press.
Wolf, Eric
   1959 *Sons of the Shaking Earth*. Chicago: University of Chicago Press.
   1967 "Closed Corporate Peasant Communities in Mesoamerica and Java." In *Peasant Society: A Reader*. J. M. Potter et al., eds. Boston: Little, Brown.
   1969 *Peasant Wars of the Twentieth Century*. New York: Harper and Row.
   1971 "Aspects of Group Relations in a Complex Society." In *Peasants and Peasant Society*. Teodor Shanin, ed. Harmondsworth: Penguin Books.

1977   "Kinship, Friendship and Patron-Client Relations in Complex Societies." In *Friends, Followers and Factions: A Reader in Political Clientelism*. S. W. Schmidt et. al., eds. Berkeley: University of California Press.

Wolf, Eric, and Edward Hansen

1967   "Caudillo Politics: A Structural Analysis." *Comparative Studies in Society and History* 9(2):168–79.

Wolfskill, George W., and Douglas W. Richmond (eds.)

1979   *Essays on the Mexican Revolution: Revisionist Views of the Leaders*. Austin: University of Texas Press.

Womack, John

1968   *Zapata and the Mexican Revolution*. New York: Vintage Books.

Worcester, Donald E.

1951   "Introduction." In *Instructions for Governing the Interior Provinces of New Spain, 1786* by Bernardo de Galvez. Donald E. Worcester, ed. Berkeley: The Quivira Society.

Wyman, Walker, and Clifton Kroeber

1957   *The Frontier in Perspective*. Madison: University of Wisconsin Press.

Yuval-Davis, N., and F. Anthias (eds.)

1989   *Woman—Nation—State*. New York: Macmillan.

Zavala, Silvio

1957   "The Frontiers of Hispanic America." In *The Frontier in Perspective*. Walker Wyman and Clifton Kroeber, eds. Madison: University of Wisconsin Press.

ABOUT THE AUTHOR

Born in Cuba, **Ana María Alonso** is an assistant professor of anthropology at the University of Arizona. Her interest in the Mexican Revolution is partly the product of her family history. Her great-great-uncle, Manuel Márquez Sterling, was the Cuban ambassador to Mexico during the Revolution, and his book, *Los Ultimos Días del Presidente Madero*, is one of the classics of Mexican historiography.

Alonso has published articles on nationalism and ethnicity, social memory, the Mexican Revolution, and gender and sexuality in northern Mexico. Her current interests include the negotiation of ethnicity and visions of national community among Hispanics in Tucson, Arizona.

CPSIA information can be obtained at www.ICGtesting.com
Printed in the USA
LVOW060314190312

273660LV00003B/3/P